RUSSIA ON THE EDGE

RUSSIA
ON THE EDGE

Imagined Geographies
and Post-Soviet Identity

EDITH W. CLOWES

Cornell University Press

ITHACA AND LONDON

Dan & Jess —
I hope you enjoy
this portrait
of post-Soviet
Russia —

Love, Edie
Dec. 17, 2011

First published 2011 by Cornell University Press
First printing, Cornell Paperbacks, 2011

Printed in the United States of America

Library of Congress Cataloging-in-Publication Data

Clowes, Edith W.
    Russia on the edge: imagined geographies and post-Soviet identity / Edith W. Clowes.
        p. cm.
    Includes bibliographical references and index.
    ISBN 978-0-8014-4856-0 (cloth : alk. paper)
    ISBN 978-0-8014-7725-6 (pbk. : alk. paper)
    1. Russian literature—21st century—History and criticism.   2. Russian literature—20th century—History and criticism.   3. National characteristics, Russian, in literature.   4. Nationalism and literature—Russia (Federation)   5. Cultural geography—Russia (Federation)   6. Territory, National—Russia (Federation)   7. Russia (Federation)—Intellectual life—1991–   I. Title.
        PG3027.C57   2011
        891.709'35847—dc22   2010042040

Cornell University Press strives to use environmentally responsible suppliers and materials to the fullest extent possible in the publishing of its books. Such materials include vegetable-based, low-VOC inks and acid-free papers that are recycled, totally chlorine-free, or partly composed of nonwood fibers. For further information, visit our website at www.cornellpress.cornell.edu.

Cloth printing   10 9 8 7 6 5 4 3 2 1
Paperback printing   10 9 8 7 6 5 4 3 2 1

CONTENTS

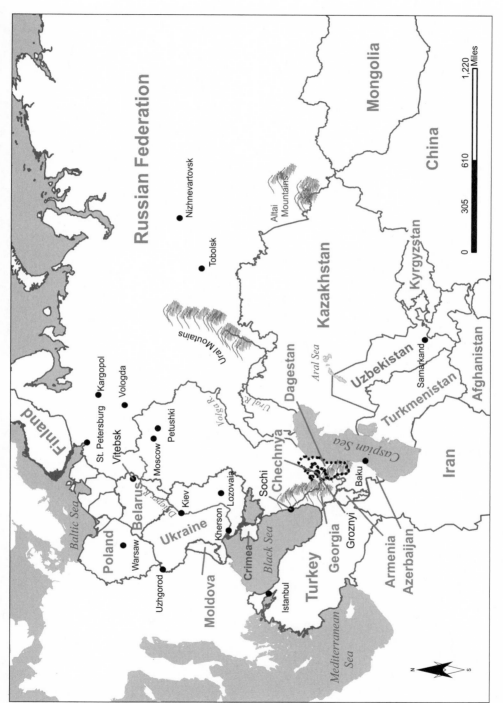

Map of Northern Eurasia, 2010

PREFACE

In January 1986, the new Borovitskaia Metro Station opened by the Kremlin wall in central Moscow. Built to remind the visitor of the low-arching hallways of the medieval Kremlin, the station's visual centerpiece is a vast, gold and burnt orange mural depicting the map of the Soviet Union and its peoples growing as a tree among the towers of the Kremlin. Fifteen impassive human figures stand for the fifteen Soviet republics. This image conveys an unconventional view of national identity, not as a grassroots formation out of which emerged a state. Rather, for the Soviets nationality was a plant cultivated, developed, and controlled by the state, symbolized here by the Kremlin.

The year 1986 is best known for the nuclear disaster at Chernobyl. In the aftermath the Soviet state in the person of Mikhail Gorbachev gave the silent Soviet nationalities a voice, the right to probe and debate painful truths, past and present. With his policy of glasnost, or openness and transparency, Gorbachev hoped to reform and revive the multinational empire he ruled. Instead, he opened the way to a remarkable debate about identity and to the eventual dissolution of the Soviet Union.

These two images—the mute nationalities on the tree-like Soviet map and people suddenly voicing their views, discussing and debating all over the Union—speak to the overwhelming power of the Russian-centered Soviet state to define, to shape, and to bestow identity. Many would say that the center was hypertrophied, that it had too much power, and various nationalities began to resist its influence. Russians, in turn, would push back, questioning their own identity. With the dissolution of the Soviet Union in 1991 peripheries and borders, both real and symbolic, would become the keys to Russians' thinking about who they are. This book investigates how and why these images became so central to Russian identity.

FIG. 1. Mural in Borovitskaia Metro Station, Moscow (1986), photo by Adrienne M. Harris, 2007, reproduced with permission.

The post-Soviet period is marked by a decisive shift in the systems of symbols and the values embedded in them—the semiotics—in which thinking about identity is expressed. In distinction to Soviet identity, which was *temporally* defined—linked to a vision of the Soviet state at the vanguard of history—the post-Soviet debate about Russian identity has been couched in *spatial* metaphors of territory and geography. This book addresses the nature of contemporary Russian identity and its relationship to the always-dominant centralized Russian state. While agreeing that the concept of a nation-state does not fit the Russian historical experience, this book examines patterns of geographical and geopolitical metaphor to understand how major cultural figures and public intellectuals construct post-Soviet Russian identity, whether in some concept of nation or ethnicity or some other kind of community.

What we find is indeed a lively give-and-take between recycled statist views and an array of public voices newly empowered by Gorbachev's, and later Yeltsin's, bold call for glasnost and public dialogue. We will hear essentialist articulations of identity, for example, in Aleksandr Dugin's neo-Eurasian imperialism and Aleksandr Prokhanov's Russian ultranationalism, as well as constructivist forms of Russianness, coming most insistently in Mikhail Ryklin's poststructuralist concept of "border," Liudmila Ulitskaia's magical realist multiculturalism, and Anna Politkovskaia's journalistic civic-mindedness. Many major voices in the contemporary debate move beyond traditional concepts of nation defined by language, kinship, ethnic group, shared history, though virtually all either cling to or interrogate a crucial characteristic of national identity—geographical territory and its symbolic meanings. Constructivist opinion sometimes advances a concept of Russianness in some ways like the so-called hyphenated identity familiar since the 1970s in the United States and in some ways like the notion of hybrid identity in postcolonial theory.[1] In contemporary multiethnic American society everyone is not just American, but, for example, African American or Chinese American, linking both juridical and ethnic self-concepts. In the Russian context a similar approach to identity will emerge through metaphors of territorial border or periphery.

In 2005—almost two decades after glasnost was introduced—President Vladimir Putin pronounced the fall of the Soviet Union to be the "greatest

1. This situation brings to mind Lorraine A. Strasheim's positive revaluation of hyphenated identity, "We're All Ethnics: 'Hyphenated' Americans, 'Professional' Ethnics, and Ethnics 'By Attraction'," *The Modern Language Journal*, 59, nos. 5/6 (September–October 1975), 240–249. A good articulation of hybrid identity can be found in Homi Bhabha, *The Location of Culture* (London: Routledge, 2004), 55.

geopolitical catastrophe of the [twentieth] century" because many of the "Russian people" (*rossiiskii narod*) suddenly found themselves "beyond the bounds of Russian federal territory" (*rossiiskaia territoriia*).[2] It is certainly not by chance that, in speaking of the "Russian people," Putin selected the juridical term *rossiiskii,* implying citizenship in the Russian Federation, instead of the ethnic term for Russian (*russkii*). In choosing this word, Putin was again constructing nation/people in such a way as to tie Russianness to the state and its authority; and he was circumnavigating ethnic constructs of nation as an ancient formation, perhaps independent of the state, based rather on language, religion, shared history, and genetic kinship. While seeming to promise civil equality for all ethnic groups under the banner of Russian citizenship, Putin's choice of words brings to mind a long statist tradition of identifying the Russian state as the dominant institution of Russianness. His words also suggest the same contradiction implicit in the Borovitskaia Metro Station mural, which alerts us to the difficulties in defining "Russian identity" in post-Soviet Russia. Is the "juridical" nation, that is a nation that has been defined by the state, the ultimate definition of national identity? Is nation defined by the territorial boundaries claimed by the state? Conversely, are all subjects, no matter their ethnic background, equally Russian in this sense and thus equally protected under the federal constitution and Russian law?

Since the mid-1980s this view of Russianness implying that as a citizen of the Russian state one is automatically Russian has been celebrated by some public intellectuals and vehemently tested by others. For some ultraconservatives, for example the neo-fascist Dugin and the ultranationalist Prokhanov, the Russian imperial state is Russians' proudest achievement. Other public intellectuals such as Ryklin, Ulitskaia, and Politkovskaia expose the state's implied claim that ethnic differences do not matter, and they insert into the post-Soviet debate the notion that all citizens, no matter what their ethnic background, have rights and should be proactive in defending them, in many cases *against* the state.

The geographical metaphors dominant in current discourse about identity convey the sense that *who* a Russian is depends on how one defines *where* Russia is. Overarching values attach to that place, however it is defined. Among the leading metaphors are traditionally imperial terms of center and periphery. Two geographical axes, north versus south, as well as the familiar east versus west, figure prominently in post-Soviet thinking. In addition, two new sets of metaphors—Eurasia versus the West and the geopolitical

<hr>

2. http://archive.kremlin.ru/text/appears/2005/04/87049.shtml.

concepts of "heartland" versus coastal power have gained considerable cur-
rency, as some try to re-establish Russia as a global power center. The image
of the "edge," where, I hypothesize, post-Soviet Russia fears that it is, bears
both geographical and psychological meaning. No longer at the hub of the
Soviet empire, many Russians in the 1990s worried about being on the margin. The "edge" also suggests an anxiety that belies the many more recent
protestations that Moscow is a powerful center and a great imperial capital.
Almost 175 years after Petr Chaadaev's famous 1836 "Philosophical Letter," in which he lamented Russia's lack of national identity, some prominent Russian commentators still write as if fearing that they are in a zone
between great eastern and western civilizations. Russia is on the edge, and
its most zealous ultraconservative boosters are on edge.

This book started as a search for continuity in Russia's speculative-
philosophical tradition after the end of the Soviet regime. My question concerned the body of thought by the great thinkers of the pre-revolutionary
Russian Renaissance—Solovyov, Berdiaev, Shestov, Rozanov, among many
others—and their possible role as interlocutors in contemporary creative
life. Theirs were not the issues and worries of public intellectuals in the late
1980s and 1990s, who were sooner attracted to various forbidden fruit of
later Russian and European thought in order to address the question of
their Russian identity. This time they were asking not "what" but "where"
Russian identity is and, to paraphrase the pop writer Pelevin, "why it is in
such trouble."[3] Among the widely ranging theories of choice were the Eurasianism of the 1920s and 1930s conceived by a group of émigré professors,
European neo-fascist thought, Buddhist philosophy, and post-structuralist
French and U.S. philosophy.

This book is structured in a "point-counterpoint" pattern to juxtapose
the chief positions in the debate about post-Soviet Russian identity. The
introduction presents the book's guiding metaphors, center and periphery,
and the possibilities inherent in each of them. I place less familiar definitions from Russian semiotic and post-Marxist thinkers in the context of
more familiar postmodernist and postcolonial definitions to show the innovative orientation toward the periphery and ideological decentering that
all of them share.

Chapter 1, "Deconstructing Imperial Moscow," deals with philosophical and literary deconstructions of Soviet Moscow and their embedded

---

3. Viktor Pelevin, *Chapaev i Pustota* (Moscow: Vagrius, 2000), 179. Aleksandr Solzhenit-
syn also asserted that "Russia is in trouble" in a 1994 interview on the TV program "Itogi."
Quoted in Wayne Allensworth, *The Russian Question: Nationalism, Modernization, and Post-
Communist Russia* (Lanham, MD: Rowman and Littlefield, 1998), 62.

assumptions about Russian identity. This discussion distinguishes between Moscow as the seat of empire and Moscow as ordinary people. I begin with three late Soviet works, Venedikt Erofeev's novella *Moscow to the End of the Line* (1969), Vladimir Voinovich's utopian satire *Moscow 2042* (1987), and Dmitry Prigov's poetic cycle *Moscow and Muscovites* (1982)—all of which challenge the centripetal force of the capital. An innovative article, "Bodies of Terror" (1990), by Mikhail Ryklin deconstructs architectural "bodies" of Stalinist Moscow, exposing the unconscious terror concealed in them. This chapter ends with the submersion of Moscow in two leading post-Soviet literary works, the brilliant short story, "Vera Pavlovna's Ninth Dream" (1992) by Viktor Pelevin and the much-discussed experimental novel *Slynx* (2000), by the scion of the Tolstoi clan Tatiana Tolstaia.

Chapter 2, "Postmodernist Empire Meets Holy Rus'," presents the main straw man in the debate, Aleksandr Dugin, the ultraconservative social commentator and political organizer whose neo-imperialist Eurasianist thinking has at times exerted some influence on Putin's Kremlin. In his chief works, *The Mysteries of Eurasia* (1996), *The Foundations of Geopolitics* (1997), and *Absolute Motherland* (1999), Dugin develops a Russocentric dream of a future Eurasian imperialist state system, centering in Moscow and the Russian north and Siberian east.

The next three chapters are devoted to significant responses to the imperialist scenario championed by Dugin, among others. Pelevin's popular novel *Chapaev and the Void* (1996) is the focus of chapter 3. Pelevin deconstructs Eurasianist thinking about the Asiatic periphery and, along with it, the authoritarian Russian-Soviet psychology. The fourth and fifth chapters consider two peripheries of the old empire that have had a crucial impact on Russian culture but have also aroused the ire of various ultraconservatives—the western border and the Black Sea littoral. Chapter 4 examines the complex concept of border developed by Ryklin in his most important works, *Spaces of Jubilation* (2002), *Diagnostic* (2003), and *Swastika, Star, Cross* (2006). Ryklin's treatment focuses particularly on the western border of the Soviet Union, and its significance both for his personal identity and for national identity in the Soviet and post-Soviet eras. The possibilities of the periphery in the literary art of Liudmila Ulitskaia form the theme of chapter 5. In her two main novels, *Medea and Her Children* (1997) and *The Kukotsky Case* (2002), as well as a number of outstanding stories, Ulitskaia unearths the cultural wealth of the Black Sea coast, a metaperiphery of many empires that tells us a great deal about the character of peripheries in general and the ways in which they interrogate the center and expand social consciousness and creative energy. A concept of Russian selfhood based on interethnic tolerance and civil law emerges in the writings of Ryklin and Ulitskaia.

The final chapter addresses the geographical blind spot of Russia's new rulers, which I call the "other South." This is the Muslim Caucasus, especially Chechnya, the site of two ruinous wars that—as Ryklin argues—beyond destroying a peripheral region of Russia, have led to the precipitous suppression of public dialogue, the silencing and recentralization of the Russian press, and the emergence of a newly empowered secret police force. The refusal to confront this blind spot, this deep-seated fear of another culture, has given Russia's controllers a pretext to recentralize power. The artistic and documentary treatment of the Chechen conflict moves through three stages—from the discreditation of outworn, Soviet-era universalism in Vladimir Makanin's novella *Captive of the Caucasus,* to the assertion of a grassroots civic universalism in a number of works, to the demonization of Chechens in popular literature and film of the early twenty-first century. This discussion of the "other South" brings the identity debate to its current troubled condition.

Many people and institutions have helped this project along its way. Appreciative thanks go to several institutions for making available free time for research and writing—the University of Kansas Center for Research and The National Endowment for the Humanities for summer stipends and the American Council of Learned Societies for a year-long Research Fellowship. I am grateful to my colleagues, friends, family, and students who supported this project. Maria Carlson, William J. Comer, Marc L. Greenberg, Eve Levin, and Irina Fediunina-Six shared their wealth of knowledge and were happy to discuss Russian identity at any moment. Rimgaila Salys, Mark Leiderman, Ben Sutcliffe, Olena Chervonik, and Alyssa di Blasio have been knowledgeable and responsive comrades in studying the post-Soviet period. Adrienne M. Harris and Sam Clowes Huneke helped with the last stages of research. Ned Huneke facilitated the final editing. Sarah Bumpus, Sidney Dement, and Adrienne M. Harris contributed photographs of the Moscow metro. I thank John Burt Foster, Jr., Joan Delaney Grossman, George L. Kline, Judith Deutsch Kornblatt, Jay Rosellini, James P. Scanlan, Nancy Tittler, and James L. West for their friendship and support. I am indebted to the anonymous readers of the manuscript for their many helpful queries and suggestions. My abiding gratitude goes to John G. Ackerman, director of Cornell University Press, for his vision and determined support of Slavic and East European studies at a time when the academic book publishing business seems to be in endless crisis as it confronts the challenges of the digital age.

ABBREVIATIONS

B   Liudmila Ulitskaia, *Bednye, zlye, liubimye* (*The Poor, The Mean, The Beloved;* Moscow: Eksmo, 2006).

BT   Mikhail Ryklin, "Bodies of Terror: Theses toward a Logic of Violence." *New Literary History* 24 (1993), 51–74.

ChP   Viktor Pelevin, *Chapaev i Pustota* (*Chapaev and the Void;* Moscow: Vagrius, 2000).

DD   Mikhail Ryklin, *Dekonstruktsiia i destruktsiia: Besedy s filosofami* (*Deconstruction and Destruction: Conversations with Philosophers;* Moscow: Logos, 2002).

DW   Anna Politkovskaia, *A Dirty War: A Russian Reporter in Chechnya,* trans. J. Crowfoot (London: Harvill, 2001).

GG   Aleksandr Prokhanov, *Gospodin Geksogen* (*Mr. Hexogen;* Moscow: Ad marginem, 2002).

I   Dmitrii Prigov, *Izbrannye* (*Selected Works;* Moscow: Eksmo, 2002).

K   Tat'iana Tolstaia, *Kys'* (*Slynx;* Moscow: Podkova, 2000).

KK   Liudmila Ulitskaia, *Kazus Kukotskogo* (*The Kukotsky Case;* Moscow: Eksmo, 2002).

KP   Vladimir Makanin, "Kavkazskii plennyi" ("Captive of the Caucasus"). *Novyi mir* 4 (1995), 3–19.

L   Liudmila Ulitskaia, *Liudi nashego tsaria* (*The Subjects of Our Tsar;* Moscow: Eksmo, 2006).

M   Liudmila Ulitskaia, *Medea and Her Children,* transl. A. Tait (New York: Schocken, 2002. [*Medea i ee deti;* Moscow: Eksmo, 2003]).

MBV   Aleksandr Dugin, *Metafizika blagoi vesti: Absoliutnaia rodina* (*The Metaphysics of the Gospel: The Absolute Homeland;* Moscow: Arktogeia, 1999).

ME   Aleksandr Dugin, *Misterii Evrazii* (*Eurasia's Mysteries;* Moscow: Arktogeia, 1999).

OG   Aleksandr Dugin, *Osnovy geopolitiki* (*The Foundations of Geopolitics*; Moscow: Arktogeia-tsentr, 2000).

PA   Aleksandr Dugin, *Puti absoliuta* (*The Paths of the Absolute*; in MBV).

PE   Aleksandr Dugin, *Proekt "Evraziia"* (*Project 'Eurasia'*; Moscow: Iauza, 2004).

PK   Aleksandr Dugin, *Pop-kul'tura i znaki vremeni* (*Pop-Culture and the Signs of the Times*; St. Petersburg: Amfora, 2005).

PL   Mikhail Ryklin, *Prostranstva likovaniia* (*The Spaces of Jubilation*; Moscow: Logos, 2002).

RV   Aleksandr Dugin, *Russkaia veshch'* (*The Russian Thing*; Moscow: 1999).

SZK   Mikhail Ryklin, *Svastika, Zvezda, Krest* (*Swastika, Star, Cross*; Moscow: Logos, 2006).

VD   Mikhail Ryklin, *Vremia diagnoza* (*Diagnostic*; Moscow: Logos, 2003).

ZCh   Anna Politkovskaia, *Za chto?* (*What for?*; Moscow: *Novaia gazeta*, 2007).

ZS   Aleksandr Dugin, "Zakoldovannaia sreda 'novykh imperii'" ("The Be-witched Milieu of the 'New Empires'"). *Khudozhestvennyi zhurnal* 54 (2004), 18–25.

RUSSIA ON THE EDGE

INTRODUCTION

Is Russia a Center or a Periphery?

THE dissolution of the Soviet empire in 1991 unleashed waves of self-doubt in many quarters of Russian life.[1] Throughout the 1990s Russians felt disempowered, politically adrift, lacking a sense of national dignity. As Viktor Pelevin joked in his 1993 novel, *The Life of Insects,* after 1991 Russians wondered whether Moscow was still the "Third Rome" [*Tretii Rim*], or, instead, had slipped into the "third world" [*tretii mir*].[2] The Russian word for "world" (*mir*) is the word for Rome (Rim) spelled backwards. Had Moscow—long a political and cultural center—now become merely a city on the peripheries of the influential cultures and booming economies of Europe, the United States, and East Asia? As a defense against such doubts post-Soviet Russia has seen an aggressive resurgence of ultranationalist and neo-imperialist thinking.

The title "Third Rome" harks back to Muscovite rule in the sixteenth and seventeenth centuries. Muscovite princes sometimes arrogated to their city the imperial title of the Third Rome, the latter-day inheritor of the Roman empire and the Orthodox Christian supremacy of the Second Rome—Constantinople. This Moscocentric nomenclature, linking Russian identity to empire and

---

1. See, for example, Lev Gudkov, "Russkoe natsional'noe soznanie: potentsial i tipy konsolidatsii," in *Kuda idet Rossiia? Al'ternativy obshchestvennogo razvitiia* (Moscow: 1994), 175–187, esp. 177, http://www.ecsocman.edu.ru/images/pubs/2006/05/12/0000277009/038. GUDKOV.pdf. For English-language discussions of post-imperial identity problems see Dominic Lieven, *Empire: The Russian Empire and Its Rivals* (London: Murray, 2000), 380–386; Karen Dawisha and Bruce Parrott, eds. *The End of Empire? The Transformation of the USSR in Comparative Perspective* (Armonk, NY: M.E. Sharpe, 1997); Andreas Kappeler, *The Russian Empire: A Multi-Ethnic History* (Upper Saddle River, NJ: Longman, 2001).
2. Viktor Pelevin, *Zhizn' nasekomykh* (Moscow: Eksmo, 2004), 81–82.

linking religion to the state, will resonate in post-Soviet Russia in the ultra-conservative discourse of Aleksandr Dugin, among many others.[3] In contrast, other voices welcome a view of Russia that embraces some of its "third world" qualities. Liudmila Ulitskaia's art, for example, works productively with the concept of the periphery—the border—with its rich multicultural and multi-ethnic social potential that challenges the chauvinism of the center. The philosopher Mikhail Ryklin theorizes the border as a crucial aspect of identity. The documentary journalism of Anna Politkovskaia places the experiences of marginalized minorities, especially the Chechens, squarely before Russian eyes, drawing attention along the way to the many instances in which all Russian citizens have been marginalized and disenfranchised by their own state. Since the early 1990s powerfully opposing views about what it means to be "Russian" have taken shape. Some focus nostalgically on reinstating Moscow as the imperial center, while others apply "eccentric" ideas of margin, periphery, and border to rethink the meaning of Moscow and to move away from the old tsarist and Stalinist paradigms and their homogenizing, russifying cultural values. Whatever their perspective on the issue of identity, we find a momentous shift since the late 1980s in the ways national personhood is articulated in Russian writing culture. In the Soviet era official identity relied on images of time, of belonging to the "radiant future," the image of the train of history or the rocket blasting into space. Post-Soviet public discourse, whether conservative or liberal, has preferred the alliance of Russianness with concepts of geographical and geopolitical space. The meaning of these spatial metaphors for conceptualizing identity forms the subject of this book. I argue that since 1991 thinking about national identity has shifted unmistakably from images of historical progress that show Soviet dominance in the race to control history, to what I call "imagined geographies"—geographical images endowed with complex post-Soviet attitudes toward self and other, tradition and change, ethnicity and multiculturalism, the state and the nature of citizenship. These metaphors include particular regions of Russia, conceptual oppositions of center and periphery, center and border, the geopolitical concept of heartland, and

3. For a discussion of the historiographic distortions around the theme of Moscow the Third Rome, see Daniel B. Rowland, "Moscow—The Third Rome or the New Israel?" *Russian Review*, 55 (October 1996), 591–614. Although this nomenclature arose in 1511, Muscovites tended rather to think of their city as the New Jerusalem or New Israel. The idea of Moscow the Third Rome became popular among Slavophiles in the nineteenth and twentieth centuries. For a thorough consideration of resurgent ultranationalism and neo-imperialism, see Wayne Allensworth, *The Russian Question: Nationalism, Modernization, and Post-Communist Russia* (Lanham, MD: Roman and Littlefield, 1998).

familiar geographical axes, juxtaposing east to west and north to south, their traditional meanings now inscribed with fresh associations.

In the late Soviet period the concept of progressive time was already failing, a development that in some ways is parallel to postmodern culture in capitalist countries. If modernity was striking for its development of temporal dyna- mism, its belief in linear progress, then in postmodernity history has sometimes seemed irrelevant. What in a closed temporal framework might have seemed like progress turns out in a broader perspective to have resembled movement along a Moebius Strip.[4] One felt one was progressing along a strategically chosen path, only to discover with the passage of time that one has arrived at or, at least, close to one's starting point. Such is the sense we might have in the Putin-Medvedev era, after hearing the Russian mantra of the 1990s that "we can't go back."[5] Granted, Russians have not returned to a country controlled by the Communist Party. They have returned to a country largely controlled by a pseudo-party and the secret police, both of which flout citizens' civil rights.

In both post-Soviet and postmodernist writing attention to space has become noticeably more pointed—even as critics and theorists speak ever more often of concepts of center and margin, center and periphery, empire, border. In the modernist era identity centered on epistemology, on the nature of knowing and the question, "How do we know the world we inhabit?"[6] Studies in postmodernism focus instead on ontological questions of place and its significance: "Which world am I inhabiting and what can be done in it?" Likewise, the "imagined communities" of the colonial and post- colonial world can be theorized in geographical terms, often along an axis juxtaposing the colonizing north and the colonized south.[7] Moreover, the

4. Francis Fukuyama proclaimed the "end of history" in his much-discussed 1989 article by the same title and book *The End of History and the Last Man* (New York: Free Press, 1992). Two earlier groundbreaking literary critical works on time in twentieth-century fiction have drawn attention to the increasing dysfunction of the concept of "history" as ritual (Katerina Clark, *The Soviet Novel: History as Ritual* [Chicago: University of Chicago Press, 1981]) and as object of parody (Linda Hutcheon, *A Poetics of Postmodernism: History, Theory, Fiction* [New York: Routledge, 1988]). For a consideration of time as Moebius strip in experimental fiction of the late Soviet era, see my *Russian Experimental Fiction: Resisting Ideology after Utopia* (Princeton: Princeton University Press, 1993), 60.

5. See, for example, the 2008 documentary by Jean-Michel Carré and Jill Emery, "CBC: The Passionate Eye: The Putin System," http://video.google.com/videoplay?docid=65809387 20868203336.

6. Brian McHale, *Postmodernist Fiction* (London: Methuen, 1987), 6–11.

7. See, for example, E. W. Clowes and J. B. Foster, Jr., eds., "Interrogating Slavic Identities: Inside, Outside, and in between...," *Slavic and East European Journal*, 45, no. 2 (2001), 195– 299; John Burt Foster, Jr., and Wayne J. Froman, "General Introduction: Thresholds of West- ern Culture," in *Thresholds of Western Culture: Identity, Postcoloniality, Transnationalism* (New York: Continuum, 2002), 2–3.

identity: as you're faced

focus of academic history and cultural studies has also shifted from the temporal to the spatial, as the more vital orientation for understanding identity. Recent innovative studies involving "imaginative geographies" of defining the "location of culture," "inventing Europe," or studying urban "texts"— the histories, landscapes, and myths of cities, or thinking about the use of maps in the medieval Russian world, operate with spatial terms.[8]

The present book uses the concept "imagined geography" to delineate a number of different approaches to speaking of Russian selfhood. In 1978 Edward Said first coined the phrase "imaginative geography" to underscore the fictional quality of territorial descriptions of the "Orient" and to focus attention on the Western process of shaping identity through distancing the West from the Islamic cultures of the Middle East.[9] These misconceptions are objects that Said wished to dispel. Drawing on Benedict Anderson's concept of "imagined communities," I use the adjective "imagined" to stress the process of creating fictional spaces of self and other as part of traditional thinking about group identity. Leading participants in the post-Soviet debate use these spatial terms in formulating contrasting identities and rethinking the question, "Who is a Russian?" not the least by answering the question, "Where is Russia?"

In these pages no geographical and geopolitical metaphor figures more prominently than the image of the periphery, which has become the crucial problem for post-Soviet Russian identity. The traditionally all-important center and the newly significant periphery have long been used to speak of imperial spaces.[10] Just as they play a crucial role in postmodernist and postcolonial theory, the parallel processes of decentering and opening of marginalized perspectives play an equally important role in another critical "post"

8. Russian research on various urban texts belongs to this trend, started in the early 1980s by V. N. Toporov. See his *Peterburgskii tekst russkoi literatury: Izbrannye trudy* (St. Petersburg: Iskusstvo-SPB, 2003). The Western dialogue about concepts and uses of geographical space has been strongly shaped by Edward Said, *Orientalism* (New York: Vintage Books, 1979). Benedict Anderson notes the significance of maps for creating a sense of colonial domain in *Imagined Communities: Reflections on the Origin and Spread of Nationalism* (London: Verso, 2002). See also Homi Bhabha, *The Location of Culture* (London: Routledge, 2004); Larry Wolff, *Inventing Eastern Europe: The Map of Civilization on the Mind of the Enlightenment* (Stanford: Stanford University Press, 1994); Valerie Kivelson, *Cartographies of Tsardom: The Land and Its Meanings in Seventeenth-Century Russia* (Ithaca: Cornell University Press, 2006).

9. Edward Said, *Orientalism*, 49–73. See also Susan Layton, "The Creation of an Imaginative Caucasian Geography," *Slavic Review*, 1986, 470–485; S. Layton, *Russian Literature and Empire: Conquest of the Caucasus from Pushkin to Tolstoy* (New York: Cambridge University Press, 1994); Harsha Ram, *The Imperial Sublime: A Russian Poetics of Empire* (Madison: University of Wisconsin Press, 2006).

10. See, for example, Dominic Lieven, *Empire: The Russian Empire and Its Rivals* (London: John Murray, 2000), 130. Lieven speaks in terms of "metropole" and "periphery."

Crisis of Identity

decentering   *opening of marginalized perspectives*

9/20/2022

concept of the late twentieth century—post-communism and the post-Soviet crisis of identity.[11] Center and periphery hold a particular meaning in the case of the dissolution of the Soviet Union on 25 December 1991. At that time the Soviet Union's dominant Russian ethnic group faced its deep-seated obsession of the modern era, its fear of being peripheral to the world's great civilizations and of losing its status as a power center. Between 1989 and 1991, Russians—who controlled the world's largest empire—lost first its central and southeast European satellites, which buffered the Soviet Union from the perceived depredations of Western capitalism, and then its fourteen republics, which provided further territorial protection against the capitalist West and the Muslim south.

As we consider the meaning that center and periphery have for the post-Soviet moment, it is helpful to review their meanings for the other "post" events, postmodernism and postcolonialism.[12] In the *Dismemberment of Orpheus: Toward a Postmodern Literature* (1982) Ihab Hassan first characterized the modern as "centering" and the postmodern as "dispersal." Over the intervening decades the "peripheral" or "marginal" does not just refer to the silenced but has become increasingly associated with the question of renewal and innovation.[13] As postcolonial thought developed, postmodernist criticism also addressed social, ethnic, and gendered "marginalized" voices, as well as the gaps and silences enforced by the center.[14] In postmodernist theory, from their "ex-centric" vantage point, these voices undermine the legitimacy of existing conceptual centralization, totalization, and hierarchy and create a decentered universe of the postmodern, challenging centers of authority, as, for example, in Michel Foucault's notion of linguistic disorder that he calls "heterotopia."[15]

Postcolonial theory has cast the relationship between power and the powerless in geographical terms of center and margin, often aligning with

11. Clowes and Foster, "Interrogating Slavic Identities," 196–203; Vitaly Chernetsky, Nancy Condee, Harsha Ram, and Gayatri Chakravorty Spivak, "Are We Postcolonial?" *PMLA*, 121, no. 1 (May 2006), 828–836.

12. Jean-Francois Lyotard, *The Postmodern Condition: A Report on Knowledge* (Minneapolis: University of Minnesota Press, 1989). Lyotard's declaration of the death of the "Enlightenment metanarrative" of the human condition and his waging "war on totality" announced an era in which the "local" would overtake the universal in importance, implying a new role for decentered space and territory.

13. Ihab Hassan, "Postface 1982: Toward a Concept of Postmodernism," in *The Dismemberment of Orpheus: Toward a Postmodern Literature*, 2nd ed. (Madison: University of Wisconsin Press, 1982), 267–268.

14. Hutcheon, *Poetics of Postmodernism*, 16.

15. Ibid., 12, 57–73; Michel Foucault, *The Order of Things: An Archaeology of the Human Sciences* (New York: Vintage Books, 1973), xviii.

the metaphorical axis between north and south.[16] The center, usually in the northern hemisphere, possesses technology, wealth, political power, and ideology, and it saps the periphery, typically in the south, of its raw materials and its own social order. The colonizing center defines cultural binary opposites of "civilization" and "barbarism," accruing to itself the authority to export its system of values to the colonized periphery.[17] In the late twentieth century this cultural one-way street became more of a two-way street as colonized groups moved to the center for education and work opportunities, and subsequently literary voices from the periphery made themselves heard. In the most optimistic scenario, cultural newness and dynamism emerge from this exchange, while in the worst social inequality and unrest explode at the center.[18]

The postcolonial margin or periphery of an empire, as Homi Bhabha defines it in *The Location of Culture*, gives us one familiar framework within which to understand the post-Soviet problem of the periphery. Bhabha equates margin with the politically disenfranchised citizenry as well as the cultural and economic "outback," which provides cheap raw materials to the center. It is frequently the most impoverished and the least nurtured part of the empire in contrast to the rich, well-educated center, the capital of the empire, which sucks the riches and energy away from the periphery.[19] Bhabha sees in the complex relationship between the colonial center and the colonized periphery forces that are crucial to the identity of the ruling nation in control of empire: the colonialized alien or Other becomes "fetishized" in the nation's identity, giving its citizens a clear sense of belonging, defining themselves against the groups of people who do not belong.[20] Bhabha posits the center as a dynamic place with a history and a future, with large historical purpose, capable of change and development. In contrast, the periphery is posited as a place without history, without an internal dynamic, whose peoples are mired in a relatively "uncivilized" and unchanging set of myths and rituals.

In the postcolonial period, Bhabha suggests, the relationship between periphery and center can become crucial to the process of cultural regeneration. His goal in addressing these opposing geo-cultural spaces is to find a way beyond the opposition through cultural exchange to a different, richer and what he calls "hybrid" form of consciousness that can benefit everyone.

---

16. Homi K. Bhabha, *The Location of Culture*, xi.
17. Ibid., 119.
18. Hutcheon, *Poetics of Postmodernism*, 12; Bhabha, *The Location of Culture*, 10.
19. Bhabha, *The Location of Culture*, xiii–xiv.
20. Ibid., 106.

He counters the traditional, center-driven prejudicial view by suggesting that the periphery is a place rich in stories and "minority discourse" that itself can spur change and regeneration when the people of the center become willing to hear them. The solution that Bhabha proposes to the rift between center and periphery is to publish these minority discourses and open them to the media, making them audible, and retrieve repressed memories that will shed fresh light on the relationship between developed and developing world.[21]

The crucial question for Russia is whether the periphery and its discourses can really provide such a source of cultural regeneration and newness. The founder of Soviet semiotics, Yuri Lotman, who himself functioned for decades on the Baltic Sea periphery, in Tartu, Estonia, gave a positive answer to this question. Working independently of postmodernist and postcolonialist theory, Lotman developed concepts of center and periphery to talk about cultural revitalization.[22] In the volume *Universe of the Mind* (1990), he conceives the two terms as crucial structural components of his overriding concept of the semiosphere, the cultural space in which mere words and things undergo semiosis or the production of meaning. He defines the center as "sections of the semiosphere aspiring to the level of self-description," that articulate normative identity. Over time the central zones "become rigidly organized and self-regulating…at the same time they lose dynamism and, having once exhausted their reserve of indeterminacy, they became inflexible and incapable of further development."[23] In Lotman's view, the weakness of the center lies in its tendency toward self-isolation and inflexibility.

In contrast, Lotman rethinks the periphery as a culturally dynamic space of new growth, altogether different from the politically and economically exploited outlying areas of empire theorized in postcolonial criticism. Here the periphery becomes the zone of ideological challenge and vital creativity, in which outlived dogmas meet resistance and words regain meaning: "On the periphery—and the further one goes from the center, the more noticeable this becomes—the relationship between semiotic practice and the norms imposed on it becomes ever more strained. Texts generated in accordance with these norms hang in the air, without any real semiotic context; while organic creations, born of the actual semiotic milieu, come into conflict with the artificial norms."[24] The periphery, newly defined, becomes the "area of

21. Ibid., 10, 13.
22. Yuri M. Lotman, *Universe of the Mind*, trans. A. Shukman (Bloomington: Indiana University Press, 1990), 134.
23. Ibid.
24. Ibid.

"the peripheral: the area of...

. . . semiotic dynamism," the "field of tension where new languages come into being," and a frontier of "contiguous spheres."[25]

Lotman's thinking parallels in some ways both postcolonial and postmodernist thinking despite the fact that he is operating with the vocabulary of semiotics, uses the idea of the semiosphere to model the dynamics of writing culture, and only implies social and geopolitical relationships. As with the other forms of contemporary cultural theory, Lotman sees the new coming from the periphery, the boundary, the margin and the center as somewhat dependent for its vitality on the periphery. This view, of a piece with both Soviet and international intellectual trends of the 1980s, provides a crucial Russian-language intellectual context for thinking about identity in the early twenty-first century.[26]

The concept of the periphery receives further attention from another leading Soviet-era thinker, the Georgian-Russian philosopher Merab Mamardashvili, whose work had a significant impact on Ryklin and Moscow Conceptualist artists and writers. Moscow-trained, Mamardashvili spent much of his career on various peripheries of the Soviet empire, including Czechoslovakia and Georgia. In 1986 he offered an "Introduction to Philosophy" that was meant to stimulate his Tbilisi University students to look beyond dogmatic Soviet notions of self. In his lectures he described human consciousness with the paradoxical metaphor of a sphere in which the center and periphery are multiple and relative: these centers and peripheries exist locally and in relationship to one another. Mamardashvili wanted to free his Georgian students from the notion that there is one center and everything else is less valuable than that center. He invited them to apprehend non-centralized notions of integrity and to embrace fullness in human existence.[27]

Mamardashvili's mobile concept of centers and peripheries helps us to see the kinds of metaphorical centers of consciousness that have come into being during the difficult post-Soviet years. It allows us to see patterns of symbolic movement of the last Soviet generation of writers and thinkers, people who helped the process of questioning and moving beyond the centralized Soviet

25. Ibid., 134, 136.

26. Ellen Berry and Mikhail Epstein, "How Does Newness Enter the Postmodern World?" in *Transcultural Experiments: Russian and American Models of Creative Communication* (New York: St. Martin's Press, 1999), 145–147. Some Russian scholars in the United States seem unaware of Lotman's and Mamardashvili's concepts of the periphery. Relying on Bhabha, Berry and Epstein argue that real regeneration in the post-Soviet moment can happen "from alternative, previously marginalized or illegitimate perspectives" and from the "intrusion of foreignness."

27. M. K. Mamardashvili, "Vvedenie v filosofiiu," in *Neobkhodimost' sebia* (Moscow: Labirint, 1996), 96, http://psylib.org.ua/books/mamar02/index.htm.

cultural paradigm. This concept anticipated two approaches to the issue of identity that are currently being explored in post-Soviet literary studies: the investigation into the changing center and the search for new voices far away from the center, on the peripheries. While a number of current identity studies are leaning toward the less-heard literary voices on the colonialized periphery, for example, in Ukraine or Georgia, this book examines public discourse about rethinking the center—particularly Moscow and central Russia.[28] It focuses on the periphery and the borderlands as they become part of the cultural and political discourse of the center. Mamardashvili, certainly one of the finest thinkers of the last Soviet generation and mentor to a number of the voices heard here, died in 1990 before the end of the Soviet empire. Still, his odd spatial image of a whole with lots of relative centers and peripheries is one that importantly anticipates those attempting to go beyond the imperial model.

In order to understand the post-Soviet debate about Russian identity we review the distinctive features of center and periphery as they took shape in Russian history. The historical construction of Russian identity differs significantly from that theorized in Western colonial relationships. Moscow as the center has been powerful to a greater or lesser degree for over 500 years (even as the second capital from 1711 to 1918) and has imposed on its peripheries a Russocentric orientation to language, religion, and ideology. The peripheries here is not a separate, economically underdeveloped space accessible only by sea, as it was for Western European colonial empires. Because the Russian empire was a contiguous territory, the periphery could be as close as a rural province in European Russia or as far as the far-flung borderlands of the empire, thousands of kilometers distant. In addition, the Russian empire neighbored with other, sometimes more powerful empires. What makes the Russian situation distinctive is the strength of cultural traditions of neighboring empires that exerted a positive, defining impact on Russian identity. One thinks of Byzantium, the Mongols, and Poland whence Russians absorbed religion, a paradigm for administration, and secular letters, respectively, and then over time annexed those areas—the Black Sea region, Central Asia, East Central Europe—as peripheries of its empire. In short, center and periphery in the Russian case is culturally more complex than it is for Western European centers and their colonized margins. The peripheries are in some cases more cultivated (Greeks, Poles)

28. See, for example, Harsha Ram, "The Sonnet and the Mukhambazi: Genre Wars on the Edges of the Russian Empire," *PMLA,* 122, no. 5 (2007), 1548–1570.

or more organized (Mongols), if not necessarily more civilized, than the Russian center.

Another point that distinguishes the Russian situation from Western centers and their peripheries is the history of Russian nationalism. Without really addressing the question of grassroots Russian national consciousness per se, which developed only in the mid-nineteenth century, Benedict Anderson argues in *Imagined Communities* that the construct of "official nationality," developed in the 1830s, became a tool with which the Romanov dynasty managed their Russian empire.[29] The result is a national consciousness based on pride of state and empire. To expand on Oleh Ilnytzkyi's question, "what is Russia without Ukraine?"—what is modern Russian identity without its imperial peripheries?[30] Since the publication of Anderson's book some have argued that Russian national consciousness is much older, dating to Muscovy and the myth of Moscow the Third Rome, although still others counter that Muscovites identified more with Orthodoxy than with the state.[31] In any case, the center of the Russian empire is quite different from European centers, such as France or Britain, which had been developing a broad national identity and a nation state before they ever had an empire. Certainly one indicator of this oddness is the decision to build a new capital on the western edge of the empire, just to compete with Europe. As the historian V. O. Kliuchevsky allegedly put it, "In Russia the center is on the periphery."[32] The argument can be made that without its peripheries Russia runs the risk of confronting its own qualities as a cultural periphery.

As national consciousness started to emerge, temporal insecurity and anxiety dominated the spatial anxiety we posit for the post-Soviet moment. At least since Chaadaev's 1836 "Philosophical Letter," Russians have worried that they lacked national dignity because they lacked a true national history.

---

29. Anderson, 83–88. For a concise discussion of national identity and empire, see Ronald G. Suny, "The Empire Strikes Out: Imperial Russia, 'National' Identity, and Theories of Empire," in *A State of Nations: Empire and Nation-Making in the Age of Lenin and Stalin,* ed. R. G. Suny and R. Martin (Oxford: Oxford University Press, 2001), 23–66.

30. Oleh S. Ilnytzkyi, "Modeling Culture in the Empire: Ukrainian Modernism and the Death of the All-Russian Idea," in *Culture, Nation and Identity: The Russian-Ukrainian Encounter (1600–1945),* ed. Andreas Kappeler, Zenon E. Kohut, Frank E. Sysyn, and Mark von Hagen (Edmonton: Canadian Institute of Ukrainian Studies, 2003), 298–324.

31. For the first view, see Geoffrey Hosking, "The Russian National Myth Repudiated," in *Nation and Myth,* ed. G. Hosking and G. Schöpflin (New York: Routledge, 1997), 198–210. For the second view, see Daniel Rowland, "Moscow—the Third Rome or the New Israel?" op. cit., pp. 591–614. The latter view is supported in Willard Sunderland, *Taming the Wild Field: Colonization and Empire on the Russian Steppe* (Ithaca: Cornell University Press, 2004), 19–21, 39.

32. "V Rossii tsentr na periferii," ascribed to Kliuchevskii, quoted in Andrei Fadin, *Tretii Rim v tret'em mire* (Moscow: Letnii sad, 1999), 212.

To the shock of most of his contemporaries Chaadaev wrote: "We do not belong to any of the great families of the human race; we are neither of the West nor of the East, and we have not the traditions of either. Placed, as it were, outside of time, we have not been touched by the universal education of the human race."[33] The consciousness that Russia lacked a linear, progressive history was a driving force in Russian thought until the late Soviet era—sometimes, as with Chaadaev, viewed as an insurmountable weakness and sometimes, as allegedly with Lenin, transformed into an advantage, allowing a backward, undeveloped Russia to spring ahead of other, more advanced nations.

Finally, Russians differ from dominant ethnic groups in other imperial centers to the west and to the east in their ambiguous social and cultural position as both colonizers and colonized. Although Europeans never actively colonized Russia per se, the modern Russian state from Peter the Great on imported European technology, manufacturing, education, and customs to render the appearance and behavior of its populace more Western and secular. This process began with the nobility, the military, and the bureaucracy, moving slowly over two centuries to the merchantry, and eventually to the peasantry. It might be said that the Russian state colonized its own subjects. To cite Chaadaev again: "on one occasion a great man [Peter the Great] sought to civilize us; and, in order to give us a foretaste of enlightenment, he flung us the mantle of civilization; we picked up the mantle, but we did not touch civilization itself.... There is something in our blood that resists all real progress."[34]

More than a hundred years after Peter's reforms, Chaadaev's voice sounds amazingly like postcolonial voices of today. His was the conscious native voice, reflecting on the situation and castigating his people, as being "like illegitimate children, without a heritage, without any ties binding us to the men who came before us on this earth." Indeed, Chaadaev's words eerily anticipate Julia Kristeva's image of the postcolonial condition when he asserted, "we Russians" are "strangers to ourselves."[35] In addition, his "Philosophical Letter" sets up something similar to the axis that Bhabha sees in colonial discourse between the historical dynamism of the colonizers and the stasis of the colonized. Chaadaev admired the historical depth of European

33. Petr Chaadaev, "Letters on the Philosophy of History: First Letter," in *Russian Intellectual History: An Anthology,* ed. and trans. M. Raeff (New York: Harcourt, Brace, and World, 1966), 162.

34. Ibid., 167.

35. Ibid., 164. Kristeva is a Kulturtraeger between Eastern and Western Europe, and her book *Strangers to Ourselves* may easily have taken its title not from Camus's novel, *L'Etranger,* but from Chaadaev's essay.

cultures and bemoaned the hapless vacuity and isolation of Russian life. Bhabha is critical of the colonizers; Chaadaev was critical of his own people, "colonized" as they were by their own state but too unselfconscious and too unwilling to grow and change.

Thus, many thinking Russians in the early nineteenth and in the late twentieth century suffered from a sense of inferiority concerning their own cultural adequacy vis-à-vis the European world. This state of affairs produces the suspicion in the Russian intellectual elite that their center is itself a kind of cultural periphery. As a historical latecomer to modernity and to the condition of being a center, this particular center has struggled to assert itself as such, if not through a deep history then through a vision of the future.

Although in the post-Soviet era the notions of center and periphery refer to the geopolitical realia of empire, in a cultural and psychological sense they strike at the very heart of Russia's—and particularly Moscow's—greatest historical fear of being nothing more than a hinterland of the world's older and richer empires to the east, the west, and the south. The story is familiar. Historically the East Slavs were on the northern edges of the Byzantine empire, from which they adopted Christianity. They were at the western edge of the Mongol empire. Through deft diplomacy and royal intermarriage and by appropriating structures of Mongol soldiering and administration, Muscovy eventually conquered rival Russian principalities and appropriated many northern territories of the Mongol empire. By adopting Eastern Orthodoxy and, after 1453, standing as the one independent Orthodox Christian state, in which a number of prominent Greeks and Southern Slavs took refuge, Moscow started to view itself as something of a center. By the early sixteenth century, when it had forcefully gathered the Russian lands under its governance, it had also assumed the ideological and symbolic trappings of empire, thus making the translatio imperii to the familiar Moscow the Third Rome conceivable.[36]

In the modern period the axis of Russian identity was redefined through its rivalry with the West, first Europe and then with the United States. This east-west axis is a construct of Russian modernity, a three-hundred-year span during which Russian national identity has become divided, complex, and highly interesting. The discourse of modern national selfhood grew from Peter's violent wresting of power from Moscow and construction of a new modern, Westernized capital, St. Petersburg, on the empire's western periphery.

36. See Michael Cherniavsky, *Tsar and People: Studies in Russian Myths* (New Haven: Yale University Press, 1961), 36–39.

The east-west orientation of Russian identity participates in a Western discourse that is fundamentally about time and history. Geographical images mark the historical progression from barbarism to civilization on a symbolic map stressing the poles respectively of East (especially Eastern Europe, symbolizing barbarism) and West (especially Western Europe, symbolizing civilization).[37] In the nineteenth century even the Slavophiles, the most Russocentric of Russian thinkers, defined themselves in terms of Europe. Even when they were resisting the European terms of the enlightenment and capitalist industrialization, they were adopting and adapting Western learning, art, technology, and the trappings of Western material culture to their own purposes.

Toward the end of the tsarist regime, the East and Asia loomed ever larger in Russian intellectual discourse. In contrast to Russian writing culture of the mid-nineteenth century, which identified Russia with the West and Europe, in the late nineteenth and twentieth centuries one finds an increasing exploration of the positive aspects of Russia's Asian heritage. Although Chaadaev recognized China as a great civilization and Japan as a viable nation, "civilized without being civilized in the European way," he still saw Europe as offering the genuine path to the future—because of its Christian heritage; the rest are "absurd aberrations of divine and human truths."[38] Until the rise of Japan in the late nineteenth century Russian interest in Asian cultures was typically channeled through Western sources. For example, Lev Tolstoy's intense interest in China, Confucianism, and Buddhism sprang largely from European writing on Asia.[39] On the occasion of General Skobelev's victory over the Turkmen army in January 1881, Fyodor Dostoevsky wrote in *A Writer's Diary*: "speaking generally, our whole Russian Asia, including Siberia, still exists as a kind of appendage, as it were, in which our European Russia seems reluctant to take any interest."[40] In contrast, Dostoevsky offered the opinion that Russia indeed has a place in Asia because the "Russian is not only a European but an Asian as well" and "it is Asia, perhaps, that provides the main outlet for our future destiny!"[41]

In the 1890s the Eurocentric philosopher and poet Vladimir Solovyov feared Asia as the source of barbaric "pan-Mongolism." His poems, "Ex Oriente Lux" (1890) and "Pan-Mongolism" (1894), predicted the apocalyptic

37. Larry Wolff, *Inventing Eastern Europe*, 4.
38. Chaadaev, "Letters on the Philosophy of History," 169.
39. Derk Bodde, *Tolstoy and China* (Princeton: Princeton University Press, 1950), 13–26.
40. Fyodor Dostoevsky, *A Writer's Diary*, Vol. 2: *1877–1881*, trans. K. Lantz (Evanston, IL: Northwestern University Press, 1994), 1368.
41. Ibid., 1369.

end of Russian-European civilization.[42] Just as Asiatic infidels had destroyed Constantinople in 1453, so pan-Mongolism would now overtake Russia. In his final work, "A Short Narrative on the Antichrist" in *Three Conversations* (1900), Solovyov quoted from his poem. He suggested that the Asian horde was a sign of the Antichrist and the Apocalypse and claimed that pan-Mongolism as a super-national movement would cause many wars in the coming century.[43] As an example, well before the Russo-Japanese War, Solovyov cited the Japanese as an aggressive military force to be reckoned with.[44]

Mention of Russia's positive association with Asia and identification of Russia's Asian qualities came, ironically, after the defeat of Russia by Japan in 1904–1905.[45] During the last years of World War I and the first years after the 1917 Bolshevik revolution, Russian literature and the arts saw a lively debate about the east-west terms of Russian identity, for example, in the novels of Andrei Belyi and in the shamanistic art of the young Vasily Kandinsky. The Scythian movement, led by major writers such as Aleksandr Blok and Evgeny Zamiatin, embraced Russia's Asian "subconscious." Russia, in this view, was partly European and partly Asian. Equating Asia with the ancient Scythian horse culture of the steppe Blok and Zamiatin associated the image of "Asia" with an unobstructed, anarchic freedom.[46] Russians, they held, enjoyed a much broader view of reality and wider vistas for their creative impulse—all of which, they hoped, would be threatening to the more self-contained, self-deluding Westerners.

The negative attitude toward the Asiatic strain in the Russian national character continued. In the first months after the 1917 revolution, one of the most popular of radical writers, Maksim Gorky, expressed deep misgivings about what he called the "Asiatic" side of the Russian character that he saw expressed in the excesses of revolution. Writing in an essay for the independent socialist newspaper *Novaia zhizn'*, Gorky called Russians "anarchists by nature," "cruel beasts," in whose veins flow "the dark and evil blood of

42. Note that Viktor Pelevin misquotes "Ex Oriente Lux" in *Chapaev i Pustota* (Moscow: Vagrius, 2000), 286.

43. Vladimir Solov' ev, "Kratkaia povest' ob Antikhriste," in *Chteniia o Bogochelovechestve; stat'i; stikhotvoreniia i poema; Iz 'Trekh razgovorov': Kratkaia povest' ob Antikhriste* (St. Petersburg: Khudozhestvennaia literatura, 1994), 459.

44. Ibid., 462.

45. For extended treatments of Russia and Asia, see Wayne Vucinich, *Russia and Asia* (Stanford: Hoover Institution Press, 1972); David Christian, *A History of Russia, Central Asia, and Mongolia* (Oxford: Blackwell, 1998).

46. Zamiatin, "Skify" (1918), translated into English as "Scythians," in *A Soviet Heretic*, trans. M. Ginsburg (Chicago: University of Chicago Press, 1970), 21–33. See also Aleksandr Blok, "Skify," (in *Sobranie sochinenii v 8-i tomakh* (Moscow-Leningrad: GIKhL, 1960), vol. 3, 360–362.

slaves, the poisonous inheritance of the Tartars and of serfdom."[47] Drawing on all the usual clichés, he claimed that Russia was founded on "Asiatic
inertness" and "Oriental passivity," and that Russians had too long "lived
by ancient Asiatic cunning," which cannot ultimately be conquered by "the
calm iron will of organized reason."[48] In order to overcome their dark, oppressive history, Gorky insisted, Russians must accept retribution "for our
Asiatic stagnation, for the submissiveness with which we bore oppression"
by the police and the bureaucracy.[49]

In émigré circles throughout the 1920s and 1930s discussion of Russia's
identity continued to be couched in terms of its relationship to Asia and
Europe. The Eurasianists, led by the philologist Nikolai Trubetskoi, the
philosopher Lev Karsavin, and the economist Petr Savitsky, were the first
public figures after Blok and Zamiatin to "cut the Gordian knot of Russia's
schizophrenic position between Europe and Asia."[50] They pictured Russia
as a bridge between Europe, by which they meant the colonizers, and Asia,
which symbolized the colonized peoples of the world. Because of its middle
position between the two continents and the two economic spheres, Russia
should serve as a natural leader following World War I, when colonized
non-Europeans were for the first time gaining an audible voice on the international stage. The Eurasian state, in Trubetskoi's view, would replace the
Russian empire but without its Russocentric ideology, building on a new
basis of multicultural governance.[51]

The Eurasian debate reemerged in the Soviet underground of the 1960s
and deepened in the 1990s. First in his novel *Cancer Ward* (1968) and later
in his samizdat volume of articles, *From under the Rubble* (1974), Aleksandr Solzhenitsyn revived the idea of a Slavic commonwealth that spanned
Europe and Asia. In his provocative tract from the glasnost era—"How

47. Maksim Gorky, *Untimely Thoughts,* trans. H. Ermolaev (New Haven: Yale University
Press, 1995), 173.
48. Ibid., 189–190.
49. Ibid., 173.
50. See Monica Spiridon, "Identity Discourses on Borders in Eastern Europe," *Comparative
Literature* 58, no. 4 (2006), 379: "to quote Mark Bassin: 'the Eurasians may be credited with
having cut the Gordian knot of Russia's schizophrenic position between Europe and Asia.'"
51. See Mark Bassin, "Classical Eurasianism and the Geopolitics of Russian Identity,"
www.dartmouth.edu/~crn/crn_papers/Bassin.pd, 9–10; see also his "Russia Between Europe
and Asia: The Ideological Construction of Geography," *Slavic Review* 50, no. 1 (1991), 1–17;
and *Imperial Visions: Nationalist Imagination and Geographical Expansion in the Russian Far
East, 1840–1865* (New York: Cambridge University Press, 1999); Nicholas V. Riasanovsky,
"The Emergence of Eurasianism," *California Slavic Studies* 4 (1967), 39–74; Otto Boess, *Die
Lehre der Eurasier: ein Beitrag zur russischen Ideengeschichte des 20. Jahrhunderts* (Wies-
baden: O. Harrassowitz, 1961); Sergei Khoruzhii, *Posle pereryva: puti russkoi filosofii (Ucheb-
noe posobie).* Series Nashi sovremenniki (St. Petersburg: Aleteia, 1994), 158–167.

Should We Restructure Russia?"—Solzhenitsyn further developed his idea of an east Slavic realm that would also embrace parts of Central Asia, particularly Kazakhstan.[52] Such neo-nationalist thinkers as Lev Gumilev (1912–1992) and in the post-Soviet period Aleksandr Dugin articulated a distinctively Russocentric idea of Eurasianism.

Recently the Asia of the mind has been reinvented in a number of films and literary works and criticism in the 1990s. Perhaps the best known is the 1991 film directed by Nikita Mikhalkov and Rustam Ibragimbekov, *Urga: Close to Eden*. Here Mongolia with its unbroken nomadic traditions emerges as more primitive but also more vital than Russia or China, which it borders. Sergei Bodrov's 2007 film *Mongol*, planned as the first film in a trilogy, deals with the early years of Genghis Khan's life. In contemporary literature, Marina Kanevskaia examines three contemporary novels, including *Chapaev and the Void*, that exhibit other aspects of what she calls an ironic *vostochnost'* or "zone of non-understanding" [*zona neponimaniia*] of the 1990s. While *Chapaev and the Void* is a serious expression of Pelevin's views, Valery Zalotukha's *The Liberation of India* (*Velikii pokhod za osvobozhdenie Indii*, 1995) and Dmitry Lipskerov's novel *Forty Years of Chanchzhoe* (*Sorok let Chanchzhoe*, 1996) playfully ironize the "eastern" fad of the 1970s and 1980s.[53]

Among the problems complicating post-Soviet Russian identity are the following oppositions—empire versus nation, first world versus third world, east-west axis versus north-south axis. The first is the issue of empire. To Ryklin, identification with empire has obliterated the conversation about a healthy national identity.[54] There are two issues at hand here—one is spatial and the other temporal. Russians have long been proud of the size of their territory, proud that the Soviet Union was and Russia still is the largest country on earth.[55] Watching their buffer zones melt away and being asked and sometimes forced to leave what used to be Soviet territory has been most painful, perhaps particularly so because of the contiguous relation of Russia to its colonized republics.

---

52. Aleksandr Solzhenitsyn, "Kak nam obustroit' Rossiiu?" *Literaturnaia gazeta*, 18 September 1990. At the end of Pelevin's *Chapaev and the Void*, after Petr's exit from the mental hospital, a Solzhenitsyn/Tolstoy figure in the form of a taxi-driver speaks in Solzhenitsyn's terms of needing to "reconstruct" or "*obustroit'*" Russia (402).

53. M. Kanevskaia, "Istoriia i Mif v postmodernistskom russkom romane," *Izvestiia RAN. Seriia literatury i iazyka*, 59, no. 2 (2000), 42.

54. Ryklin, *Vremia diagnoza*, 21, 102.

55. See, for example, Walter Benjamin's description of Russians' love of maps in *Moscow Diary*, ed. G. Smith, trans. R. Sieburth (Cambridge, MA: Harvard University Press, 1986), 50–51; Kivelson, *Cartographies of Tsardom*.

Since 1991 Russians have been thrown back on their own resources, pushed back to the still-spacious boundaries of the Russian Republic. Along with the east-west axis of authority there has emerged another axis of economic power, linking Russia to two of the imagined geographies of European colonialism, the north-south axis and, alternatively, the images of "first world" and "third world." In the early 1990s, as the Soviet economic order collapsed and Russian cities became dumping grounds for imported goods from capitalist countries, one frequently heard the fear expressed that Russia was little more than a "banana republic," a new colony supplying raw materials, in this case largely oil to the developed capitalist economies of the world. Sergei Romashko, writing in 1997, focused on Russia's fundamentally peripheral nature: "In our time it has not only become extremely clear, but, still more important, directly, painfully palpable, how very fragile that delicate construction is which we call civilization. This is especially true for us in Russia, which has remained, as in the first centuries of its existence, a peripheral country [*pogranichnaia strana*], a province [*krai*], as if hanging above the Eurasian steppes."[56] The social commentator Andrei Fadin talks about the inherent process of "third-world-ization" [*tret'emirizatsiia*] of Russia, against which most ordinary Soviet people rebelled and continue to rebel.[57] Fadin identifies a serious problem in the "deep ideological vacuum," which saps people of their motivation to work, to do positive things, save money, and build a life.[58] This shift from the relatively protected second world down the hierarchy of wealth and power to the third world ironically put Russians—among the northernmost people of the world—in the position of an impoverished, exploited (southern) colony with relation to its imagined (northern) colonizers.

Writing culture of the post-Soviet period features a vital debate about identity that merits the attention of the rest of the world. Ours is a time when it is easy to believe that the only thing that happened in Putin's Russia is the reestablishment of the police state and the return to the bad old times, now under a nationalist neo-imperialist guise. In the terms of this study the Putin-Medvedev government has strived to re-erect the old walls between the center and its peripheries. Other thoughtful voices would concur with critics as diverse as Julia Kristeva and Homi Bhabha who assert that in the postmodern, postcolonial world there are no more simple centers and

---

56. Sergei Romashko, "O Nine Sadur i ee knige," in *Sad* (Vologda: Poligrafist, 1997), 6. It is worth noting that the Russian word for periphery, *krai*, also means "edge," once again suggesting anxiety at no longer being a center.
57. Fadin, *Tretii Rim*, 90.
58. Ibid., 96.

peripheries. As Bhabha puts it: "The 'locality' of national culture is neither unified nor unitary in relation to itself, nor must it be seen simply as 'other' in relation to what is outside or beyond it. The boundary is Janus-faced and the problem of outside/inside must always itself be a process of hybridity, incorporating new 'people' in relation to the body politic, generating other sites of meaning."[59] Instead of just saving the center for people who look a certain way, speak a certain standard of Russian, and profess to believe in an ossified form of Orthodox Christianity, these voices take as a more productive goal the rich possibilities for creative interaction between the center and the periphery.

59. Homi Bhabha, *Nation and Narration*, 4.

1 DECONSTRUCTING IMPERIAL MOSCOW

> Look, Orlov, since we don't live forever,
> It would be a shame to miscalculate
> That you and I live at the edge of the world
> And that somewhere out there really is Moscow
> With its gulfs, lagoons, mountains
> With its events of global import
> And its Muscovites, proud of themselves
> But no, Moscow is where you and I are standing
> Moscow will abide where we tell it to
> The real Moscow is wherever we put it!
> That is—in Moscow.
> —DMITRY PRIGOV, *Moscow and Muscovites* (1982)

CREATIVE moments in the lives of the world's major cities often come during times of identity crisis. Even before the return of Soviet Russia's capital to Moscow in March 1918, the imperial Russian capital, St. Petersburg, experienced a crisis of identity—it had always been, as the great historian V. O. Kliuchevskii allegedly remarked, the "center on the periphery."[1] In his path-breaking novel *Petersburg* (1916), Andrei Belyi brought to the surface the fissures in identity that had been widening throughout the nineteenth century—Asia versus Europe, center versus periphery, Mongol versus Slav, revolutionary versus bureaucrat. In Belyi's rendition, St. Petersburg as center is full of borders and rifts that render it dysfunctional. New life would open up, the novel's young characters dreamed, through detonating a bomb and assassinating a highly placed government bureaucrat in whom these divisions were personified. In another famous novel, Evgeny Zamiatin's *We*, written during the Russian Civil War, the dystopian One-State—based in part on Andrei Belyi's novelistic portrait of Petersburg and the realia of revolutionary Petrograd—is depicted as a center that has walled itself off from its periphery and has the most repressive relationship to that periphery.[2] By the 1960s and 1970s when Andrei Bitov wrote his experimental novel

---

1. Quoted in Andrei Fadin, *Tretii Rim v tret'em mire* (Moscow: Letnii sad, 1999), 212.
2. Robert Maguire and John Malmstad, "The Legacy of *Petersburg*: Zamiatin's *We*," in *The Silver Age in Russian Literature*, ed. J. Ellsworth (New York: St. Martin's Press, 1992), 182–195.

Pushkin House (1978), the old capital had become a moribund, former center on the periphery, now a city-museum, stunning but fixed in time, and surrounded by a wasteland of crumbling, prefabricated Soviet apartment houses.

Like St. Petersburg in the early twentieth century, Moscow of the late twentieth century experienced an identity crisis, and along with it a creative surge. Starting in the 1980s Moscow, the Soviet capital and imperial hub of the communist universe, the so-called second world, was a center starting to worry about its increasingly peripheral nature. The deconstruction of Moscow myth—Muscovite, Soviet, and otherwise—was becoming prominent as both a literary and a critical theme. This chapter investigates this literary and critical deconstruction of Moscow, which opened the dialogue about Russian identity.

Historically, in contrast to St. Petersburg, Moscow has rarely suffered a debilitating crisis of identity. Since its founding in 1147 it gladly played the role of the upstart, the youngest, the most dynamic, and aggressively militant of Russian cities. In the early sixteenth century Muscovite propaganda arrogated to Moscow the position of inheritor of the recently fallen Constantinople and the center of the Eastern Orthodox world. Even when Peter the Great moved the imperial capital to St. Petersburg in 1712, Moscow remained the capital closest to Russian hearts and, with the founding of Moscow University in 1755, the intellectual center of Russia. By the 1830s it had become the home base for Russia's nationalist Slavophiles, bent on preserving distinctive qualities of Russian history and culture against the incursions of Peter's and Catherine's Westernization.[3]

The current crisis of identity arose in the late-Soviet literary and critical resistance to the city of Moscow as a people-crushing imperial center, following the Soviet invasion of Czechoslovakia in August 1968 and the subsequent repression of the Czechoslovak experiment in liberal socialism, the Prague Spring. The invasion marked the end of the post-Stalinist wave of utopian hopes. Rethinking Moscow played out in variations on two utopian themes—the myth of the insular community and the Atlantis myth of the lost, sunken city.

One approach to rethinking Moscow can be found in late- and post-Soviet satires portraying the center as an island unto itself possessed of remarkable centripetal force, which blocks relations with the periphery. The first example is Venedikt Erofeev's brilliantly playful 1969 novella *Moscow-Petushki* (*Moskva-Petushki*), written directly after the Soviets crushed the

---

3. Nikolai Gogol', "Peterburgskie zapiski 1836 goda," *Sobranie sochinenii v 6-i tomakh*, vol. 6 (Moscow: GIKhL, 1953), 107–108.

Prague Spring.[4] Russia's premier satirist Vladimir Voinovich, working in exile, framed his hilarious futuristic spoof *Moscow 2042* (*Moskva 2042*) in 1982, the year of Leonid Brezhnev's death.[5] Most recently the island/isolation motif combines with the motif of the hidden city in Tatiana Tolstaia's postmodernist utopian parody, *Slynx* (*Kys'*, 2000).[6] Instead of dealing with the oppressive imperial overlay in Moscow, as the "sunken city" works do, these works focus on the issue of the center's self-isolation from all peripheries and neighbors and its subsequent degradation.

The Atlantis myth builds on a concept of the psychologically or politically repressed, the forgotten, and the authentic. It often appears as the image of a hidden community, in some way remembered and revealed, which undermines the oppressive center, exposing its inauthenticity. I take this image of the "sunken Atlantis" from Galina Belaia's series of conversations and essays published in *Ogonek* in 1991 under that title.[7] The sunken city motif emerges in 1982, in the cycle *Moscow and Muscovites* (*Moskva i moskvichi*) by the Moscow Conceptualist artist and poet Dmitry Prigov (1940–2007). Around 1990 it reappears in the cultural criticism of the deconstructionist philosopher Mikhail Ryklin, particularly in his seminal essay on the Moscow metro, "Bodies of Terror" (1990).[8] Near the same time Viktor Pelevin in his 1991 story "Vera Pavlovna's Ninth Dream" (*Deviatyi son Very Pavlovny*), gives the motif another twist, combining it with the biblical myth of the flood. In all these works what is underground, hidden, or sunken becomes an important challenge to the outer and visible signs of empire above ground.

As a center, Moscow differs from concepts of the center in postmodern and postcolonial theory. Paradoxically—since it is geographically contiguous with its peripheries—Moscow is relatively disconnected from its hinterlands. It stands out because of its disconnectedness from its peripheries. In this way it resembles the utopian and dystopian traditions of the island or insular city that we find, for example, in Thomas Moore's island of *Utopia,* Campanella's seven-walled city on a hill in *City of the Sun,* Nikolai

---

4. Venedikt Erofeev, *Moskva-Petushki* (Paris: YMCA, 1971). Translated into English as *Moscow to the End of the Line,* trans. H. W. Tjalsma (Evanston, IL: Northwestern University Press, 1997).

5. Vladimir Voinovich, *Moskva 2042* (Ann Arbor: Ardis, 1987). Translated into English as *Moscow 2042,* trans. R. Lourie (New York: Harcourt Brace, 1990).

6. Tat'iana Tolstaia, *Kys'* (Moscow: Podkovka Inostranka, 2001). Translated into English as *Slynx,* trans. J. Gambrell (Boston: Houghton-Mifflin, 2003).

7. Galina Belaia, "Zatonuvshaia Atlantida," *Biblioteka Ogonek,* no. 14 (Moscow: Ogonek, 1991).

8. Mikhail Ryklin, "Bodies of Terror: Theses toward a Logic of Violence," *New Literary History,* 24 (1993), 51–74.

Chernyshevsky's glass and aluminum palace in *What Is To Be Done?*, and Zamiatin's glass-walled city in *We*. At other moments it resembles an encircled camp. The "metautopian" experimental fiction of the last three decades of the Soviet period—to which Erofeev and Voinovich contributed—did a great deal conceptually to break apart the closed, fixed utopian borders of the Soviet state and to open up this "utopian" zone of fixed thinking to the fluidity of other perspectives and alternatives.[9]

It is important to point out that the two late-Soviet works that begin the process of deconstructing Moscow as a self-isolating city, spinning in its own sphere, are written from an "eccentric" perspective, by émigrés who were looking in at the center from the outside. The internal émigré, Venedikt Erofeev, and the more usual kind of émigré, Vladimir Voinovich, both view the totalitarian center from the periphery and focus on the overwhelming centripetal force of the center that allows for no real periphery or, at most, just the fantasy of a periphery, which is ultimately smashed.

The drunken narrator of *Moscow-Petushki*, Venichka, tries to escape Moscow, the Kremlin, and its oppressive ideology, to Petushki. Although a real town outside Moscow, Petushki represents for Venichka a private, pleasurable land of Cockaigne. He imagines taking the suburban commuter train (*elektrichka*), only to realize at the end that he never left the Kursk Station in Moscow. In the last four chapters settings in Petushki overlap with familiar locations in Moscow—Kursk Station Square, the Garden Ring, and finally the Kremlin. In distinction to the "progress" or journey on which it is loosely modeled, Aleksandr Radishchev's eighteenth-century *Journey from St. Petersburg to Moscow*, there is no "progress"; there is only a mental journey that ends up in the same place it started. At the end Venichka imagines his own death, like Evgeny in Aleksandr Pushkin's poem, "The Bronze Horseman," chased down by the twentieth-century equivalent of the Bronze Horseman, Vera Mukhina's 1937 statue of "The Worker and the Collective Farmer."[10] Absurdly, given that he has just died, he manages to write about the moment of his death.

Moscow in this work is a space of squalorous liquor stores and dark, dirty stairwells, a city inhabited by the dark shadows of thuggish policemen

---

9. For a full treatment of the term meta-utopia as it applies to late-Soviet underground fiction, see my *Russian Experimental Fiction: Resisting Ideology after Utopia* (Princeton: Princeton University Press, 1993). For a discussion of *Moscow-Petushki* and *Moscow 2042*, see especially, 46–68, 79–82, 132–140, 192–197.

10. It is probably no coincidence that Erofeev, as author of the foundational work of the late twentieth-century Moscow text, emphasizing Moscow as a centripetal force without a serious peripheral counterbalance, alludes to the foundational work of the "Petersburg text," Pushkin's "Bronze Horseman." One might even see here, however ironically, an intentional *translatio imperii*, or at least a transferal of the imperial city text.

and dominated by a powerful nerve center—the Kremlin. Venichka claims never to have seen the Kremlin; when he goes in search of it, he ends up at Kursk Station, which opens the way to his imagined escape from Moscow's centripetal force to his own private utopia in the village of Petushki. At the end, confused by the impression that his destination of Petushki looks suspiciously like familiar parts of Moscow, Venichka finally arrives at the Kremlin, even as he is being chased and beaten by thugs. There is no escape.

In Voinovich's novel *Moscow 2042*, Moscow is an isolated enclave, walled off from everywhere, even its suburbs; nominally ruled by a despot; and entertaining false pretensions to being cutting-edge and high-tech. The protagonist and first-person narrator Vitaly Kartsev, who has been living in emigration in Munich for several years, time travels in 1982 to Moscow sixty years hence in order to do research for a science-fiction novel he is planning about the future Moscow. Arriving in the Moscow of 2042, he finds a foul, dirty city, masked by a healthy dose of self-delusion. Although everything is built of plastic and cardboard and food is made of excrement, citizens believe that they are living in an advanced society. This future Moscow is built around three ring roads known as the "Communist Rings" or "KK" (*Kol'tsa Kommunizma*), which resemble the three ring roads familiar in present-day Moscow. To go across each ring requires a special visa. The further one gets from the small inner sanctum inside what we know as the Boulevard Ring, the more unbearable life becomes.

It is significant that *Moscow 2042* marks the shift in the conceptualization of identity from temporal categories to spatial, territorial ones. Here, as in many postmodernist works, the interaction of history, time, and power becomes the object of parody. Control over Moscow's isolation extends beyond physical barriers to temporal barriers. Deliberately planning (or having planned, depending on one's temporal perspective) his science-fiction novel to end with the fall of the regime current in 2042, Kartsev finds himself being strongly pressed during his time-travel visit to alter his version of history. Incongruously, Moscow's 2042 rulers already have the published version of the book that Kartsev has come to "research" and insist that he change the ending so that their "utopia" will not be invaded by a Solzhenitsyn-like, underground leader, Karnavalov. Even through time these rulers absurdly attempt to hold writers, even exiled writers, under control and to preserve Moscow's independence and isolation.

The point in both of these tales is that Moscow as a centripetal force has isolated itself in three ways: ideologically, through its closed, single-minded leadership; physically, through building walls and barriers; and temporally, by controlling the narrative about its history. Moscow is so powerful vis-à-vis its periphery that it sucks in everything around it to its center, leaving the periphery all but non-existent, even in the minds of those attempting to escape it or change it. There is no place to escape.

⤚

The sunken or hidden city theme in Dmitry Prigov's *Moscow and Muscovites* hints at the opposition of the hidden "imagined community" of thinking, creative people and the visible "imperial" city with its stone monuments and buildings and ubiquitous police force. *Moscow and Muscovites* plays with the myths underlying what cultural historians now call the "Moscow text," that complex of city mapping, history, creative images, interpretations, and narratives that give the city its particular identity.[11] In a brief prose foreword the poet mock-seriously states his immodest culturological goals: "This book undertakes to lay the methodological groundwork for the study of the Moscow theme through poetic media in correlation with the historiosophical concepts of our time" (I, 28).[12] That this preface is a parody becomes clear in the sentence immediately following: "Like any first effort, it is completely possible that it will almost immediately become an anachronism." Just as St. Petersburg has its weighty academic studies linking the city's history, topography, and high cultural production to its mythic narratives, now Moscow will have a most engaging satire on late Soviet mentalities and attitudes. The poems themselves are voice-masks—sometimes the banter of the poet with his good friend, Orlov, and sometimes the defensive self-justifications of ideologues of various political and cultural stripes. With these voice-masks Prigov makes light of Moscow's load-bearing narratives and symbols of identity, which constitute the city's "mystique" (*mistika Moskvy*).

At the core of Prigov's cycle is the conflict between the image of Moscow as imperial capital with its stone monuments and state institutions and Moscow as a community of thinking, creative individuals. Here we encounter a defining contrast between translatio imperii from St. Petersburg back to Moscow—characterized by images of empire that carry both Byzantine and Central Asian/Mongol overtones—and the poet's insistence on the personal

11. "'Moskovskii tekst' russkoi kul'tury," in *Lotmanovskii sbornik,* vol. 2 (Moscow: Russian Humanities University (RGGU) Press, 1997), 481–835; G. S. Knabe, ed., *Moskva i "moskovskii tekst" russkoi kul'tury: Sbornik statei* (Moscow: Russian Humanities University (RGGU) Press, 1998). For a limited introduction in English to the concept of the "Moscow text" see, for example, Ian K. Lilly, ed., *Moscow and Petersburg: The City in Russian Culture* (Nottingham: Astra Press, 2002); Ian K. Lilly, "Conviviality in the Pre-Revolutionary 'Moscow Text' of Russian Culture," *Russian Review,* 63 (July, 2004), 427–448. Prigov's cycle echoes the popular book with the same title by V. A. Giliarovskii, written in 1926. Giliarovskii's goal was to describe old Moscow even as it was disappearing under Soviet bulldozers.

12. Dmitrii Prigov, *Izbrannye* (Moscow: Eksmo, 2002), 28. Citations to this book are given in the text, using the notation "I" and page number(s).

definition of Moscow as a place of the heart and the mind.[13] In its imperial hypostasis Moscow is full of heavy monuments to its own power. It is conceived as a mythical heaven, the imperial hub, from which its inhabitants look at the earth of the rest of the empire. In contrast, there is the idea of a mobile, hidden Moscow made up of people who create a Moscow for themselves. The cycle consists of twenty-three poems divided into three parts. The first seven poems play with originary myths of Moscow power and the nation. Poems in the second group explore the interaction of person and city, and the third group asserts the poet's agency in recreating this city.

After asking the question about the Moscow mystique in the first poem, Prigov continues his Moscow cycle with six more poems that point to key features of Moscow mythology. The second poem, "My Ancient Moscow Is Splendid," brings to bear the twin imperial heritage—the Byzantine and the Mongol—upon which Moscow originally designed its military, political, and religious bid for power. It sets the stage in the streets of Moscow, on which are blended images of north and south; the sands of southern, Central Asian deserts swirl in Moscow's streets and the snowy northern air blows them around. There ensues a mock battle between two symbols of empire— the eagle with the porphyry-bearing wings of the Byzantine empire and the snow leopard of Central Asian mountains, which to this day is a symbol of numerous Central Asian cities, as well as the Tatar Autonomous Republic. Muscovites, now merely passive spectators, cheer on the victor. In Prigov's patently absurdist style it remains unclear which imperial animal will take the upper hand, so the Muscovites stand on the sidelines rooting for one of the animals, and we never find out which one.

The next poem, "When Napoleon's Measure Surpassed Europe's Scale," points to the modern myth of a Russian nation formed through the defense of Russian territory against invaders. Here Prigov offers the romantic concept of nation as ethnos, the "fabulous Russian people" (*russkii skazochnyi narod*). Prigov highlights the Russian people's qualities of mobility and flexibility, traits notably absent in the imperial version of Moscow. Moscow as home of the people can shift and change when it needs to, for example, to defend against Napoleon. Ever ironic, Prigov undermines the notion of the *narod*. The Russian nation emerges in a process of grammatically impersonal thinking: for example, "it was thought" and "it was imagined." The poet does not divulge who exactly is doing the thinking and planning, though it would seem to be some state or military entity, since what is being discussed is where to place field fortifications, batteries, General Bagration, and then

---

13. See Sidney Dement, "Empire and Identity in D. A. Prigov's 'Moskva i moskvichi,'" paper presented at AATSEEL, Philadelphia, 30 December 2006.

the nation. The "fabulous Russian people" are just that—they are just an image in someone else's narrative. They do not belong to themselves.

The following two poems address two Muscovite traits—the demand for total fealty and the belief in Moscow's divinely ordained indestructibility. The fourth poem, "And What Is Moscow," moves away from the invader theme to emphasize Moscow's remarkable centripetal quality, which forces a foreigner to choose either to fight or switch allegiance, either be "beaten to death" or "come over to our side and become a Muscovite" (I, 31). The fifth poem, "Thus Everyone Designs to Insult [Moscow]," reiterates Moscow's force of attraction for the territorially ambitious and its special relationship to divine force. Even as they stumble home, foreign invaders dream of a new attack: "To Moscow! To Moscow! Back! O, Drang nach Osten!" (I, 32). The reason that Moscow is a bastion that resists conquest is that "apparently, God is preserving Moscow" (I, 32). The poet, now adopting a chauvinist tone, asserts that Moscow indeed enjoys divine favor.

Having outlined—and undermined—the myths of national personhood and the forging of "imagined community" through the defense of Moscow from other countries in the modern era, Prigov turns, tongue-in-cheek, in the next two poems to Moscow's imperial psyche, the twentieth-century myth of Moscow as the hub of a multiethnic Eurasia. The sixth poem, "You'll Find One of Every Kind in Moscow," pictures Moscow as the sacred multiethnic homeland (*pervorodina sviataia*), the origin of "Germans and Poles / Chinese and Mongols, and Georgians / Armenians, Assyrians, Judeans," all of whom arose here in Moscow and then in ancient times went their separate ways and founded new states throughout the world. In the end, these nations ask to be ruled by "the ancient hand of Moscow," and "Moscow affectionately takes some back / But not all" (I, 33), because some of these peoples "have not understood, deserved / Grown enough" (I, 33). Russians are far from belonging to just one ethnic group—Russianness embraces amoeba-like anyone willing to be loyal to Moscow.

The seventh poem, "When in This Place Ancient Rome," is a child-like spoof on the Third-Rome myth of Muscovy. Prigov switches cities, imagining the first Rome arising in Moscow. Instead of recounting the well-known myth of the White Cowl that traveled from Rome to Constantinople to Holy Rus', or Filofei's 1511 letter to Tsar Vasily III that ends with the much-quoted lines, "Moscow is the Third Rome—a fourth there will not be!"—Prigov imagines ancient Rome actually arising in "this place."[14] He pictures

---

14. See Peter J. S. Duncan, *Russian Messianism: Third Rome, Holy Revolution, Communism and After* (London: Routledge, 2000). Duncan's book does not go as far as the post-Soviet moment, dealing only with Gennady Ziuganov.

Muscovites going "to the senate in togas / Crowned with a laurel wreath" (I, 34). The poem ends with another vestimentary metonymy, focusing on modern clothing as a sign that perhaps Muscovites are still the "envy of the world" (I, 34). The poet admits that although Muscovites wear other kinds of clothes nowadays, the "heart of proud Muscovites still beats" as if they were wearing togas.

The second third of the cycle complicates the relationship between the contrasting ideas of multiethnic empire and a Russian nation, and the final part of the cycle asserts poetic agency in conceiving Moscow. In the eighth poem, "When a Movement Arose," an imagined movement for an independent Moscow is nipped in the bud by the state, the poet claims, by marshaling other ethnic groups—the Mongols, Poles, Germans, and French—who presumably help to put down rebellion. Importantly, here in the eighth poem, we find a slight hint of the theme of the hidden city. This poem ends with lines very similar to the preceding poem but quite different in implied meaning of personal pride in Moscow: "Whether in the style of a young woman's walk, or in her word / Flickers the mad flame / Of Muscovite national pride" (I, 34). Hidden signs of pride and loyalty emerge subtly through gesture and word. That being said, it is worth noting here the strange and somewhat baffling choice of the Latinate adjective *natsional'nyi,* which refers not to the Russian-rooted word for people, *narod,* but to the foreign-sounding word, *natsiia.* This choice suggests not grassroots community but the allegiance to an institution relating to the state, for example, a national theater or a national team.

Poems in the middle of the cycle make fun of images of imperial Moscow and its territorial claims. For example, the tenth poem, "When Muscovites Go for a Walk," draws repeated attention to the Third Rome motif, seeming to exalt Moscow above all other cities. It describes strolling Muscovites watching the "Heavenly Moscow" with its "views of Rome, Constantinople / Poland, Peking, the whole universe" (I, 35). The eleventh poem, "And the Moscow of the Epoch of My Life," also focuses on the heavenliness of Moscow and the mere earthliness of the rest of the "whole disenfranchised world" (*ves' bespravnyi mir*). This Moscow is heavy with landmarks and monuments of political and cultural power, "Leninskii Prospekt and the Mausoleum / The Kremlin, Vnukovo, the Bolshoi Theatre and the Malyi / and the policeman at his post" (I, 36). This imperial Moscow, with its firm police presence, lives only to expand: "Moscow continually grows and breathes / Toward Poland, toward Warsaw it grows / Toward Prague, toward Paris, toward New York / And everywhere, if you look impartially / Moscow and its peoples are everywhere" (I, 36). At the end, Prigov undermines this imperialist pride when the poet's mock-imperialist voice proclaims self-importantly: "Wherever Moscow is not, is simply emptiness" (I, 36). Here, as in Erofeev's and Voinovich's visions of the insular Moscow, there is no significant periphery that offers a counterweight to the centripetal force of the capital.

In distinction to Moscow as the seat of imperial power is the appealing, alive, but hidden Moscow, the Moscow invented by ordinary people. This is a Moscow we have not yet encountered. Of the twenty-three poems in *Moscow and Muscovites* nearly half of them make reference to the quality of mobility and changeability first presented in the Napoleon poem. The seventh through the ninth poems deal with the Moscow hidden in people's hearts and minds, the site of "national" pride. We have briefly touched on the first two of this group. The ninth poem, "When Moscow was still a She-Wolf," draws the contrast more starkly between the imperial city with its claimed link to divinity and Russian people, now as a "clan." According to Prigov's pseudo-legend, Moscow is not Rome but the she-wolf from pagan Roman legend who fed and raised Rome's founders, Romulus and Remus. The Moscow-as-she-wolf bears "a large clan [*plemia*] of white-toothed Muscovites" (I, 34), who absurdly both watch and participate in the miracle that makes them disappear—a flame [*plamia*] descends from heaven and takes everyone with it back to heaven so that "Moscow stands—but there aren't any Muscovites" (I, 34). The phonetic proximity of the word for clan [*plemia*] and the word for flame [*plamia*] disguises the brutal fact that the heavenly flame, associated with higher divine right, destroys the people of Moscow while exalting them. Without its living, breathing people Moscow is accursedly empty. This theme of emptiness echoes the well-known curse visited by Tsaritsa Eudoxia on Russia's other imperial capital, that "St. Petersburg will stand empty!" Prigov thus strengthens his implied preference for Moscow as a community of people in contrast to the imperial state with its bureaucracy, police, massive stone buildings, monumental statuary, and chauvinist attitudes. Tragically that community is simply absent.

Most of the poems in the last third of the cycle, particularly sixteen through twenty, revisit the hidden, mobile Moscow. In the sixteenth poem, "When Mass Arrests Passed Throughout the World," the poet pictures the various ethnicities that make up Moscow taking refuge in the woods beyond Moscow and founding their own Moscow. He then decides that this legend is probably just a lie because "people have only rarely heard of [this city] / and never saw Muscovites alive" (I, 39).

The eighteenth poem, "Sometimes Unjovial Pictures," stresses the role of language in forging identity. We are reminded that Muscovites create meaning in their difficult lives and carry on to educate their "descendants" through language, by "finding the right word," "filled with meaning" (I, 40).

The cultural, spiritual life of language and invention is paramount for identity, overcoming otherwise brutal physical conditions. The nineteenth poem, "They Exchanged Moscow," cycles back to the theme of the hidden Moscow. It is worth quoting this crucial poem at length to give a sense of Prigov's logic:

> Here they switched [*podmenili*] Moscow
> And hid it from the poor Muscovites
> And beneath the earth It sits and cries
> All in cupolas and small standing towers
> All in the transparent portals of the Parthenon
> And in the straight statues of the Erechtheon
> And in the enormous statues of Echnathon
> And in the waters of the Nile, Ganges, and Yangtse (I, 40)

This ancient Moscow, by implication, was made to disappear by the sleight of hand of its Soviet rulers, taken from its citizens and replaced with something else. All the same, it survives under the earth, under the water, and absurdly in ancient architecture and statuary.

Although Prigov acknowledges the overwhelming power of the imperial image of the capital and its ability to form, coerce, and dispose of its residents, he also defends the imaginative power of each resident. After again spoofing the foundational myths of Moscow, he returns repeatedly to the idea expressed in the final poem of the cycle: "Moscow is where you and I are standing / Moscow will abide where we tell it to / The real Moscow is wherever we put it! / That is—in Moscow" (I, 42). In his foreword to the cycle Prigov urges, "let enlightened Moscow become a monument for all of us" (I, 28). He replaces the stolid statues that dot the landscape of Soviet Moscow with a more abstract and perhaps playful notion of a monument that heralds an "enlightened Moscow," something like the personal, inventive Moscow of his cycle, one that makes fun of police and stone symbols.

We can now return to our original question concerning *Moscow and Muscovites*: What is the "Moscow mystique" that at the start Prigov asks his friend Orlov to define? It is partly the hidden Moscow created and recreated by its inhabitants and partly the wielding of imperial state power. True to Moscow Conceptualist style, Prigov's "Enlightened Moscow" is possible only when all Moscow myths become the objects of play, thought, and creative agency.

⤶

In his critical essays the philosopher Mikhail Ryklin uncovers another "sunken Moscow." Ryklin focuses on Stalinist Moscow and deconstructs it through bringing it into an uncomfortable closeness to what he sees as its psycho-social hidden reality, the Soviet Russian mass unconscious. Ryklin is interested in this psychic underground within the heart of Moscow, with its "blank spots and carefully kept secrets" of Soviet history and ideology.[15] In his view, the Russian unconscious is embodied in the physical underground beneath Moscow, the Moscow metro, which serves as a series of metaphors for the trauma of Stalinist terror and its repression.[16] In iconography of the early metro stations, first built in the 1930s, one encounters a disturbing combination of national, rural, and agricultural images of comfort and harmony, and images of observation, control, and implicit terror.

Ryklin derives his approach to "reading" the Moscow metro in this light from basic premises he finds in Mikhail Bakhtin's famous study, *Rabelais and His World*. Bakhtin shows that political terror hides behind icons of ethnic and national identity, or *narodnost'*, which he calls "collective corporeality." Behind this mask the forces of terror become invisible to the unaided eye. In his ingenious article "Bodies of Terror," Ryklin turns images in the Moscow metro into "objects of contemplation." This approach, he claims, is "an extremely aggressive act," given that the Soviet masses were simply meant to use the metro, to absorb the celebration of themselves in these underground temples, their statuary, and their murals, but not contemplate the psychological messages hidden in its iconographic symbolism. Ryklin comments, "These images concentrate in themselves the imaginary realm of the crowd—that is, the sole unconscious reality, from which they derive their right to existence." They are symbolic of the "traumas brought on the masses, to the masses, through the masses, and the images do not yield to rational interpretation" (BT, 58).

At first glance, the décor of these stations is meant to create a sense of belonging to a group that is rising to great heights and achieving wonderful things. "What strikes you," Ryklin writes, "is not the dense piling of bodies, but the impossibility of contemplating it at all, the ontological profundity of the elimination of loneliness" (BT, 58). The statuary and murals "incarnate the reigning ideology of publicness, bringing the non-individuality of the masses to its logical conclusion" (BT, 58). The desired effect is the forceful celebration by the crowd of itself and implicitly the denial of the critically thinking, creative individual person. Thereby the masses, having been

---

15. Mikhail Ryklin, *Vremia diagnoza* (Moscow: Logos, 2003), 9.
16. Mikhail Ryklin, "Bodies of Terror: Theses Toward a Logic of Violence," *New Literary History*, 24 (1993), 58. Further citations to this article are given in the text, using the notation "BT" and page number(s).

terrorized and traumatized through revolution and collectivization, themselves become a force of terror, rejecting the reflective human self.

The symbolic figures in the first metro stations, Ryklin tells us, have two origins—rural and urban. The first relates to the rural roots of most Stalin-era Muscovites, who had recently moved to the capital from the countryside, escaping the horrors of collectivization. For example, mosaics in the Kiev Metro Station (1953) construct the rural Ukrainian folk and the abundance of nature, masking the horror of collectivization and war, more brutal and murderous in Ukraine than anywhere else. Many murals with a rural theme feature motherly figures, conveying a mood of "total rejoicing, inseparable from the earth and fertility" (BT, 59).

The second group of figures discussed by Ryklin relates to the "trauma of urbanization" following the unspoken and unspeakable suffering of collectivization. Ryklin argues that "in this vision is unleashed the criminal energy of the masses, untranslatable into the idyll of a rural holiday" (BT, 59). Panels at Avtozavodskaia (1943) showing steel workers with a technician observing them imply "labor as an insurmountable obstacle—whose continual overcoming [by the Party] takes the form of violent action, in a climax of terror" (BT, 59). The Avtozavodskaia Metro mural suggests to Ryklin the control of labor by the figure to the right who is both observing and measuring (Fig. 2). Although Ryklin does not clarify which features disclose the experience of terror, we may assume that they are to be found in two gaps—one between rural fruitfulness in other murals and dark, heavy industrial labor in this mural, and the other between the laborers and the controlling gaze of the technician.

Although Ryklin's argument concerning the trauma of urbanization is intriguing, it suffers from a dearth of concrete examples. Nonetheless, it certainly invites further study of the Moscow metro and other Stalin-era monuments. My discussion below adds some examples that appear to me to show similar characteristics.

Mosaics of "creative workers" or, for example, the stained-glass painters at Novoslobodskaia Station (1952), convincingly document Ryklin's claim of the forced etatization of art, of the "Party's seizure of the energy of artistic creation" (BT, 62).[17] In a stance close to that of ancient Egyptian figures, the painter is shown dressed in something close to business clothes, a tie and jacket, his face clean-cut, shaven, and completely impassive. He is painting a canvas, the subject of which we cannot see. The emphasis, thus, is on

17. Pavel Rakitin, ed., *Moskovskii metropoliten* (Moscow: Interros, 2005).

Fig. 2. Metro Station Avtozavodskaia, fall 2008, photograph by Sarah Bumpus, reproduced with permission.

Fig. 3. Novoslobodskaia Metro Station, spring 2010, photo by Steven Jug and Adrienne Harris.

the painter's appearance, not on the quality of his thought or his artistic production.

Another leaded glass image in Novoslobodskaia Station supports Ryklin's argument about the etatization of the arts (Fig. 3). It shows a more casually dressed painter, though still very much overshadowed by two images of state power, the small white towers to the left and the large towers outside the artist's window.

Ryklin remarks that many faces in metro statuary and wall decoration bespeak anything but a jubilant mood. When one looks closely, those faces are impassive and even gloomy. Ryklin argues that: "Such faces appear in Russian culture only after the trauma of violent urbanization." They speak of the masses' vacillation between "imagined rejoicing" and "the wretched reality of the endless duty of labor" (BT, 59). Ryklin discusses the statue of the student with a book at Revolution Square Station as an example that expresses this hidden experience. The student's impassive face and bent body, far from expressing joy of learning, convey the (hidden) "trauma of forced urbanization" (BT, 63).[18]

One might also point to the statue of a crouching father holding his child, also at Revolution Square Station. Although both figures exude trust and calm, here again there is no "jubilation." There is a certain slippage between how they are dressed (or undressed) and their pose and facial expression. Although both are relatively undressed, suggesting leisure time and fun, there is no joy or merriment in their faces. One wonders what it is that the pair is looking at, what the father is showing the baby, whether a parade or the metro. Although not depicted, one senses something marvelous within view that the father wants to show the baby—perhaps the brilliant future of communism? Or Stalin?

If the experience of terror is the point that Ryklin ferrets out from his deconstructive reading of the gaps and silences of the metro, among the most open, obvious messages of metro décor and architecture is that of the grandeur of empire. As Ryklin puts it, "The empire is fully actualized in the architecture and makeup of the metro" (BT, 68), and he predicts that: "This imperial quality, I would say, transcends the actual empire and will necessarily survive it" (BT, 68). Various stations from the Kiev Station to the Borovitskaia Station (1986)—with its enormous map of the Soviet Union shaped like a tree growing in the Kremlin (Fig. 1)—celebrate the demographic and geographic reach of the Soviet empire.

Ryklin's deconstructive analysis of the function of collective psychological repression of terror in the magnificent halls of the Moscow metro, built overtly as a series of temples to celebrate the power of the Soviet masses, is an act of reinstating the force of the individual thinking person after the Stalinist collective body had wiped it out. His reading fits well with Prigov's images of the hidden Moscow, displaced by Soviet purges and massive internal strife. For both, Moscow is the place where, as Prigov puts it, the inhabitants define it: "Moscow will abide where you and I tell it to."

A different, cruder but highly humorous deconstruction of Moscow comes in the brilliant short story by Viktor Pelevin, "Vera Pavlovna's Ninth Dream" (1991).[19] Here, in contrast to the conceptualists who deconstruct

18. Ibid.
19. Viktor Pelevin, "Deviatyi son Very Pavlovny," in *Sinii fonar'* (Moscow: Tekst, 1991), 140–156.) Available at http://pelevin.nov.ru. Translated into English in "*A Werewolf in Moscow Region*" *and Other Stories,* trans. A. Bromfield (New York: New Directions, 1998), 36–58.

the imperial Moscow to uncover the hidden or sunken Moscow, Pelevin starts with an underground setting, in the Moscow metro, but then also sinks Soviet and perestroika-era Moscow beneath the waves. Somewhat like Prigov, Pelevin writes in an absurdist, philosophizing vein, asking ontological questions about the nature of the Moscow world.

"Vera Pavlovna's Ninth Dream" is the dream of an elderly lavatory attendant in the Moscow metro during the perestroika period of the late 1980s. The story's title and the protagonist's name recall the most important nineteenth-century literary precursor to Soviet socialist realism, Nikolai Chernyshevsky's ideological novel *What Is To Be Done?* (1863). Pelevin's story parodies Chernyshevsky's novel, with the heroine's four dreams opening the future paradise on earth and the liberation of women. In Pelevin's story this discussion is set in a Schopenhauerian-Wittgensteinian dialogue between two bathroom attendants, Vera Pavlovna and her good friend Manyasha. They debate the nature of reality and solipsism and whether the world is actually as we imagine it. Vera Pavlovna is a solipsist, who worries about the nature and mystery of existence and wonders to what degree the world reality is the function of our own consciousness.

Like Ryklin's article Pelevin's story focuses on the metro, though certainly the least beautiful space in it, and then moves to the event of actually submerging all of Moscow. The theme that Prigov, Ryklin, and Pelevin share is the voluntarist notion that their beloved Moscow—not the Moscow constructed by its Soviet overlords—is wherever thinking, creative people are, and it will become whatever they make of it. Finally, with Pelevin, as with Prigov and Erofeev, we find a literary *translatio imperii,* taking from St. Petersburg writers Pushkin, Chernyshevsky, and Dostoevsky the themes of self-will and state-enforced change and replanting them in Moscow. We encounter by the end of the story a fantasized end to Moscow and the Soviet empire that only a bathroom attendant could dream up: excrement wells up from under the city and sinks Moscow beneath its slime.

This ending represents a strange version of the biblical flood story from Genesis. In Genesis God is unhappy with the created world. God salvages two of each creature and Noah's family in an ark. Noah and the animals float for an eternity on the flood, only then to land on Mt. Ararat and repopulate the earth. In Pelevin's story Moscow is flooded with excrement after two events. First, the lavatory is turned into a kiosk during perestroika of the late 1980s. People start enriching themselves by selling merchandise which, following Freud, Vera Pavlovna imagines to be lumps of excrement. Second, in her dream Vera Pavlovna murders her friend and mentor after a philosophical disagreement over the role of individual human will in effecting social and economic change. Although guilty of murder, Vera Pavlovna is one of two people to survive (the other is an Asian dictator Pot Mir Soup, who had visited Vera's bathroom). Finally, instead of Mt. Ararat, the only sign of firm land is one of the key symbols of the Soviet empire—the red star atop one of the Kremlin towers. At the end of the dream all signs of earthly life, including the star, disappear. There will be no repopulating of this world.

As with the other deconstructions of Moscow, in Pelevin's story the imperial periphery figures only symbolically, as part of Moscow. All that really exists is Moscow and its symbols of empire. As Vera Pavlovna paddles through the slime, she latches onto the globe that has broken loose from the Central Moscow Telegraph on Tverskaia Street. The Soviet empire has always meant to Vera Pavlovna only the map, which reminds her of a side of beef hanging in a butcher shop.

The Moscow of Pelevin's story is a world in flux, changing from the capital of an empire to a city ruled by forces that had been repressed since the revolution—individual will and enterprise, as well as the uncensored depiction of scatological aspects of human existence. There is a strong carnival aspect to this deconstruction, a topsy-turvy revolution in which powerful people and their symbols end up on the bottom and the powerless rise to the top. The all-powerful imperial Soviet Moscow has now sunken beneath the waves of excrement, and the will of "small people" becomes dominant. The Soviet order has toppled, and the lower, grotesque phenomena of human existence have taken over.

The most complex literary deconstruction of Moscow is rather the *destruction* of Moscow in Tatiana Tolstaia's post-utopian novel *Slynx* (2000).[20] *Slynx* belongs most obviously to the self-isolating view of Moscow of Erofeev and Voinovich, though we can also point out some signs of the sunken-city "return of the repressed." Two hundred years after an enormous explosion Moscow as such exists no more. On the same territory stands a primitive settlement with a "Big Man" complex that changes its name according to the tyrant currently in power. The current despot Fedor Kuz'mich, names the town Fedor-Kuz'michsk, using the name to enhance his personality cult. By the novel's end the name will have changed to reflect the name of the new tyrant, Kudeiar Kudeiarich. The time frame of 200 years echoes the

20. Tat'iana Tolstaia, *Kys'* (Moscow: Podkova, 2000). Also available online at http://lib.ru/ PROZA/TOLSTAYA. Further citations are given in the text, using the notation "K" and page number(s). Where indicated, I borrow Gambrell's clever translations of Tolstaia's neologisms. Tatyana Tolstaya, *Slynx,* trans. Jamey Gambrell (Boston: Houghton Mifflin, 2003).

time frame in Zamiatin's classic dystopia, *We,* in which the seemingly om-
nipotent One State has existed for 200 years. Zamiatin's city is exceedingly
high-tech and futuristic, while Tolstaia's town is primitive—what one could
call "no-tech." Both are defined by the motif of self-isolation.

This post-Muscovite "nowhere," far from directly engaging the issues
of empire, is filled with timorous, xenophobic people who want only to
be left alone. The explosion has left almost everyone a mutant, except a
few "oldeners" (*prezhnie*), who survived the blast and can only die if they
are murdered. This much smaller settlement has become a "city of fools."
Inhabitants worship the past and gather strange texts, anything from in-
structions for operation of a meat grinder, to classical Russian poems, to
an encyclopedia, all of which call forth the same adulation. These strange
characters think they value culture and books but can barely read. They
have no appreciation of the passage of time, no method of interpreting
the texts that remain, and are generally lacking larger historical, cultural,
and lexical frames of reference that would make it possible for them to
interpret anything they read. Indeed, their worlds are controlled by what
one might call folkloric structures—legends, rituals, superstitions, and
totems.

The former Moscow stands on seven hills—an ironic reference to Rome
and to the imperial myth of Moscow the Third Rome, a reference that only
the reader but none of the characters can appreciate. Thanks to the efforts
of one of the oldeners, the settlement still sports a few street signs from
the old Moscow. The settlement embodies the very essence of self-isolation,
now turned idiotic. Although geographically it appears to be isolated from
everything around it, guarded by a watchtower, the mutant citizenry bear
within themselves a self-isolating spirit and the imagined geography to
go with it. They are ignorant, fearful, self-oppressing, and oppressed by
their ruler, first by the relatively liberal, Khrushchev-like Fedor Kuz'mich,
and by the end by the paranoid, terrorizing, cruel "Chief Sanitation Man"
(*General'nyi Sanitar*), Kudeiar Kudeiarich Kudeiarov.

The townspeople live in terror of the environs, isolating themselves still
further and leaving themselves at the mercy of the current dictator. They
have erected a watchtower with four windows each facing a different direction (K, 9). From its top one gains a perspective on the physical look of
their world. One sees "the whole pancake of the earth, the whole roof of
the sky, the whole cold december, the whole city with its ghettos, with its
dark crooked huts—empty and opened wide, combed through with the fine
combs of the sanitation men's hooks and still lived in, still swarming with
absurd, scary, obstinate life!" (K, 338). The outlying areas around the town
arouse paralyzing fear of "limitless fields, unknown lands" (K, 7). There is

no sense of the town being a center of power that rules these areas as part of a domain; just the opposite, the political structure, such as it is, is oriented inward toward controlling the townspeople and what they know.

Each direction of the compass elicits a different attitude and is associated with a different set of symbols (K, 7–15, 338). For example, the north is a fearsome, impassable place, associated with the mythical, wild, cat-like beast, the slynx [*kys'*]. It is covered in "slumbering forests, storm-fallen trees, branches have woven together and you can't get through, the thorny bushes catch on your foot cloths, the twigs rip your hat from your head" (K, 7). The west seem more open and accessible but strangely senseless to the townspeople: it seems like there is a path leading westward from the town, but the path leads nowhere, and one forgets why one went that way. Following that path seems like a great idea at first but then enthusiasm gives way to doubt: "then suddenly, as they say, you stop and stand there. And think: where is it I'm going? What for? What's there that I didn't see already? Is it really better over there? Then you start feeling sorry for yourself!" (K, 8) The residents of the settlement see no reason to leave and explore the west. They prefer their life where they are, however terrifying it may be, so they stay.

Like the north, the south presents something of a threat. One can encounter people there, which the protagonist Benedict calls "Chechens": "You can't go south. That's where the Chechens are. First it's all steppe and more steppe—your eyes fall out for looking,—and beyond the steppe are the Chechens" (K, 9). Perhaps the friendliest of directions is the east. Townspeople like to go to the east of town because of the "bright woods, long grasses, shiny-glazed" (K, 15). Azure-colored flowers grow there that are at once tender and useful: one can make threads and cloth from them. The most magical aspects of the eastern direction are the so-called elfir (*klel'*) trees, which produce honey-like "firelings" (*ognets*).[21] The elfir is widely held to be the best tree both because of the sweet firelings and because it has wonderful nuts in its cones (K, 17).[22]

At the beginning of the novel the town has three moats encircling it, just as the old Moscow had three ring roads around it. By the end Kudeiarov (whose name recalls the terrifying cult leader in Andrei Belyi's novel, *The Silver Dove*) builds three walls around the city to isolate it further from the

21. Gambrell translates *klel'* as elfir. Because *klel'* is actually a combination of maple [klen] and fir [el'], perhaps "mafir" would work better.
22. It is important to note that Benedict's oldener mother dies of poisoning by a fireling; it is possible and even likely that she was poisoned by someone in power who felt threatened by her.

outside. He builds additional walls inside the city to keep the populace from defacing favorite monuments, such as the wooden "pushkin."

The implication of Tolstaia's novel is that the xenophobic, self-oppressing mentality that has historically characterized Moscow—that all the writers discussed in this chapter also underscore—continually reinvents itself by legitimating acts of terror as acts of nature. Myths and legends are built around these acts in such a way as to mask the act itself behind a façade of historical legend and fairytale images and characters. To begin with, to give themselves some semblance of history and pride the characters reinvent a version of Moscow's Third Rome legend and a number of aspects of high Muscovite culture. For example, they invent the story about the meat grinder as something "developed by the slaves of the Third Rome" (K, 159), implying that their forebears, even the slaves, were exceedingly clever. These references, of course, are pathetic echoes of the Muscovite imperial legend.

What Tolstaia's de(con)struction of Moscow shares with Ryklin's is her attention to the psychological-cultural operation of masking terrorist rule with icons—and in Tolstaia's novel, myths—of origin or survival. At the heart of the novel is the central myth of the slynx, a figure of terror. The word *kys'* is a neologism, connecting the Russian word for lynx (*rys'*) with the Russian diminutive used to call a cat (*kis*). The legend is recounted a number of times, starting at the very beginning of the novel with the story passed down from the old people (K, 7). The slynx, who allegedly lives near the settlement, jumps on the neck of an unsuspecting wanderer. When it "cuts through the main vein with its claw and all a person's reason comes out," the person turns into a moron (K, 7). The person stops eating, the neighbors mock him, treat him cruelly, and eventually he dies.

The protagonist Benedict obsesses about the slynx. At night when it is dark, he terrifies himself, imagining the slynx prowling in the impassable northern woods. He is horrified at the thought of the slynx scratching open his vein with its hooked claws. Now the horror at the slynx becomes a crisis of identity: the slynx so terrifies one that, as Benedikt thinks, "it's just as if you were a stranger to yourself [*sam sebe chuzhoi*]: what is this? Who am I? Who am I?!...That's what it does, the slynx...sniffs you out...over the long distances, through the blizzard, through thick-beamed walls, and what if it were right next to you?" (K, 66). Benedict has worked himself into a frenzy.

Eventually the reader relates the legend of the slynx to the General Sanitation Man Kudeiarov and his family, who indeed are the slynx. The Kudeiarov family has cat-like eyes that light up, illuminating the way on a dark night; those eyes can also burn the people to whom they are speaking, and they have claws on their feet that scratch the floor as they sit at the dinner table (K, 181). As the conversation grows lively, the scratching increases (K, 184). Kudeiarov's title as Chief Sanitation Man plays irreverently on his real function as chief secret policeman. During nocturnal raids on townspeople's huts he confiscates any pre-explosion books, claiming disingenuously to be healing the community. In the dark of night he dresses, oprichnik-like, in a hooded robe, takes a hook with which to grab books, and rides his Red Sleigh through town, in a razzia-type action. This action drives terror into the hearts of the populace. Benedikt recounts an incident in his childhood, very much like incidents during the Stalin and Hitler eras, when his drunken father took his oldener-mother's "old-print" book from before the explosion and burns it out of fear of the razzia (K, 54).

Although Benedikt is intellectually challenged, he senses the link between the Red Sleigh and the slynx. He engages in rituals to ward off the Red Sleigh, just as he does the evil eye or the slynx, which makes him feel entirely alone and defenseless. Benedikt cannot articulate the connection consciously and refuses to think about it (K, 172). Benedikt eventually marries Kudeiarov's daughter Olga, and allies himself with the Chief Sanitation Man to overthrow Fedor Kuz'mich. Benedikt, who has the stump of a tail (like a lynx), and Kudeiarov, whose eyes light up and has cat-like claws, accuse one another of being the slynx. Kudeiarov, who has assumed power, throws Benedikt out of his *terem,* and, at least until the whole town is blown up at the very end, the connection between the legend of the slynx and the terrorizing, oprichnik-like Kudeiarov is hushed up.

In this novel, there is no imagined community; indeed, there is hardly any community at all. There is neither nation, nor empire, just the age-old, repeating drive to use violence, to repel strangers, to oppress one's own fellow citizens, and to censor oneself, to control information and learning, and to accept directives from a tyrant who cloaks himself in a leader cult.

The sunken-city theme in *Slynx* concerns the sense of a higher level of culture and civilization of an era now long gone. The artifacts left from the old Moscow are preserved by the oldeners who are the intelligentsia of the post-explosion settlement. If there are any thinking people in this moronic community, it is they. Still, they have insurmountable impediments to understanding the things that they cherish. Benedikt, whose mother was an oldener, cannot understand the meaning of the word steed, thinking of it as some kind of mouse (K, 32). There is such a thing as a "schopenhauer," which Benedikt thinks is a "story, only you can't tell a damn thing from it" (K, 97). The townspeople absurdly misinterpret the artifacts they love; for example, a wooden post that becomes known as the "pushkin." The oldener Nikita Ivanovich thinks of a pushkin as a black "beriawood" memorial, "a rebellious and angry spirit; his head bent, two meat patties on the sides of his face—old-fashioned sideburns" (K, 151). The settlers in Fedorkuzmichsk cannot understand what it means and use it to hang out their laundry.

Tolstaia completely undermines the hopefulness of the thought that hidden or submerged there exist the remains of a better life. There are two points to be made about Tolstaia's darkly humorous treatment of the sunken city theme. The first is that the Moscow of the "bad old days" of the Soviet era is now for the residents of Fedorkuzmichsk the shining light of high civilization. The sunken city, Tolstaia implies, should stay sunken. The second point is that there is no way back even to that relatively higher civilization. None of the citizens, not even the oldeners, have the intellectual, interpretive tools to figure out the meaning and use of the artifacts they have preserved. This isolated community is degenerate and focused on itself. Afraid of the outside world, it can only degenerate into further terror and tyranny.

In conclusion, the "Moscow text" of the late- and post-Soviet moment is a psycho-cultural complex of narratives and metaphors that project an embedded set of values and an ingrained mentality. Prigov, Ryklin, Pelevin, and Tolstaia psychoanalyze this complex and expose the values and attitudes that have become second nature throughout the Soviet era. The common concerns among these writers and thinkers are an overriding solipsism, isolation, xenophobia, and a penchant for inward-directed physical violence and control of citizens themselves.

In a 1993 article on Russian identity, "The Russian World," Tolstaia underscores the need to keep channels of communication open to the outside:

> For me Russian nationalism, national-patriotism is terrible—not just for the obvious reason, that it lethally and unmistakably smells of fascism, but mainly because its idea and goal is to lock up the Russian world on itself, to plug up all the chinks, holes and pores, all the little windows, through which come draughts of the jolly springtimes of other cultures, to leave Russians alone with themselves. That is not the kind of nationalism that prefers fellow citizens because they share language and blood but the type that wants to bolt the doors and pound the neighbors and the next of kin, pronouncing them to be strangers [chuzhak]. In this "pure Russian" milieu we can all suffocate, go mad from claustrophobia, senselessly, and squander the flights of fancy and gifts that we have from nature. In a mixed, open, constantly self-renewing milieu we could live and move in a considered fashion, and think, and work, naturally, remaining Russian, but not sinking into a drugged sleep [durmaniashchaia spiachka].[23]

23. Tolstaia, "Russkii mir," *Den'* (Moscow: Podkova, 2003), 412. "Russkii mir" was commissioned by the *Guardian* as part of a series by non-English writers on the subject of national identity and nationalism.

All the writers discussed here would agree with Tolstaia's expression of the vital need to resist Moscow's tendency toward self-isolation, toward denial of its peripheries, and to hold open the channels of communication and interaction. And each makes literary or critical gestures to clear space for this sort of post-authoritarian life, in part by putting the thinking, speaking self back at the center of defining what Moscow is. As Prigov articulates in his final poem in *Moscow and Muscovites:* "But no, Moscow is where you and I are standing / Moscow will abide where we tell it to / The real Moscow is wherever we put it!" (I, 42) The voices in these writings are all voices of rejection that break apart the isolated imperial capital and leave space for fresh concepts of what it means to be a Muscovite and, more broadly, a Russian.

Finally, we return to Galina Belaia's perception in *Sunken Atlantis* that the image of the sunken city is temporal in nature. In Belaia's view, the sunken city represents pre-revolutionary culture with its refined language and its broader, more discerning consciousness.[24] All the works discussed here show that the pre-revolutionary culture is no longer a usable past—indeed, it is no longer reclamation of *time* but redefinition of *space* that demands contemporary attention. What will emerge in the following chapters is that the temporal dominant of modernity has yielded in the ensuing post-Soviet years to a spatial and geographical dominant: "newness" happens when Muscovites acknowledge the reality of various peripheries and develop a relationship with them, admitting difference and otherness into the life of the center. Four prominent public figures—Dugin, Ryklin, Pelevin, and Ulitskaia—will envision or symbolically enact a number of solutions to the self-isolating, solipsist, centripetal Muscovite mentality described in this chapter—some focusing on concepts of nationhood, others focusing on a multiethnic empire, and others focusing on still other kinds of imagined community.

24. Belaia, "Zatonuvshaia Atlantida," 12. It is worth mentioning that Ryklin in his study of Moscow in *Spaces of Jubilation* (Prostranstva likovaniia, 2001) brings up the "sunken city" theme again, but this time in spatial terms rather than temporal ones. He discusses the post-Soviet restorations of pre-revolutionary architecture. Probably the most famous of these restorations is the Church of Christ the Savior, which had been destroyed by Stalin to make way for his monumental but failed project of the Palace of Soviets. The church was rebuilt on its old site using an enormous number of donations from private citizens. Ryklin notes that this strange post-Soviet restoration has progressed according to a "postmodern image" of pre-revolutionary Moscow, which itself actually remains an Atlantis, a "sunken city" (*Prostranstva likovaniia* [Moscow: Logos, 2002], 151–152). The pre-revolutionary past is grasped naively merely as a place to restore and to re-enter.

2 POSTMODERNIST EMPIRE MEETS HOLY RUS'

How Aleksandr Dugin Tried to Change the Eurasian Periphery into the Sacred Center of the World

I am a Muscovite, root and branch, I am pathologically in love with Moscow and the Muscovite period of our history. I am a consistent and radical opponent of westernizing, liberalism, the profane way of life.
—ALEKSANDR DUGIN, *Pop Culture and the Signs of the Times* (2005)

"If the European New Right chooses us [Russians], that means it chooses the barbarian element, and therefore it must choose our methods of action," [Dugin] says. He notes that the New World Order will not come about by means of "aging gentlemen meeting in seminars." He advises the following: "You must take a knife, put on a mask, go out of the house in the evening and kill at least one Yank." He adds, "I do not know whether any of the New Right activists have ever been under artillery siege, but our people do not only go to meetings or fight at the barricades, they also go to real wars, for instance to the Dniestr district [Moldova], or to Yugoslavia.... The New Right is only a project, and we are its architects. The future is truly ours."
—Interview with Dugin (1998)

Russia is a country with an unpredictable past....everyone thinks up his own past, his own history for this madhouse, and one narrative is no better and no more correct than another, there are as many pasts as you like.
—TAT'IANA TOLSTAIA, "The Russian World" (2003)

Citations for Dugin's works are given in the text following the relevant quotation. The following notations are used:

ME: *Misterii Evrazii* (1996, Moscow: Arktogeia, 1999).

MBV: *Metafizika blagoi vesti. Absoliutnaia rodina* (1994, Moscow: Arktogeia, 1999).

OG: *Osnovy geopolitiki. Geopoliticheskoe budushchee Rossii. Myslit' prostranstvom* (1997, Moscow: Arktogeia-tsentr, 2000).

PA: *Puti absoliuta* in *Absoliutnaia rodina* (1989, Moscow: Arktogeia, 1999).

PE: *Proekt "Evraziia"* (Moscow: Iauza, 2004).

PK: *Pop-Kul'tura i znaki vremeni* (St. Petersburg: Amfora, 2005).

RV: *Russkaia veshch'* (Moscow: 2001).

ZS: "Zakoldovannaia sreda 'novykh imperii'," *Khudozhestvennyi zhurnal* 54 (2004), 18–25.

SINCE the late 1980s the fringe ultraconservative Aleksandr Dugin has become prominent in the public sphere, at first speaking from the far right of the Russian cultural and political spectrum, later merging into the mainstream, masquerading as a geopolitical theorist. Since 2000 he has enjoyed an audience among some right-wing, pro-Kremlin ideologues and more recently he has rebranded himself as a cultural critic. Stung by Russia's post-Soviet regression into the background of world events, he has vociferously asserted outrageous ideas about Russian identity, using neo-imperial metaphors of Eurasian geography and territory. Dugin's chief concern is the revival of Russian identity based on an all-powerful Russian state and its reconstructed Eurasian empire. Of interest for those who study Russian cultural identity is Dugin's neo-Eurasianist movement, founded in 2001 on an idea of Russianness that combines a strange mix of Slavophile values, Eurasianist thought from the 1920s, neo-fascism, and, finally, a wildly different orientation toward what he calls postmodernism.

Although the neo-Eurasianist movement is just one of many rightist movements, in the framework of this study Dugin makes a good starting point for a discussion of post-Soviet Russian identity and its self-definition through imagined geographies, if only because his diatribes have drawn so much public response.[1] Among ultraconservatives, he has been the most persistent in theorizing Russia's return from its post-Soviet position as a cultural and political backwater back to its accustomed position as a center of power. He places the problem of national identity squarely within his own *imagined* geography, the imagined geography of northern Eurasia, arguing for the "undoubtedly profound reality of national psychology, the 'inner continent' [*vnutrennii kontinent*], that synthesizes in itself the world view of the gigantic nation" (ME, 576). Within each true Russian, Dugin implies, there is an "inner continent," seeking self-realization in the actual physical continent of Eurasia.

Each of the other three principals in this study responds, if not to Dugin himself, then to various aspects of the neo-imperialist Eurasianism that he represents. Viktor Pelevin exposes Eurasia as an imaginary space. Liudmila Ulitskaia transfigures the symbolic geography of the "north" with which Dugin defines Russia. Mikhail Ryklin uses the liminal space of the Western border to diagnose anxiety underlying neo-imperialism. Even toward the

---

1. Marlene Laruelle, *Russian Eurasianism: An Ideology of Empire*, trans. M. Gabowitsch (Baltimore: Johns Hopkins University Press, 2008), 9. Note that the second epigraph comes from *Sarmatian Review* (January 2000), 687; and the third comes from Tolstaia, *Den'* (Moscow: Podkova, 2003), 404.

end of the Putin presidency, the frequent appearance of Dugin as the object of literary-political satire signals his continued relevance in the dialogue about identity.

Educated in religious studies at Moscow University with a candidate's degree from Rostov University, Dugin has always been fascinated by various forms of national myth. In 1988 he joined the right-wing group Pamiat' (Memory).[2] When the Afghan War journalist, Aleksandr Prokhanov, launched the ultraconservative magazine *Den'* in 1990, Dugin became a faithful contributor.[3] In the mid-1990s he helped to form the National Bolshevik Party, joining the neo-fascist writer, Eduard Limonov.[4] Here Dugin played the role of ideologue and specialist on fascist theory. Once the party failed to garner the 5 percent of the vote needed to win representation in the Duma, he moved to other projects. After writing his "textbook" of geopolitics, *The Foundations of Geopolitics* (*Osnovy geopolitiki*, 1997), Dugin injected himself first into the Duma as an adviser to its speaker Gennady Seleznev (who wanted the book to become part of the school curriculum), and then moved closer to the Putin Kremlin through Gleb Pavlovsky, a pro-Kremlin political scientist.[5] Dugin continued his activities in extreme nationalist venues, editing the journal *Elementy*, and developing a cultural website (www.arctogaia.com), which he started in 1998. He managed to build legitimacy as the spokesperson for the far right wing of Russian public opinion, receiving invitations to speak in such academic centers as the Johns Hopkins University School of Advanced International Studies.[6] In 2001 Dugin founded the social-political movement Evraziia (Eurasia), which was fully endorsed at its founding ceremony by the influential political scientist and

2. For a readable historical overview of Russian nationalism see Wayne Allensworth, *The Russian Question: Nationalism, Modernization, and Post-Communist Russia* (Lanham, MD: Rowman and Littlefield, 1998).

3. Eduard Limonov, *Moia politicheskaia biografiia* (St. Petersburg: Amfora, 2002), 69.

4. Stephen D. Shenfield, *Russian Fascism: Traditions, Tendencies, Movements* (Armonk, NY: M.E. Sharpe, 2001).

5. John B. Dunlop, "Aleksandr Dugin's 'Neo-Eurasian' Textbook and Dmitrii Trenin's Ambivalent Response," *Harvard Ukrainian Studies*, 1–2 (2001), 91–129. For more on Prokhanov, see Barry P. Scherr, "After Perestroika: The Era of Rasstroika," *South Central Review*, 12, nos. 3/4 (Autumn–Winter, 1995), pp. 153–167. For an excellent discussion of Dugin's intellectual heritage see Laruelle, *Russian Eurasianism*, 107–144.

6. Mark N. Katz, "Policy Watch: Moscow's Multipolar Mirage" (2005), http://www.spacewar.com /reports/Policy_Watch_Moscow's_Multipolar_Mirage.html. Also, http://www.marknkatz.com /Russian_Foreign_Policy.html.

TV journalist Aleksandr Panarin.[7] Dugin has made every effort to hold himself in the limelight, writing in intellectually serious venues, such as *Literaturnaia gazeta* and *Krasnaia zvezda,* and popular venues, such as *Ogonek.*[8] Depending on which commentary one reads, he has either had significant or quite minimal success in making himself heard.[9]

According to various reports, Dugin exerted some influence on social attitudes and on political life in the Putin administration. As Marlene Laruelle put it in 2001, Dugin "claims to be the new [Putin] government's 'shadow counselor'."[10] In 2000 he argued that his neo-Eurasian thinking had a direct impact on Putin's foreign policy, when the latter used the word "Eurasian" in a speech to refer to Russian identity: "Russia has always felt itself to be a Eurasian country."[11] A friend of Dugin's, Dmitry Riurik, has served as ambassador to Uzbekistan.[12] Other leaders in the former Soviet states, for example, the president of Kazakhstan Nursultan Nazarbaev, have expressed interest in Eurasianism and a possible Eurasian Union.[13]

It is unclear what sort of following Dugin actually enjoys. He is certainly his own best promoter: he claims without any clear proof that *The Foundations of Geopolitics* found "serious resonance" among Russian readers (OG, 6). Fearless and undaunted by facts, Dugin welcomes attacks by the mainstream press, perhaps operating under the same assumption that prompted some

---

7. Andreas Umland, "Toward an Uncivil Society? Contextualizing the Decline of Post-Soviet Russian Extremely Right-Wing Parties" (2001–2002), http://www.ciaonet.org/wps/uma01/uma01.pdf, 32.

8. See, for example, his grossly anti-liberal editorial, "Svoboda dlia," in *Literaturnaia Gazeta,* 9 (March 5–11, 2003), 2; see also his conversation in *Ogonek,* "Filosof ot sokhi," 6 (2003), http://ogoniok.ru/archive/2003/4798/19-18-25/.

9. Dunlop, "Aleksandr Dugin's 'Neo-Eurasian' Textbook." See also Marlène Laruelle, "Alexandre Dugin: Esquisse d'un eurasisme d'extrême-droite en Russie post-soviétique [Alexandre Dugin: A sketch of a far-right Eurasianism in post-Soviet Russia]," *Revue d'études comparatives Est-Ouest,* 3, no. 32 (2001), 85–103, esp. 92. Laruelle sees the communist leader Ziuganov taking inspiration from Dugin in his *Geografiia pobedy: Osnovy rossiiskoi geopolitiki* (Moscow: Partiinaia pechat'kprf, 1997). Matthew Schmidt, "Is Putin Pursuing a Policy of Eurasianism?" *Demokratizatsiya* (Winter, 2005), *http://www.findarticles.com.* Umland, "Toward an Uncivil Society?" Note that Dugin has a line of textbooks on politics meant to seem scientific. As of this writing, the latest is *Obshchestvovedenie dlia grazhdan novoi Rossii* (Moscow: Evraziiskoe dvizhenie, 2007).

10. Laruelle, "Alexandre Dugin," 85. For an opposing view, see Schmidt; Dugin wanted to be power behind Putin throne. See, also, Umland, 33.

11. Quoted in Schmidt. See, also, Andrei Kolesnikov and Aleksandr Privalov, *Novaia russkaia ideologiia: khronika politicheskikh mifov, 1999–2000* (Moscow: Gos. universitet, Vysshaia shkola ekonomiki, 2001), 362; Kolesnikov in his *Izvestiia* column made fun of Dugin for rushing to take credit for Putin's apparently shifting foreign policy. Note the discrepancy in year with Laruelle (2008), 7, who mistakenly says Putin delivered this speech in 2001.

12. Laruelle, "Alexandre Dugin," 93.

13. Ibid., 89, note 3.

Kazakhs to welcome the 2006 film *Borat*—that even harshly negative press is better than none at all. That his name is widely familiar to Russians who pay attention to the media is incontrovertible. But whether he is recognized as a trustworthy expert on Russian affairs is another question. According to a poll taken in February 2003, he did not count among the 100 most trusted political experts in Russia.[14] Although there is nothing genuinely new in his portly body of writing, it is important to pay heed to it because it expresses a yearning for high national self-esteem widespread in today's Russia.

Dugin's thinking belongs to a long line of Russian rejections of Western liberalism. His ultraconservatism shares little with the thinking of the original Slavophiles, Ivan Kireevsky and Aleksei Khomiakov, or with genuine neo-Slavophile nationalists Aleksandr Solzhenitsyn and Valentin Rasputin, who found the remnants of pure Russianness in what is left of the Russian peasantry following collectivization. Nonetheless, Dugin's talk of *sobornost'* (spiritual community), his adoration of Moscow and medieval Muscovy, his interest in *Domostroi* (the sixteenth-century Muscovite book of domestic order), his deeply primitive, patriarchal vision, and his high valuation of Orthodoxy as Russia's state religion—all are traits he shares with Slavophile thought. Shown in priestly garb in a photograph for *Ogonek*, Dugin even professes to be an Old Believer (Fig. 4).[15] Somewhat reminiscent of Slavophilism is Dugin's desire to revert to a new medievalism, to return Russia to a nostalgic image of Muscovy blessed by the Holy Spirit, and to a concept of the Russians, anointed as a chosen people (MBV, 385).

Dugin disdains empirical science and careful scientific thinking in general and espouses an archaic ideal of the "sacral society," but he also embraces scientific rhetoric and high-tech media when they help him to legitimize and spread his word. Hallmarks of his style include fuzzy, contradictory thinking, criticizing the "objectivity" of modern science, while taking full advantage of Internet technology. He affirms subjective mythical thinking, while callously dismissing personal feelings, experiences and relationships, and private rights.

As a number of studies have argued, neo-fascism is much more prominent in Dugin's writing than Slavophilism.[16] In his imagined world we encounter the anti-modern, anti-scientific, conservative-utopian views that mark fascist thought. Among the fascists whom Dugin admires are the German Nazi ideologist Karl Haushofer, who gave geopolitics a bad name; Sicilian

14. See http://vibori.info/rating/02-07-2003.shtml.
15. See http://www.ogoniok.ru/archive/2003/4798/19-18-25/.
16. See, for example, Laruelle, "Alexandre Dugin"; Dunlop, "Dugin's 'Neo-Eurasianism'"; and Umland, "Toward an Uncivil Society?"

Fig. 4. Aleksandr Dugin, *Ogonek*, 19 (May 2003), 18.

thinker Julius Evola, whose concept of "tradition" Dugin adopted; René Guenon, the French intellectual who converted to Islam; and the French Nouvelle Droite thinker Alain de Benoist. Dugin takes inspiration particularly from the French Nouvelle Droite, wanting to achieve for Orthodox Russia what the theorists of the New Right in France envision for Catholic Europe. Among contemporary Russian nationalists, he particularly singles out for praise Iury Mamleev, Evgeny Golovin (PA, 7), and one or two rightist Central Asian thinkers close to militant Islamic nationalism, for example his so-called teacher Geidar Dzhemal (PA, 7), and Timur Pulatov, author of the novel *Floating Eurasia* (*Plavaiushchaia Evraziia*, 1991).

Dugin's political plans focus on the grand geopolitical picture, on power and empire at the expense of the ordinary person. His amoral megalomania and his indifference to human suffering speak loud and clear: "I deal in big categories, categories of space—heartland, rimland, world island, the continent of Eurasia, Atlanticism… in my professional work I deal in global numbers, that is, not just one baby, but all the babies in the world, or not just one person with his anatomy, arms and legs, but 250 million arms or 500 million eyes, that is the approximately minimal object for geopolitical consideration" (PK, 95). Repeatedly, he reminds his audience that individual people and their welfare are of little importance to him—and to Russia. What matters to him is the massive aesthetic of whole continents and peoples and Russia's power and influence within that global scenario. This scornful anti-humanism also fits his fascist paradigm: "The nation is everything, the individual—nothing" (OG, 257). His fascist-imperialist appetite is best felt in his slogan, "Eurasianism above all" (OG, 777), which echoes the pan-Germanic hymn, "Deutschland über alles."

Dugin exalts the state and scoffs at the efforts of citizens in civil society to secure and defend individual rights. He holds to a mystical cult of the strong leader, imagined as the "White Tsar" and a strong secret police (ME, 579).[17] He admires the secret police and their terrorist tactics, even blaming "the liberals" for diminishing the prestige of the profession of spy, information gatherer, and secret agent (PK, 103). He praises the Soviet-era KGB for anticipating his Eurasianist project by investigating the sacral geographies of peoples of Eurasia "for the creation of an Asiatic strategic bloc under Moscow's control" (ME, 610). In a radio interview Dugin asserts that people actually benefit from being terrorized (PK, 99–100), and even suggests that Russia needs a new *oprichnina,* the secret police of Ivan the Terrible.[18]

Most important in Dugin's writings is his blending of geopolitical theory and the Eurasianism of the 1920s, which won a certain following in the 1980s in the Soviet Union. In the 1920s Eurasianist thinking developed among Russian émigré intellectuals interested in Russia's Asiatic heritage, most notably the philologist Nikolai Trubetskoi and the economist Petr Savitsky. The movement initially emerged in Symbolist and Scythian literary circles before the Revolution. The Eurasianist thinkers wanted to reconstitute the Russian empire, though without the repressive Russification of the nineteenth century and at the same time fully embrace the Asiatic aspects of

---

17. Note Dostoevsky's use of the term "White Tsar," in his *A Writer's Diary.* Dostoevsky was of the opinion that "the name of the white tsar should stand far above those of the khans and emirs, far above that of the empress of India, far above that of the caliph himself." Fyodor Dostoevsky, *A Writer's Diary,* Vol. 2: *1877–1881,* trans. K. Lantz (Evanston, IL: Northwestern University Press, 1994), 1369.

18. Aleksandr Dugin, "Russkii orden: sovremennoi Rossii nuzhna oprichnina," *Ogonek,* 5 (2005), www.ogoniok.com/archive/2005/4890/11-27-27.

Russian history, economy, and culture. Among the myriad republications of works of early twentieth-century Russian philosophers since the beginning of glasnost in 1986, thick volumes by various Eurasianists saw the light of day.[19] At the same time works by nationalists close to the Eurasianists, such as the ethnologist Lev Gumilev (1912–1992), started to appear. In his *From the History of Eurasia* (1993) Gumilev fleshed out the opinion of the earlier Eurasianists that Rus' was first built on a natural coalition of Turkic, Mongolian, and Slavic peoples, and that the Mongols exerted an influence on Russian history much more positive than the usually assumed disaster.

In concept, Dugin's neo-Eurasianism embraces the geopolitical theories of the British geopolitical theorist Sir Halford Mackinder, who, in a 1904 article, "The Geographical Pivot of History," developed a view of Eurasia as the geopolitical heartland of world history.[20] To establish post-Soviet Moscow as a world center, Dugin appropriates Mackinder's terminology. In *Democratic Ideals and Reality*, published in 1919, Mackinder used the concepts of "world island," the Eurasian "heartland," and the coastal "rimland" to distinguish continental and seafaring political cultures. In Mackinder's view, the heartland (Siberia, and more generally Eurasia) was the locus of ascendant power, while the influence of the rimland (primarily Britain and the United States) was waning.[21] In addition, Mackinder saw a strong possibility for a Eurasian alliance between Russia and Germany, which, he argued, should be forestalled at all costs. Anticipating the eventual formation of NATO, Mackinder stressed that the job of the rimland was to contain the heartland.

Dugin adopts Mackinder's terms, adding that the heartland is a positive concept in terms of archaic world culture and civilization (OG, 215). Into this picture Dugin injects his own reappropriation of the old Third Rome myth of Moscow and Holy Rus' as the homeland of true, unadulterated Christianity and of the good empire (PE, 11). With the shift of power, first, from Byzantium to Muscovy and, second, from the Mongols to Muscovy, Russians made the northeast of the Eurasian continent the locus of a great political power. The Russian state became an important actor in world affairs or, as Dugin puts it, a "leading subject of world history" (PE, 30).

Mackinder's geopolitical vocabulary was later adopted by a variety of intellectuals whom Dugin finds attractive—the Russian Eurasianists, Karl

19. N. S. Trubetskoi, *Istoriia. Kul'tura. Iazyk,* ed. V. M. Zhivov (Moscow: Progress/Univers, 1995); P. N. Savitskii, *Kontinent Evraziia,* ed. A. G. Dugin (Moscow: Agraf, 1997).

20. Sir Halford J. Mackinder, "The Geographical Pivot of History," *Geographical Journal,* 23, no. 4 (1904), 421–437.

21. For a discussion of Mackinder's views, see Arthur Butler Dugan, "Mackinder and His Critics Reconsidered," *Journal of Politics* 24, no. 2 (1962), 241–257.

Haushofer, and U.S. naval officer Admiral Alfred Mahen, who developed the concept of "sea power" (OG, 75). Dugin's understanding of Mackinder's theory relies partly on its use by the Russian Eurasianists, Petr Savitsky and Nikolai Trubetskoi, who in their *Europe and Humanity* (*Evropa i chelovechestvo*, 1920), embraced Mackinder's distinction between Atlanticism and continentalism to denote two different spheres of geopolitical influence. For them Russia was the great Eurasian continental power that had replaced the original Eurasian empire of the Mongols. Dugin adopts Savitsky's and Trubetskoi's conviction that the Mongols taught medieval Russians their political habits and gave them the geographical template for building empire.[22] As Dugin articulates this idea, Russians "seemed to change places with the Tatars" and eventually assumed control over the Eurasian space (PE, 29). Dugin's project of re-establishing Moscow's power throughout the vast expanses of the Eurasian continent aims at eventually shutting out the so-called liberal Atlanticist states of Western Europe and North America. We can see on the maps posted in 2002 on the Evraziia website that Dugin calls Russia the "ultimate world periphery" or the "black hole space" in the configuration of world power. He envisions Russia as becoming the "nucleus of multipolar resistance" to the Atlanticists and the hub of several axes, linking Moscow to Tokyo, Southeast Asia, India, Iran, and Berlin.[23]

Embracing Russia's dual European and Asian character and thus justifying regathering the old tsarist empire, Savitsky and Trubetskoi emphasized the interaction of Turkic and Iranian cultures with Slavic cultures. They borrowed Mackinder's term "Turanian" to describe the mix.[24] Dugin takes from Trubetskoi and Savitsky their post-Slavophile ideology of a "third way," which creates an imagined Eurasia built on Iranian-Turkic-Slavic bonding: "in [the Eurasianists'] conceptions the geographical location of Russia between East and West plays a central role. For them Eurasia is basically Russia, and the Russian ethnos (in the supranational sense of that word) is seen as today's bearer of Turanism [the general Turkic and Iranian heritage], a particular imperial psycho-ideology, conveyed to the Rus' by the Turkic-Mongolian tribes of the Horde. Thus, in distinction to the monarchist camp, the Eurasianists were less 'pan-Slavists' than they were Turkophiles" (ME, 591). Beyond Mackinder's idea of the Turanian, Dugin uses Eurasianist vocabulary of empire, itself derived from Byzantine imperial phraseology, that

22. See, for example, Trubetskoi, "Nasledie Chingiskhana: Vzgliad na russkuiu istoriiu ne s Zapada, a s Vostoka" (1925), *Istoriia. Kul'tura. Iazyk*, 239.

23. http://images.evrazia.org/images/map-3-small.jpg.

24. Trubetskoi, "O turanskom elemente v russkoi kul'ture," *Istoriia. Kul'tura. Iazyk*, 141, 156.

pictures the imperial state as a "symphony" embodying "imperial harmony and justice." Most important, he agrees with his Eurasianist forebears that on balance the Mongols had a beneficial effect on Russia and provided the geopolitical model for Muscovite imperial expansion (OG, 85).[25]

⤳

Perhaps the strangest term in Dugin's disturbingly eclectic mixture is the "postmodern." Immediately we must ask what this concept has to do with Dugin's anti-intellectual, anti-civil, historically backward-looking imperialism. To Dugin, the postmodern means essentially coming after the modern time, with its secular, rational, universalist worldview, and replacing it with a crude, newly reconstructed "medieval" view, featuring the cult of the White Tsar, an admiration for rule by force and terror, and a contempt for science, evidence, civil society, and human rights.

Dugin's interrogation of scientific fact links tangentially to Western postmodernist cultural criticism. Dugin sports a cavalier attitude toward scientific claims to truth, neither offering concrete, observed fact nor addressing the question of true judgment or truth. His arguments rely on rhetoric and repeated assertions in the hope that they will gain an aura of legitimacy. In *The Mysteries of Eurasia,* he cynically abuses postmodernist inquiry into the nature of fact to assert that there is really nothing one could call scientific fact:

> Disillusionment with the positive sciences operates on all levels—the discoveries of depth psychology and psychoanalysis showed the degree to which a supposedly "rational" person is under the influence of dark forces and impulses, walled up in the abysses of the subconscious; linguists and psycholinguists have revealed...the direct dependence of thought on the specifics of languages; positivist philosophers realized to their surprise that there is no such thing as an "isolated fact," and that outside of interpretation there can be no mention of facts; and finally, physicists studying the paradoxes of quantum mechanics came to the conclusion that the presence or absence of the "observer" exerts a direct influence on the course of quantum processes, introducing the subjective factor to a rigorous discipline, such as physics. (ME, 603)

In Dugin's view, the observer's personal interests, as well as his cultural, psychological, and linguistic conditioning, undermine the validity of science, suggesting that the whole pursuit of scientific knowledge is a waste of time. In short, Dugin calls for a return to non-scientific epistemic systems based on

25. See Nicholas Riazanovsky, "The Emergence of Eurasianism," *California Slavic Studies,* 4 (1967), 39–72, esp. 49, 55. Charles J. Halperin, "Russia and the Steppe: George Vernadsky and Eurasianism," *Forschungen zur osteuropäischen Geschichte* (Berlin), no. 36 (1985), 55–194, esp. 92, 96.

intuitive or revelatory insight, which, he realizes, will be jeered by scientists as "benighted," as "holdovers from the dark middle ages" and "savage aberrations of primitive humanity." His goal is to appeal to his rightist cohorts whom he hopes to bring forth from the countercultural shadows (PA, 11) with the bombastic thought: "It's time to return to myth. And that means a return to the magical, sacred and amazing country—Bright Rus'" (ME, 604).

Although he dismisses scientific knowledge, it is worth noting that Dugin makes pseudo-scientific arguments when it comes to ethnology, linguistics, or political theory. In keeping with his disdain for science, Dugin defines his "expert" knowledge in anti-scientific ways, linking this mode of thinking to the postmodern, as well as to fascist thinking. For example, he claims his adopted area of expertise, geopolitics, as a postmodern science, a "pack of intuitions, bound by an expectation of cognizing reality in an utterly new aspect" (OG, 4). Geopolitics claims no "scientific rigor" (OG, 13), but Dugin calls this theory a "leading, privileged discipline [sic] of the postmodern...a top-priority science of our new, post-industrial society" (OG, 6). In his twisted reworking the major benefit of geopolitics is a justification for Russian leadership in Central Asia.

Dugin employs a number of rhetorical tactics to create a sense of authority and credibility. Ironically, in the light of his dismissal of scientific inquiry, he sets great store by his academic credentials, which include two degrees, a claim to broad erudition across many disciplines (e.g., religious studies, political geography, popular culture), and a claim to fluency in at least nine languages. Dugin's style, at first glance, would seem to be that of an academic, although he writes almost entirely without sources and citations. He rarely gives concrete examples to prove an abstract point.

Dugin produces his reams of writing so rapidly and carelessly that dozens of factual errors—not to mention sloppy logic—creep into his writing.[26] For example, he loves to draw on etymologies, nearly always fake, to support his fascist values—mystical knowledge accessible only to the initiated, assertion of the sacredness of the Russian lands, male intellectual superiority, and women as a lower life form.[27] In his first book, *The Ways of the Absolute*

26. Dugin's mistakes include careless ones and grave misrepresentations. In *The Mystery of the Gospel*, he calls Muscovite rulers "tsars" even before the fall of Constantinople (MBV, 383), and he has the fall of Constantinople happening in 1454 (MBV, 385). He miscalculates the number of years between the Schism and the fall of Constantinople (MBV, 386). In a more significant error, he confuses the fifteenth-century Russian *hesychasts,* who were oriented toward a life of inward meditation, with the Possessors or Josephites, who were strongly inclined toward theocracy (MBV, 384).

27. Fake etymologies were also used by Eurasianists, such as George Vernadsky (see Halperin, "Russia and the Steppe," 125) and Nikolai Trubetskoi (see Riazanovsky, "The Emergence of Eurasianism," 49).

(*Puti absoliuta,* 1989–1990), while speaking of forms of mystical knowledge, Dugin links words that have no morphological or etymological relationship. For example, he links the Sumerian word *me* ("mystical force"), with the Indo-European root for "power," *mag* (for which Dugin gives no meaning, but which, in fact, does relate to notions of "power" or "force") and the Hindi *maya* ("illusion") (PA, 35–36).[28] Sumerian is a completely different language group, unconnected to Indo-European languages. And the Hindi *maya* is unconnected to the root for "power."

Elsewhere, Dugin justifiably relates the Sanskrit word for knowledge, *jna,* to the Greek word, *gnosis,* and German *kennen,* but insists that all of these words denote knowledge understood as "initiation" and actually "touching the principle of *sacred knowledge*" (PA, 66). Though some words for mystical knowledge, such as "gnosticism," arise from these roots, they relate purely to the realm of the mystical or sacred only in Dugin's imagination.

More important for our goal of interrogating geographical metaphor are Dugin's attempts to use etymology to establish the Russian lands as ancient and sacred ground, even before the Slavs ever arrived. He links the Russian word for "Swedish" (*shvedskii*) to Russian words for "light, white, bright" (*svetlyi*) and to the word for "holy" (*sviatoi*) (ME, 577). It has been established that the *shvedskii* came to Russian as a German borrowing and has nothing to do with either the much older Russian words *svetlyi* or *sviatoi*.[29]

Dugin's worldview combines an extreme religious-fanatical mentality with a conservative utopian temperament. Dugin revels in reimagining a

28. What most people would call Indo-European, Dugin following Nazi usage calls "Indo-Aryan." I would like to thank Marc L. Greenberg for untangling these and following fake etymologies.

29. Max Fasmer, *Etimologicheskii slovar' russkogo iazyka* (Moscow: Progress, 1986), vol. 3, 576, 585. According to Fasmer, *svetlyi* and *sviatoi* have no direct connection. *Svetlyi* has roots in the Indo-European word for "white" (*çvetás*) and *sviatoi* in the Indo-European word for "blooming" (*çvantás*). Although not directly relevant to this study, it is worth noting that Dugin uses particularly implausible etymologies to argue the superiority of the male sex and the inferiority of the female sex. This example shows how insubstantial Dugin's thinking is. In *The Russian Object* (*Russkaia veshch'*, 2001), an odious book with a neo-Nazi style down to the Fraktur-like font used on its title page, Dugin employs false etymologies to argue that because the Russian words for woman, *zhena* and *zhenshchina,* do not have etymological roots in the words for human being [*chelovek*] and man [*muzhchina*], women are not even the female of the human species but are something else quite different (RV, 2: 482). (In fact, *zhena* is related to the Indo-European word **gwen-* and the English word "queen." Fasmer relates *zhena* to the root **gna-* or "goddess" (Fasmer, *Etimologicheskii slovar',* vol. 2, 46). "Man" and "*muzh,*" which Dugin relates to *mysl'* or "thought" (RV, 2: 484) are related to the Indo-European "manu" but also the root for "testicle."

deep past, a past beyond textually provable history, that offers meaning for Russian existence. He anchors his Russian identity in archaic myths that color and distort the twentieth-century geopolitical terrain to which he subscribes in his more "scientific" works. To repeat Dugin's anti-scientific credo: "It's time to return to myth. And that means a return to the magical, sacred, and surprising country—Bright Rus'" (ME, 604).

In order to grasp Dugin's religious, political, and social project, which he calls "traditionalism," and his goal of defining an archaic Russian identity as a guide to charting Russia's future, it makes sense to outline Dugin's national-imperial myth, its setting in world geography and history, and Russia's place in it. A literary-critical account of Dugin's writing—particularly *The Ways of the Absolute* (1989), *The Metaphysics of the Gospel* (1994), *The Mysteries of Eurasia* (1996), and *Project Eurasia* (2004)—will delineate value-bearing images of space and time, main characters, and the significant plot functions of his mythic master plot, all leading to a more palpable summary of his vision for Russia.

The key factor in Dugin's thinking about identity is geographical space. In this point he follows the lead of Nazi geopolitical thinkers, the Eurasianists, and the Soviet-era ethnologist Gumilev, who theorized that identity and mentality are determined by geographical and meteorological environment.[30] Russian space in Dugin's writings is always pictured in terms of two geographical regions, the far north and northeast of Eurasia. His first concern is to establish the north's—and especially Moscow's—significance as "sacred ground," extending from prehistoric pagan times to the post-Soviet present, as the political, economic, and cultural center of all Eurasia. In *The Mysteries of Eurasia* Dugin emphasizes the central importance of the geographical north as a sacred source of all great peoples and civilizations. Drawing on a number of ancient myths—Greek, Hindi, Iranian—Dugin defines the north as the area above the large mountain ranges that stretch from east to west, where a number of major peoples find their mythical origins. For example, he claims, in Hinduism the north (or the east, depending on the variant) is the dwelling of the god Indra (ME, 587). In Greek myth the northern land, Hyperborea, is the birthplace of "sunny Apollo" (ME, 587). In Aryan myth, adopted in Nazi ideology, the North Pole is the birthplace of the Aryan race (ME, 577). Although in many mythologies the

30. Lev Gumilev, the son of famous poets Anna Akhmatova and Nikolai Gumilev, was interested in Eurasianism. Gumilev, Dugin alleges, met Savitskii in the Stalinist camps of the 1940s and became inspired by his theories (Dugin, OG, 83). (Note: Laruelle (*Russian Eurasianism*) disproves this allegation; see p. 56.) He developed the "passionary" theory, linking mentality and systems of value to geography, climate, and ecosystem.

north is a source of evil, Dugin insists that those initiated into the northern realm, open for themselves a paradise: "only by making a spiritual journey to the center, to the pole of the beyond, does the doom of the 'guards of the threshold' disperse, and the radiant [*presvetlyi*] polar garden of paradise is revealed" (ME, 606). In his maps of Eurasia Dugin shows the Russian north as that world periphery from which will emerge a new, powerful order.

Because the Internet plays a vital role in Dugin's effort to disseminate his views, it is important to mention the symbolic geography implicit in the name of his website, http://arctogaia.com. The URL, which uses Greek roots to convey the idea of the northland, connotes a virtual geographical north. The banner on the webpage informs us that we are visiting "Arctogaia, the whisper of the Absolute Motherland." Here one can find a virtual library of rightist reading matter, including Dugin's own works, his interviews, as well as a picture gallery with photographs of himself, his family, and close sympathizers.

We have already mentioned Dugin's fake-etymological hints as to the sacred and racially white nature of the northern steppe and forest that eventually became the Russian lands, wrongly linking the word Swedish to Russian words for light, white, bright (*svetlyi, belyi, svetovoi*) and to holy (*sviatoi*) (ME, 578). Dugin ties the root word for Russian (*rus*) to the Germanic word *rot* (red) which, translated into the Russian *krasnyi,* also means beautiful (ME, 578). Thus, the symbolic meanings of Holy Russia (*Sviataia Rus'*) derived by Dugin, include both "white and red" and "bright and beautiful."

Dugin's sense of time is oriented toward crisis and apocalypse, toward the revelation of the new temporal order, what he calls the coming "time after time." Drawing partly on Francis Fukuyama's 1990s mantra of the "end of history," which he quotes often, Dugin believes that humanity is at the end of time, after which there will be a wholly new order.[31] He finds a parallel between our time and his version of the apocalyptic medieval Muscovite mentality. At both times, so goes his story, Moscow provides a sheltering cloak against the apostasy of the rest of the world. In Muscovite times Dugin finds the roots of Russians' sense of being a chosen people. Medieval Muscovy was seen by its citizens as an "'island of salvation' chosen by providence" (MBV, 385). Muscovy was allegedly directly linked to the Holy Spirit and its "correct order" (*domostroitel'stvo*), which was to be revealed in the near future (MBV, 385).

---

31. Francis Fukuyama, *The End of History and the Last Man* (London: Hamish Hamilton, 1993).

Dugin's sense of time can be called counterutopian, which means the op-posite of a forward-looking, futuristic utopian time.[32] His sensibility leads him backward into deep history, which can mean either the archaic past "outside of time" or merely the past before recent centuries dominated by the European Enlightenment and modernity, which he wholly rejects for its universalist view of the human condition. Dugin takes this deep-past mythol-ogy as a usable conceptual basis, a tradition, as it were, for future social and political development. In his picture of the ideal future he sees the "coinci-dence of possibility with principle [*nachalo*]": "[I]n Tradition what is meant by the spiritual source [*istok*] or principle [*nachalo*] is not the actual past but the past 'outside of time,' the paradisal, the past of the golden age, and therefore is nearer to the future than to the actual past, or more exactly, to the 'eternal present,' to 'all ages' existing at once" (PA, 35; see also PE, 11).

In Dugin's geopolitical myth there are three kinds of heroes—the original Eur-asianists, fascist and European new-rightist thinkers, and his neo-Eurasianist contemporaries. He admires intellectuals who he believes share one of his passions, whether for Eurasian imperialism or for mythologies of the deep past. These heroes offer Dugin aspects of his ideology of traditionalism, which is vociferously negative—anti-personalist, anti-individualist, anti-civil rights. Traditionalism stands for the "rights of nations" but without saying who can claim those rights and act on them, who belongs to a nation, and who is to make that supreme decision as to who belongs.

Dugin's villains are whole classes of people—primarily the Jews and the Catholics, followed by Westerners—with whom Dugin disagrees, who stand for civil social values, representative democracy, and enlightenment ratio-nalism. In a "neo-pagan" mystical work, *The Metaphysics of the Gospel,* Dugin offers us a retread of the traditional Muscovite-Slavophile Orthodox expressions of hostility vis-à-vis Western Catholicism and Judaism. He re-cycles old anti-Semitic prejudices, calling Judas's purported "theocide" the "collective crime of the Hebrews [*iudei*]" (MBV, 365), which for all time defined Jews as an "accursed people" (*prokliataia natsiia;* MBV, 367).

Over against the "bad" humanism of his villains, Dugin idolizes Eastern Orthodoxy and its emphasis on "metaphysics"—by which he means kenosis, meditation, and mystical revelation.[33] The "mystical soul" of Orthodoxy, ac-cording to Dugin, "draws to itself the ray of apotheosis" of the "non-divine [*nebozhestvennyi*] through grace" (MBV, 265–266). By the "non-divine"

---

32. Karl Mannheim, *Ideology and Utopia: An Introduction to the Sociology of Knowledge* (1929), trans. by L. Wirth and E. Shils (San Diego: Harcourt Brace Jovanovich, 1985), 230.

33. Here Dugin uses the ancient Greek term *hesychasm,* which means inner spiritual calm and tranquility.

Dugin means Mary Mother of God and, through her, all of humanity. Politically Dugin sees Orthodoxy as the "imperial Christianity of Byzantium" (MBV, 289) and the true religion of empire. In contrast, he claims, "Judeo-Christian" Catholicism focuses on the salvation of the individual soul (MBV, 265) and on earthly, theocratic rule (MBV, 289).

In his attacks on Europeans Dugin uses the pro-Mongol, anti-Western Eurasianist terminology of Nikolai Trubetskoi—and before him, of the nineteenth-century nationalist, Nikolai Danilevsky—referring to the Europeans as the "Romano-Germanic tribes" and referring to the rule of European colonizers as the "Romano-Germanic yoke" (PE, 33). Peter's new order and his Westernized aristocracy of the eighteenth and nineteenth centuries become homegrown villains, the " 'colonizers' of barbaric lands," and ordinary Russians "take on the role of the 'exotic natives' " (PE, 34). Dugin also calls West Europeans "Atlanticists" formed into NATO and led by the United States, which—in Dugin's view—as the single superpower of the 1990s was trying to spread its liberalism, civil society, individual rights, and democratic ideals across the globe.

It is worth noting the irony in the fact that despite his hostility toward the West Dugin accepts European ideological models. He cites and debates far more European and American thinkers than he does his "heroic" Central Asians of Turkic and Iranian descent. Eurasia has virtually no voice in Dugin's world, while the mythic villains of the West have many varied voices that are much more interesting to Dugin.

The goal of Dugin's mythmaking is to restore a sense of Russia's legitimate control over its former geopolitical space and with it a feeling of national pride and identity: his story will end with the return of the physical Russian empire and public consciousness of the empire as sacred ground. Although he claims just the opposite—that he seeks a "multipolar free world with a 'flowering complexity' of cultures and civilizations" (PE, 133)—Dugin forces the issue of Russia as center for the unification for Eurasia. "Russians should always insist on the geopolitical 'moscocentrism' of Eurasia, that is, move tirelessly toward the realization of a 'panasiatic' or 'euroasiatic' project, the strategic integration of the eastern part of the continent, which exactly corresponds to the logic of Russia's territorial development and its mission in the framework of sacral geography" (ME, 613). As he puts it, empire is "Russia's geopolitical idea, its calling, its fate" (PE, 133). "Eurasian centrism" will return to Russians a sense of their historical importance. Russia will no longer be a periphery.

We can now reconstruct the main events informing Dugin's search for a new iteration of a Eurasian order. The plot moves through five main stages—pre-modern Orthodox society, pre-modern Mongol rule, the two modern Russian empires, and postmodernity. The pre-modern offers Dugin the template for the mystical mindset and the simple social order that he wants for building a new traditionalist Eurasia. Ancient religions as different as Hinduism and Judaism, Dugin argues in *The Ways of the Absolute,* are built on a first principle of the "inexpressible," access to which is hindered by "solid form," the body of the physical world (PA, 18). Cognition here is oriented toward salvific liberation from matter:

> Liberation of the form of things from the shell of matter is the task of reasoned [*razumnyi*] existence (as understood by the Tradition), where gnoseology strictly identifies with soteriology [doctrine of salvation], that is, the cognition of the material object, the process or phenomenon is at the same time their "salvation," their essential removal from the material burden of flesh. The task of cognition is in the transfiguration of the flesh of the cognizing person. (PA, 59)

This relation to the body and matter will shift in Dugin's "postmodern" rendition, but the fascination with the archaic and the mystical and inexpressible remains a crucial aspect of building a new basis for political authority.

Pre-modern traditionalist society gives Dugin the social castes on which to model a contemporary traditionalist "sacred empire." Recycling nineteenth-century stereotypes used by Nietzsche, he sees warriors and priests as the elite castes who hold power in traditional societies (MBV, 373). As he puts it, the "Sacred Empire...is a synthesis and the acme of the adequate combination of the priestly and the warrior principles" (MBV, 375). Medieval Russia, Dugin continues, inherited from Byzantium a concept of the "sacred empire" and combined it with a balance between two kinds of kingdom, the Kingdom of God (*tsarstvie*) and the Earthly Kingdom (*tsarstvo*) (MBV, 375). Dugin claims—without any historical foundation—that this Orthodox balance between earth and heaven forestalls the extremes of theocratic governance, which, in his view, is the fate of the Jews (MBV, 379), and tyranny, which is the weakness of the pagan system of rule by the warriors. In Dugin's view, the Byzantine empire provided a "unique synthesis of the Kingdom of God and the Earthly Kingdom, having become that providential *thousand-year kingdom*" (MBV, 379). In Eastern Europe, in Dugin's view, this pre-modern spiritual and social order was first embodied in ancient Kievan Rus', which was "in a certain—spiritual—sense, the province of the Byzantine empire" (MBV, 383), the northern edge of the "Orthodox *oikumene*," the inhabited world of Orthodox Christianity (PE, 25).

Although ethnic identity is decidedly underplayed in Dugin's picture of pre-modern life, he explicitly views ethnic amalgamation as a crucial aspect of building the Eurasian imperium. In *Project Eurasia* Dugin cites Lev Gumilev's theory, based in part on the Eurasians' speculations, that the Kievan population was a combination of Slav, Iranian, and Turkic peoples (PE, 13, 15). Importantly, it is in the pre-modern era that Russians become not one ethnic group but a mix of various Slavic, Turkic, and Finno-Ugric groups (PE, 82). Here is the model for the supra-nationality that Dugin hopes to reconfirm in the new multicultural, multiethnic Eurasian state.

Russian princes at the northern periphery of Eurasia eventually transferred to themselves the imperial authority of its two precursors, the Byzantine and the Mongol, thus redefining the Russian lands as the center of the world. Muscovy appropriated the military and political means to build empire from the Mongols and the mantle of empire along with the Third Rome myth and the myth of "Holy Russia" from Byzantium (ME, 576). From an ideological point of view, Dugin puts a slightly different slant on the three traditional pillars of the autocracy, emphasizing all pre-modern Russian history as the "history of Orthodoxy," which fused "the people and the state" into one whole (MBV, 383). In this version of medieval Russian history, for Dugin as for Gumilev and his Eurasianist predecessor Petr Savitsky, the Mongols became a much more positive force than in the traditional, west-leaning narrative of Russian history. Dugin holds Muscovy as the pinnacle of Russian greatness.

The modern era perverted true Russian identity, as the medieval deep past and its so-called traditions are its ideal. Dugin wholly rejects modern concepts of evolution and progress (PA, 10) and the tendency over the last few centuries to build "anti-traditional" societies (PA, 179). In Russia this trend, embodied by the late seventeenth-century Schism and Peter's ascension to the throne, led to the ruin of what Dugin sees as the fine balance in medieval Muscovy between the Kingdom of God and the Earthly Realm. By the early eighteenth century, in Dugin's historical mythologizing, Russia fell from grace (MBV, 305). Indeed, Dugin sees the act of moving Russia's capital from Moscow to St. Petersburg as the destruction of the "symphony" of forces among Russian state, church, and people (MBV, 390). This move meant the "secularization (*obmirshchvlenie*) of Russia" (MBV, 390).

The postmodern, which Dugin understands to be the present time, suggests rich possibilities for moving "back" to the future. From one perspective, the postmodern can be seen as both further spiritual destruction brought by the demons of modernity—rationalism, capitalism, universalism, and liberalism. From another, postmodernity rejects the modern and lays bare archaic aspects of the human psyche, thus paving the way for a re-engagement with the "time before time." Dugin sees the postmodern as a two-pronged development. The main branch of the postmodern, as he puts it in a 2004 interview in *Khudozhestvennyi zhurnal,* is a radicalization of modernism as the "hypermodern" or the "ultramodern." This form of the postmodern means *"total nihilism,* full desemanticization of the substantial [*soderzhatel'nyi*] historical process, in which the human person becomes irrelevant and has no replacement" (ZS, 19). In *Project Eurasia* Dugin describes this postmodernity in economic and political terms:

> The postmodern is globalism, ultraliberalism, domination of the unipolar [U.S.-dominated] world, the domination of the network, the loss of validity of all traditional forms of identity—of states, religions, nations, ethnic groups, even families and sexes. Instead of the state there is the "open society," instead of traditional confessions—sectarianism and indifference [*indifferentnost'*], instead of peoples—individuals, instead of sexes—clones, cyborgs and performance of transsexual operations. (PE, 498)

This branch of the postmodern is a *"process of realizing the exhaustion of the modern* as such" (ZS, 19). As Dugin claims in *Pop Culture and the Signs of the Times,* this form of the postmodern functioned as an important tool of colonization of post-Soviet Russia by the West in the 1990s (PK, 450).

In answer to this concept of the decadent postmodern Dugin defines another, "eastern" postmodern, a fusion of the old left and the old right in a new "active postmodern." In his definition it is the "radical antithesis of post-history, the active dissolution of the existing System, the loud and victorious assertion of the emptiness [*pustotnost'*] of its center.... active postmodernism will become reality only if the contemporary world falls into the emptiness of its own center, will be eaten up by awakened chaos" (PK, 433). Dugin believes the decadent postmodern will become a cultural, economic, and political black hole that will suck everything into itself, leaving room for the backward reaching, eastern branch of the postmodern—Dugin's solution to the Russian identity crisis.

Dugin sees this eastern branch of the postmodern as recapturing the premodern. He cites French rightist Jean Parvulesco's conceptualization of the postmodern as *nettoyage par le vide* or cleaning house, as a result of which the *"fundamental archaic traits"* of culture begin to shine through (ZS, 19). Now, at the "end of time," Dugin hopes for a new "initiation" into the ancient "center," the sacred wholly other, returning from the "periphery," in which humankind resides (PA, 78). In *Project Eurasia* Dugin defines the "postmodern of the East [*postmodern Vostoka*]" as a process of fusing the postmodern with particularly Russian traditions: "Russia *must absorb the parameters of the postmodern,* but use them for its own historical goals, reformulating in postmodern terms its historical mission (just as the Soviet period was a formulation of that same mission in terms of the New time, the modern" (PE, 163). If the Western postmodern means the end of history, a nonsensical ethical void, the lack of an absolute valuative center, then the eastern postmodern points toward the "return to the synthetic, integral style that on this new historical level reconstructs wholeness, characteristic of traditional societies" (PE, 164). Thus, in a number of writings Dugin points toward an ideal traditionalist society, a "utopia," as it were, and a new human type.

In distinction to pre-modern spirituality, which views the corporeal world as a barrier to unutterable mystical truths and attempts to tear down that barrier, in Dugin's postmodern world, the corporeal will have a distinct place in a "metaphysics for the earth" (PA, 15). In a 2004 interview Dugin announces: "We are standing on the threshold of a global *conservative revolution,* on the threshold of a new humankind, a shift in the anthropological code" (ZS, 20). His book, *Pop Culture and the Signs of the Times* (2005), offers a clearer, though still vague, view of how that conservative revolution might start. He foresees the merging of the new left and the new right (PK, 424), even as Atlanticism and Western globalization force the world community to accept an anti-utopian, liberal "brave new world" (PK, 121). The new right, he claims, has rejected "statism," the concept of the nation-state, the xenophobia and social-ethnic elitism of the old right and is now seeking "wholism," a sense of wholeness rooted in ancient sacral life newly rediscovered (PK, 425). Those on the new left have liberated themselves from the "terror of reason" and now seek a new version of the dissolution of hierarchy and the "orgiastic festival of revolution" (PK, 425). Dugin claims that the difference between right and left is superficial and that both will benefit from passing through chaos to find a better order, which includes the "return of the sacral": "the chaos of the 'new left' becomes the embryo of the order of the 'new right'" (PK, 426).

Russia will offer an attractive alternative to the Atlanticists' anti-utopian scenario, by forming a Eurasian Union "with its neighboring civilizations [through] a complex, many-leveled, dramatic dialogue" (PE, 123). Dugin anticipates a federalist order with economic, religious, and cultural autonomy permitted to local communities in great measure (PK, 143). The new economy allegedly will be anything but centralized, characterized by autarchism, featuring many sovereign local economies, which will not be ruled by a unifying theory (PK, 146). A seeming contradiction here is Dugin's insistence on a "patriarchal model" (PK, 153) in which there will be local autonomy but only with the cooperation of the overriding state centered in Russia, indeed, in Moscow. These local and regional economies are to be coordinated and integrated through the state, which would be another way of describing a new economic centralization and colonization.

Thus, this ideal Eurasian society is both patriarchal and hierarchical, despite the fact that Dugin tries to have it offer some measure of liberation of peoples "oppressed" by the Atlanticists. Without defining what a people is and how it is decided who belongs to what people, Dugin outlines a social and political order based on "rights of peoples," of national communities, not of the individual (PE, 156). In many ways, Dugin appears to be recycling the old Soviet nationalities policy, only now making it sound liberationist.

Along with political hypocrisy comes religious hypocrisy. Dugin combines a desire to seem tolerant of all ethnic groups and religions, particularly ancient ones, with an affirmation of the superiority of Russian Orthodoxy as the state religion. In Eurasia there are several dominant religions—Christianity, Islam, Buddhism, Judaism, Taoism, as well as "archaic cults." Eurasianism, Dugin claims, welcomes ethnic and religious difference (PK, 165, 169), while at the same time asserting the "universal mission of the Orthodox Church" (PK, 167). As with the multicultural economy that requires coordination of the "state," in the religious sphere there needs to be an interfaith council run at the center that settles conflicts between religions (PE, 169).

Inscribing a counterutopian dream in the playful irreverence of postmodernism as we know it, Dugin dwells on the issue that worries him most—Russian identity. He claims that being Russian is primarily defined by messianism, the sense of being a godbearing, chosen people, inhabiting the "sacral geography" of Eurasia and conscious of being at the earth's center. At base, Dugin associates being Russian with embracing the northern Russian lands as paradise. He claims fuzzily that all one has to do to be Russian is merely to feel the sacredness of Russia: "Russians call 'Russian' anyone who agrees with their profound intuition about the sacred quality of the lands on which they live" (ME, 589). In Dugin's world, the Russian lands occupy that source, that *"central* place" pictured in so many ancient mythologies. It is this sense of inhabiting a sacred space that lends Russians their sense of "uniqueness" and defines "Russian patriotism" (ME, 589). Russia's mission, Dugin concludes, is the "deep realization of the necessity of uniting the giant territory of the Eurasian continent" (PE, 348).

This link of Russian identity to the sacral center translates into a reassertion of imperial space: there is no Russian identity without empire. There is no Russian ethnicity per se and no personhood outside of the ruler. There is only space. Other than the iconic image of the leader, the "Russian White Tsar," there are no selves, no individuals. There are only the masses: "The nation is everything, the individual—nothing" (OG, 257). Now, in our postmodern time, Dugin reasserts a tie between Russian identity, state, leader, religion, and empire that recalls medieval Muscovy: "Russia never identified itself as its population as something only ethnic—it was rather a reality of a higher level, a reality of geo-sacral Tradition, in which various nations had their own appropriate place" (ME, 579). The tsar is the leader of all ethnic groups in the empire and is always more important than any one ethnicity (ME, 579).

Dugin apparently senses that most Russians will balk at his horribly simplistic, anti-humanist, and oppressive definition of identity, because he starts to treat them as if they were children who need to be taught who they are: "One has to impress (*vnushit'*) upon all Russians the basic idea that personal identity of each separate person is of secondary importance, a derivative of national identity." To this didactic thought he adds, almost comically—if it were not such a threat to Russian intelligence: "Russians must realize that in the first place, they are Orthodox, in the second—Russians, and only in the third place—humans" (OG, 255). In *Project Eurasia* he repeats his radical motto: "The nation is everything, the individual is nothing" (PE, 416).

Dugin is different from conservative and extreme nationalist Russian precursors and contemporaries. His thought has been called, justifiably, an "eclectic Russian version of far-right thought rather than...a new variant on traditional Eurasianism."[34] Although some differences between the conservative traditions of Solzhenitsyn and Rasputin and Dugin's views have already received mention, it is worth dwelling on similarities and differences in their forms of imagined geography. Although both embrace the north and the northeast as the homeland of pure Russianness, the neo-nationalists in no way anticipate Dugin's vague mystifications and contradictory thinking.[35] Solzhenitsyn sees development of the Russian northeast as a choice for a *national* rather than *imperial* future and a move toward much greater economic and technological strength. Solzhenitsyn urges national self-definition in the spirit of humility, while Dugin arrogantly urges the expansion of Russian influence wherever possible.

Although he trumpets the "rights of the nation," Dugin is neither a populist nor a nationalist in any traditional sense; he has no admiration for the Russian peasantry or any other social group as the defining center of Russian identity. He dismisses Solzhenitsyn's proposals for local autonomy presented in the latter's much-discussed "How Should We Restructure Russia" (1990).[36] Here Solzhenitsyn draws on a Swiss model of cantons to build decentralized local

34. Laruelle, "Alexandre Dugin," 85.
35. In *From under the Rubble* [*Iz-pod glyb*] (Paris, 1974), in the article titled "Repentance and Self-Limitation as Categories of National Life," Solzhenitsyn defines the north and the northeast of Russia as the Russian "home" [*dom*]. The future of Russia is the "Russian Northeast," which Solzhenitsyn defines as the "North of European Russia...and the middle region of Siberia" (148).
36. A.I. Solzhenitsyn, "Kak nam obustroit' Rossiiu?" *Literaturnaia gazeta,* 18 September, 1990, 3–6.

governance into the Russian political order. Dugin rejects this autonomous model in *The Foundations of Geopolitics,* when he discusses Russia's economic "third way," which suggests that security and "national flowering" are most important and cannot be achieved by Swedish or Swiss models (OG, 281).[37]

Since 2005 Dugin's vision of the Eurasianist empire has shifted away from political science toward what one might call strategic dreaming in what Dugin dubs "Internet Eurasia." In *Pop-Culture and the Signs of the Times* he writes: "It is time to understand that Eurasia has a place not only in physical, economic, and political geography, but also in virtual, internet geography" (PK, 488). He appears to have shifted away from an actual, political solution to make Russia the center of the world and world events. Now we encounter what may be called "Dugin-lite," that is, Dugin trying to sound more like a Bakhtinian, or even a Lyotardian, in his praise of polyphony and the decentralization that the Internet brings. This new and entirely hypocritical realization of the Eurasian project is happening in the virtual medium of the Internet, which, against all his earlier rhetoric, is seen as good because it is liberating, democratic (which even for Dugin is "good" when one is waging war with Western liberalism). The Internet is a powerful tool because it gets rid of what he now calls the "authoritative [*vlastnyi*] center," and allows a place for Dugin and others' extremist views to be aired. The Internet has changed our accustomed view of the "center which sends forth the word, and the enormous passive majority of consumers who are forced to be silent or recycle the same stupidity that they had heard on the TV screen the night before" (PK, 482). He proclaims the Internet the "weapon of the disenfranchised of this world" (PK, 489) because "in the Internet everyone is equalized—both the marginalized and the System, both rich and poor, both rulers [*vlastiteli SMI*] and users of information" (PK, 490). The Internet gives life to "ideal democracy" which, he adds, "in reality has never existed and will never exist" (PK, 482).

Dugin enthusiastically acknowledges the help that the Internet gives to his extremist cause. He asserts that in the vocabulary of the Internet, "'anarchy,' 'narcotics,' 'fascism,' 'maniacs,' 'bomb,' 'nationalism,' 'extremism'…far outstrip the quiet politically correct [words] 'market,' 'human rights,' 'Soros,' 'open society'" (PK, 482). For Dugin the revolutionaries of today are the Internet hackers and pirates who transgress against Western

37. In a 2006 interview Solzhenitsyn expressed strong concern about Russia's future and regretted that his model had thus far received no attention from political leaders (*Der Standard,* 14–15 October 2006, p. 2. Thanks to Jay Rosellini for bringing this article to my attention). It is interesting to note that Fadin does draw positive attention to a moderate Solzhenitsyn-inspired conservatism around the newspaper, *Grazhdanin Rossii,* founded in 1993 (Andrei Fadin, *Tretii Rim v tret'em mire* (Moscow: Letnii sad, 1999), 209–210).

copyright laws. In some places, he notes, with cookies one can trace where a user has been and protect copyright, but in Eurasia—for example, in Russia and the former republics of the Soviet Union, in China, India, and Iran—there is a whole industry of Internet piracy that is challenging the monopolar world of the Atlanticists. The volume of piracy and production of pirating programs has an important strategic value and defines this part of the world as the geographical zone of "anti-copyright" (PK, 485). Dugin calls on anti-Western, anti-liberal activists to wage war through the Internet: "no one can just sit through [modernity], and, however much we might just wish away the 'world-wide web' [*mirovaia pautina*], sooner or later we will find ourselves swaddled in it, and then it really will be too late" (487). Dugin urges conservatives not just to sit back but to take control of the conservative revolution on all its fronts, including the digital one.

The Internet thus provides Dugin with a postmodern, post-industrial medium for his counterutopian theorizing. How to evaluate this recent move toward the Internet is a crucial question. Does the development of this virtual Eurasia mark a retreat from the political scene, an admission that the actual return of the Russian empire and the full authority of the Russian Orthodox Church will not soon become state policy? Or does Dugin's move signify a strategy for building a political network, something like the quite successful moveon.org on the liberal side of the U.S. political scene?[38] Very likely, given Dugin's tenacity, we should view it as the latter—as a way of marshalling a segment of public opinion that eventually could be moved to realize the neo-Eurasianist dream.

It has been argued that Dugin's Russocentric empire-building and his heralding of Russian national identity are fully at odds with one another. Solzhenitsyn made the point in 1974 in *From Under the Rubble*, that the two contradict one another. As *Kommersant* journalist Andrei Fadin notes, "our whole imperial tradition can be viewed in essence as a variant of this kind of self-assertion, rebellion against the consciousness of our own quality of being second-rate [*vtorichnost'*] and peripheral [*periferiinost'*], an inferiority complex turned inside out."[39] This imperial effort to insert Russia into the world system has defined Russian culture and "popular consciousness" throughout the modern era.[40] Fadin and many others take the opposite view: the imperial myth destroyed the national myth and the "basis of our self-perception, self-understanding, our way of fitting into the world."[41]

38. Umland argues that Dugin is involved in the quiet stage of building a rightist following.
39. Fadin, *Tretii Rim*, 86.
40. Ibid., 87.
41. Ibid.

Dugin's anti-Westernism has prompted considerable debate. Writing in 1999, *Izvestia* journalist Andrei Kolesnikov parried: "As we come to an understanding of ourselves, we also need to understand the sense of American or, more broadly, western geopolitics. Its goal is not to invade, subdue, or weaken Russia. The point is rather to preserve the influence of western civilization."[42] Kolesnikov also mimics Dugin's political vocabulary, mentioning Samuel Huntington's "clash of civilizations" and Russia as a "zone of indeterminacy." He asks whether Russia will stay in the zone of Western influence or whether it will go some third way. Mocking Dugin's dream combining the primitive and the high-tech, Kolesnikov asks, "Will [Russia] return to the status of an empire in bast shoes, but with rockets, or will it develop as a democratic state oriented toward a market economy and generally civilized standards of living?"[43] After the Kursk submarine accident in 2000 Kolesnikov accused the Kremlin of starting to talk in the language of Aleksandr Prokhanov's rightist newspaper *Zavtra,* to which Dugin is a contributor:

> No one should be surprised that Aleksandr Dugin, the prominent geopolitical philosopher of the extreme right, the regular contributor to Prokhanov's paper, is making an appointment with [Gleb] Pavlovsky [the pro-Kremlin political scientist]. Extreme rightist ideology is now becoming more than dominant in national [*otechestvennyi*] social commentary and government rhetoric—it is becoming "in." Dugin even seems fit to join the team of Kremlin speechwriters: he writes wonderfully, although sometimes a bit mistily.[44]

Kolesnikov quips that with the acceptance of Dugin in Kremlin circles, "we can now finally conclude that government ideology has taken shape" and asks ironically "how is Dugin worse" than Mussolini's speechwriter Giovanni Gentile.[45]

In conclusion, Dugin's writings capture three themes prevalent in contemporary Russia. One is a backward-looking nostalgia for empire. The second is a fascination with the mystical and the arcane. And the third is a love of high-tech chic. Interestingly, this and other rightist efforts to re-establish Russian imperial pride have aroused a series of important creative efforts to incorporate the periphery in a number of alternative articulations of post-Soviet Russian personhood.

42. Kolesnikov, quoted from *Izvestia* (27 March 1999), in Andrei Kolesnikov and Aleksandr Privalov, *Novaia russkaia ideologiia* (Moscow: GU-VshE, 2001), 44.
43. Ibid.
44. Ibid., 323.
45. Ibid., 323–324.

3 ILLUSORY EMPIRE
Viktor Pelevin's Parody of Neo-Eurasianism

> It is not difficult to detect behind this forgery, now more than 70 years old, the activity of well-financed and aggressive forces which were interested in concealing the truth about Chapaev from the peoples of Eurasia....the very discovery of the present manuscript seems to us a clear indication that the balance of power on the continent has shifted.
> —PELEVIN, *Chapaev and the Void* (1996)

Among the most popular novels in post-Soviet Russia, Viktor Pelevin's *Chapaev and the Void* (*Chapaev i pustota*, 1996), starts with a preface by an imaginary editor, who addresses his readers as the "peoples of Eurasia"—they are not Russians nor is Russia a place on the map.[1] The novel's title refers to the popular Civil War hero Vasily Chapaev, the commander made famous in a 1923 novel, a 1930s film, and hundreds of jokes. Pelevin's editor wants to bring his readers the "truth about Chapaev," that "has been hidden for too long from the peoples of Eurasia" (ChP, 9). The novel about Chapaev that then follows consists of the edited notes of the avant-garde poet-philosopher Petr Pustota (whose name means Peter Void or Peter Emptiness)—whom the historical Russian world knows and loves as Chapaev's soldierly sidekick Petia. Against all expectations, this playful novel portrays Chapaev as a cultivated Buddhist guru just playacting as the headstrong but brilliant cavalry officer Chapaev of Soviet times.

Pustota claims to have finished his notes between 1923 and 1925 in the Central Asian (fantasy) locale of Kafka Yurt, close to the same time as Dmitry Furmanov wrote his canonical Socialist Realist epic, *Chapaev*. Pustota's story is complicated by the fact that it proceeds in two different historical moments, though we readers are never fully sure which time, if any, is the "real" one. Although Petr wants his readers to believe that his story takes

---

Citations from Viktor Pelevin's *Chapaev i Pustota* (Moscow: Vagrius, 2000) are given in the text, using the acronym "ChP" and page number(s). The title of the English translation is *Buddha's Little Finger*, trans. A. Bromfield (New York: Penguin, 2001). All translations are my own.

1. Konstantin Kedrov, "Knizhnyi reiting," *Izvestiia*, 4 July 1997), http://dlib.eastview.com. www2.lib.ku.edu:2048/sources/article.jsp?id=3159193.

place in 1919, he has to deal with a competing story that makes him an inmate in a Moscow mental hospital around the time of the fall of the Soviet
Union in 1991.

The same is true of space depicted in *Chapaev and the Void*. The editor
never mentions Russia as such, and in the novel Petr mentions Russia only
once in a heated philosophical debate about consciousness, mind, and body.
The familiar territory of Russia and its twentieth-century counterpart, the
Soviet Union, is replaced by a number of dislocated spaces, both real and
recognizable (e.g., Moscow) and imaginary (e.g., Eurasia), which will turn
out to be a disparate handful of imagined spaces in someone's fantasy.

It is important that the editor thinks of the anticipated readership for Petr
Pustota's story as Eurasian rather than Russian. Russia as such exists here
more or less as a sad joke in a philosophical dialogue. The reference to Eurasia
in the preface recalls the post-Soviet surge of enthusiasm for neo-Eurasianism
among some ultraconservative political circles. Just the mention of this
marked geographical space invites a reading of the novel as a response to
Aleksandr Dugin's loud neo-Eurasianist expressions of imperial nostalgia,
of a renewed desire for geopolitical centrality, for power and security.[2]

This chapter focuses on themes crucial to Pelevin's *Chapaev and the Void*,
the deconstruction of the Soviet mass psyche and the search for identity.
Contemporary neo-Eurasianism with its national-imperial idea is an ideological straw man that receives wonderful philosophical and psychological
satirical treatment in this novel. Among its delightful features are a series
of zany philosophical dialogues variously about consciousness, ethics, and
metaphysics—and always about identity. The post-Soviet tendency to link
identity to spatial-geographical metaphor, becomes here the object of a fundamental philosophical challenge.

Set partly in a Moscow mental hospital, Pelevin's Chapaev parody lends
itself to a psychoanalytic challenge to the repressive neo-Eurasianist view
of human nature. Here the focus is on the constructions of self of the four
inmates in the psychiatric hospital story, each of whom is viewed as an allegorical component in something we can call the "national-imperial psyche."
What might once have been presented as a cohesive, mass self, celebrating
the myths and symbols of Soviet power, has now crumbled into separate
parts, each searching for identity and meaning. The fantasies of each display
the detritus of a fragmenting order in which symbols of power mix comically with those of other, invasive, cultures. In the balance of each psyche we
find a dominant psychological component—whether super-ego, ego, or id.

---

2. "Eurasia" is a term one encounters elsewhere; for example, in Vladimir Sorokin's conceptualist porno satire, *Blue Lard* (*Goluboe salo*) (1999).

Two characters cannot bear their newfound independence and "seek the master," to use a Russian term (*ishchut khoziaina*). These are the cross-dressing weightlifter, Merely Maria, who takes his name and identity from a Mexican soap opera, and the mystically minded Mafioso Vladimir Volodin. The consciousness of each inmate is dominated by hyper-awareness of authority. In them the Lacanian Symbolic Order dominates, speaking to the self's acceptance of and interaction with authoritative symbols, sets of rules, and leaders in society. The third is the late-Soviet student, drunkard, and would-be suicide victim Semyon Serdiuk, in whom a seemingly inexplicable sense of loss, nostalgic mourning for Stalinist militarism, and a yearning to die for a noble, military cause symbolize a sort of national-imperial unconscious—that inchoate, terrifying "Real" that threatens the contemporary male Russian psyche. The inmate who fittingly demands the most attention from the reader is the purported author of *Chapaev and the Void,* Petr Pustota, a young intellectual who imagines himself both an edgy, avant-garde poet and a Civil War hero. His fantasy act of picturing himself as philosophical interlocutor beside the massively popular hero Chapaev during the consciousness-defining historical moment of the Civil War, can be said to embody the national-imperial Imaginary Order.

To understand Pelevin's satire of neo-Eurasianism, it is helpful to summarize the aspects of Dugin's thinking that interest Pelevin. Dugin stands for a view of Russia as an imperial nation, with Moscow designated as the center of all Eurasia. One of his main ideas is that nations, not individuals, have personhood and rights. The only individual who has value is the leader, the "White Tsar." Finally, Dugin supports the idea of a police state. He approves of the use of violence and terror, particularly against his enemies, the liberals, who believe that individual people have civil rights. One of Dugin's favorite historical tyrants, the White officer Baron Ungern von Sternberg—who in 1921 conquered and briefly ruled a part of Mongolia—is featured in Pelevin's novel as Baron Jungern.[3]

Pelevin makes reference to neo-Eurasianist geography, with Moscow as the center of an enormous empire and Eurasia as its massive periphery. The Eurasia of Pelevin's novel is nothing more than the focal point of an obviously imagined geography. In total, *Chapaev and the Void* features five imagined geographical settings—two in Moscow and three in peripheral Eurasian spaces. Petr's story starts in Moscow of early 1919, that is,

---

3. Aleksandr Dugin, "Misterii Evrazii" (1996), *Absoliutnaia rodina* (Moscow: Arktogeia, 1999), 600. Baron Ungern von Sternberg, a Baltic German, was the dictator of Mongolia for six months in 1921. Known as the "Black Baron" for his cruelty, he was betrayed to the Red Army by his own troops and shot.

Moscow soon after it regained its status as Russia's capital. It transfers to post-Soviet Moscow, sometime in the early 1990s. Petr Pustota's 1919 Civil War fantasy, which weaves throughout and occupies half the novel, continues in three settings that we can call "psychic spaces," all of them in fantasy Central Asia: Altai-Vidniansk, Inner Mongolia, and a psychedelic version of the Ural River.[4]

The two Moscows in Pelevin's novel are historically based and can be traced on a map. In Pelevin's symbolic geography there is no actual, existing geographical periphery that is other or alternative to the center Moscow. What we have are psycho-geographical spaces, spaces of the fragmented national-imperial mind, that deconstruct the Stalinist center and its mythologies, for example, the epic history of the Civil War, of which the Chapaev legend is a key example; the youth cult and the military prowess of Stalinist youth; and the greater-than-human power of the police state.

Moscow, thus, exists as an appendage to characters' consciousnesses, particularly that of Petr Pustota. Petr both starts and ends the novel with a stroll through Pushkin Square and the Boulevard Ring by Strastnoi and Tverskoi boulevards in the northwest part of central Moscow (Fig. 5). At the start we find two important landmarks and symbols of Russian identity: "Tverskoi Boulevard was almost the same as two years ago when I last saw it.... The bronze Pushkin seemed a bit sadder than normal, probably because it had a red apron hanging from its chest, with the inscription, 'Hail to the first anniversary of the Revolution'.... it was already beginning to grow dark. Strastnoi Monastery was barely visible through the snowy gloom" (ChP, 10).[5] The two symbols of identity, of course, are the Pushkin Statue and Strastnoi Monastery. The Pushkin Statue was unveiled in 1880 with great fanfare and made into a national symbol through Dostoevsky's famous Pushkin speech. Opposite the Pushkin Statue, on the other side of Tverskaia Street, Moscow's main artery leading northwest from the Kremlin, stands Strastnoi Monastery. A clear symbol of Russian Orthodoxy, Strastnoi Monastery was one of the monasteries closest to the center of Moscow (Fig. 6).

At the end of the novel, the old spaces containing Pushkin Statue and Strastnoi Monastery are empty, showing clearly that changes have taken place and we are in a different time. Petr remarks: "Tverskoi Boulevard was almost the same as last time I last saw it.... Still, there was one difference

4. Angela Breitlinger, "The Hero in the Madhouse: The Post-Soviet Novel Confronts the Soviet Past," *Slavic Review*, 63, no. 1 (Spring 2004), 43–65. Breitlinger argues correctly that in *Chapaev and the Void* there are only "psychic" and "psychiatric spaces."

5. Breitlinger, "The Hero in the Madhouse"; Marina Kanevskaia, "Istoriia i Mif v postmodernistskom russkom romane," *Izvestia AN. Seriia literatury i iazyka*, 59, no. 2 (2000), 37–47.

FIG. 5. The Pushkin Statue at its original site at end of Tverskoi Boulevard (1891, from
N. A. Naidenov's album), reproduced in *Moskva zlatoglavaia v starykh fotografiiakh i
graviurakh* (Moscow: Planeta, 1989), individual picture.

which I noticed as I came to the end of the boulevard. The bronze Pushkin
had disappeared. The yawning emptiness that arose in place of the statue
seemed strangely to be the best of all possible monuments. And where
Strastnoi Monastery used to be was now nothing but emptiness, barely
disguised with sickly trees and tasteless streetlights" (ChP, 400). Strastnoi
Monastery was razed in 1937, the year of the Great Terror as well as the
100th anniversary of Pushkin's death. At this time the Pushkin monument
was transferred to the Strastnoi side of Tverskaia Street. Tverskaia, now re-
named Gorky Street, was widened to accommodate parades and cavalcades
to celebrate the cult of the dictator, Stalin. The Pushkin Statue in its new
location became famous after Stalin's death as a meeting place and a place
of non-violent political protest.

The Moscow at the end of *Chapaev and the Void* is post-Stalin Moscow
in which beloved cultural and religious monuments have disappeared—we

FIG. 6. Strastnoi Monastery, nineteenth century, photograph by E. V. Got 'e-Diufaje (n.d.), from reproduction in *Moskva zlatoglavaia v starykh fotografiiakh i graviurakh* (Moscow: Planeta, 1989).

are not told why, though other characters hint at various reasons. The heart of this Moscow is no longer Pushkin Square but something else—or perhaps it has no real heart. As Petr perceives it, Moscow of the 1990s breathes an emptiness suggesting loss, in which these two signals of educated Russian national identity (great literary art and Orthodox Christianity) are noticeably absent (Fig. 7). Petr rejects this contemporary Moscow, continually recreating the 1919 Moscow of his dreams. It is worth noting that the other three mental hospital patients also have lost their Moscows with their treasured symbols. What remains in post-Soviet Moscow could be called a "semiotic void" filled with objects that have little meaning.

The peripheries of the empire exist only in Petr Pustota's epic geographical illusions. The first is the town of Altai-Vidniansk, which in contrast to Moscow appears on no map. Convalescing after his imagined heroic deeds

Fig. 7. An underpass under Tverskaia Street at Pushkin Square now has a nostalgic reproduction of Strastnoi Boulevard with the monastery to the left side, finished in stone (photograph by E. Clowes).

at the Battle of Lozovaia Station, Petr imagines himself literally in a small hole in time and space, the town Altai-Vidniansk, with its trashy restaurant significantly named "Heart of Asia."[6] The name of the restaurant echoes Dugin's favorite geopolitical designation for Russia as the heartland. Altai-Vidniansk has no geographical reality, it exists in characters' consciousness outside of historical time and physical space. It embodies that key theme of *Chapaev and the Void,* emptiness—not in the Buddhist sense of potential, but as the absence of events, time, and value. It is in Altai-Vidniansk, however, that Chapaev, Petr, and the cocaine-sniffing officer Grigory Kotovsky have their ontological conversations, and Petr first experiences Inner Mongolia, the ultimate psychic space.

Inner Mongolia is the central space in Petr's spiritual searchings. Far from being the actual geographical region with the same name, this Inner Mongolia is a spiritual "no place." Defined by Chapaev's Buddhist guru, the

6. Lozovaia is a place in the Eastern Ukraine repeatedly conquered during the Civil War by the Ukrainian anarchist Makhno, who had nothing to do with Chapaev. See Martin Gilbert, *Atlas of Russian History,* 2nd ed. (New York: Oxford University Press, 1993).

shadowy Baron Jungern, Inner Mongolia is a completely private cosmos with qualities defined by the degree of one's inner enlightenment. Petr asks where it is, and Jungern explains:

> That's just the point, it's nowhere. You can't say that it exists somewhere in a geographical sense. Inner Mongolia isn't called that because it is inside Mongolia. It is inside the person who sees emptiness, although the word "inside" is completely inappropriate in this case. Neither, in fact, is it Mongolia, people just call it that. It would be silly to try to describe it to you. Just believe me when I say that it is well worth striving for it your whole life. And there is nothing better in life than to end up there. (ChP, 292)

Note that this Inner Mongolia and Baron Jungern mimic the Eurasia and Baron Ungern von Sternberg, though in the completely different key of Buddhist enlightenment.

It is also worth noting how Petr comes to experience the paradoxical nonspatial space of Inner Mongolia. The Inner Mongolian episode happens in what one can only call a "rip" in the fabric of time, as if shifting from the narrative into a parallel space. Briefly, it happens during an argument between Chapaev and Kotovsky about whether the afterlife is a return from a physical form to formless essence. In his frustration at Kotovsky's philosophical dualism, Chapaev shoots an inkwell and the droplets of ink hang in midair, not yet splattering on the map table. Forty pages later we encounter the ink droplets again suspended in midair, this time after the inkwell has been shot not by Chapaev but by Baron Jungern (suggesting that Chapaev and Jungern are different forms of the same person). The droplets then splatter all over the same map table. During this moment Petr has for the first time experienced, as Chapaev puts it, something like "eternity" (ChP, 296).

In the Inner Mongolia episode Petr goes with the Baron to a Valhalla for former warriors to observe people in their self-created dream worlds, each of which looks like a campfire on a pitch-black plain. The historical Baron Ungern von Sternberg conquered the town of Urga by lighting a large number of campfires at night around the town and convincing the inhabitants that they were being besieged by an enormous army. In *Chapaev and the Void* this dark, featureless plain dotted with campfires becomes a metaphor for cosmic emptiness filled with numberless private consciousnesses and worlds. We recognize one of them as the fantasy of Pustota's fellow inmate in the psychiatric hospital, the Platonist Mafioso Volodin (ChP, 269).

The third Eurasian peripheral space is the Ural River. Although the Ural River does exist on the border between Europe and Asia, this Ural River is a psychedelic flood and can only be viewed as a figment of the imagination. As in Furmanov's 1923 novel, the Ural River is the last new setting of the Civil

War portion of Pelevin's novel, and the death of Chapaev at the Ural River is its final event. In contrast to Furmanov's story, here it is the Red weavers, not the White Army, who commit the final crime of killing Chapaev. The workers burn down the manor house in which Chapaev, Petr, and Anna the machine gunner are living. The three escape, when Anna uncovers her special "Buddhist" machine gun with which she destroys the weavers and the whole physical landscape. As in the Furmanov novel, Chapaev dives into the river and disappears.

This setting links to the post-Soviet setting in the psychiatric hospital. The 1919 image of the Ural River as psychedelic flood that engulfs everyone can be viewed as an emanation of 1990s Petr's desire to escape the mental hospital. Petr's psychiatrist, Timur Timurovich Kanashnikov,[7] interprets the Ural scene with its destruction of all the 1919 characters as Petr's renunciation of his alternate 1919 self and a healthy recognition of that self as a mere fiction. At this point Timur Timurovich considers Petr to be healthy and releases him from the hospital.

The center-periphery dynamic created between Pelevin's Moscows and their Eurasian peripheries is entirely different from the liberated discursive space theorized by Linda Hutcheon for "ex-centric" postmodernist fiction, the political and cultural "hybrid" claimed by Homi Bhabha for postcolonial fiction, or the source of massive grandeur imagined by Dugin in his neo-Eurasian political deliriums.[8] In *Chapaev and the Void* there is no physical-geographical periphery that becomes the source of a renewing energy or that does anything but reconfirm the centrality of Moscow. Because there is no dynamic, the center remains dysfunctional, physically isolated, concentrated only on itself. The fantasy status of the various peripheral settings reconfirms the "reality" of Moscow: in Pelevin's Russia there simply is no other physical place with the fascination of Moscow. According to postmodernist and postcolonial concepts, which posit the periphery as the place from which new energy and life comes to the center, what Pelevin dramatizes is hardly a regenerative situation.

Having exposed the geographical claims of neo-Eurasianism as the fantasies of the Moscow-centered mind, Pelevin turns to a philosophical spoof on the generally post-Soviet tendency to link identity with space. The philosophical dispute about consciousness and space between Petr and his highly refined commanding officer and Buddhist spiritual mentor Vasily Chapaev comes

7. Timur Timurovich's last name, Kanashnikov, may refer to the infamous Stalin-era psychiatrist, Semyon Kanatchikov, whose notorious Moscow insane asylum was euphemistically called "Kanatchikova dacha" (Breitlinger, "The Hero in the Madhouse," 47).

8. Hutcheon, pp. 57–73, esp. 73; Homi Bhabha, *The Location of Culture* (London: Routledge, 2004), 55.

as a delightful injection into the epic world of the Civil War of a comic philosophizing spirit. Pustota and Chapaev are standing in a shed at a table laden with military maps. Mimicking the most famous scene in the popular 1934 film *Chapaev,* in which Chapaev develops military strategy by placing potatoes in crucial positions on the map, Pelevin's Chapaev uses onions to argue about ontology. Structurally this dispute occupies a marked position in the center portion of the novel, in the fifth of ten chapters.

In this dialogue, Pelevin sets forth his philosophical argument with Eurasianism through considering the paradox of consciousness and space. Chapaev forces the conclusion that it is virtually impossible to say conclusively who "I" am and where my consciousness resides: does my consciousness exist in space, or does space exist in my consciousness? On the one hand, what "I" call "my" personal perception of space appears to have created the spatial entities that give me my sense of being and belonging (in other words, space exists in my consciousness). On the other hand, the world seems physically to exist and to lend us the framework for our consciousness (that is—my consciousness exists in space).

The defining link between space and consciousness is as old, at least, as Kant's *Critique of Pure Reason,* in which Kant posits time and space as two pre-existing "forms of sensible intuition" or "properties of mind" that are crucial for any knowledge.[9] Petr refers to Kant, asserting that humans can be conscious and think only by means of structures of space and time.[10] In his discussion with Chapaev about the locus of consciousness Petr reiterates this thought: "The concept of place is one of the categories of consciousness" (ChP, 179). Thus, answering the question, "Who am I?" depends on answering the question, "Where am I?"

In contrast, Chapaev supports a generally Buddhist view of the self as what has been characterized as a "composite of various aggregates, a series of psychophysical reactions and responses with no fixed center or unchanging ego-entity."[11] Consciousness, in his view, is a state existing beyond the single mind that, as such, exists nowhere. Committed Buddhist though he seems to be, this Chapaev is very well versed in Western philosophy, even (comically) making intelligent philosophizing a requirement for serving as an officer in his unit (ChP, 181). He scoffs at Kant, misquoting the famous

9. Quoted in Monroe C. Beardsley, ed., *The European Philosophers from Descartes to Nietzsche* (New York: Modern Library, 1992), 388.

10. Petr does suggest that consciousness might be susceptible to comparison to Leibniz's concept of the monad, the cosmos writ small, but Chapaev dismisses the comparison with a vulgar pun, suggesting that consciousness might be dependent on male sexuality: instead of respecting Petr's term monad [*monada*], Chapaev calls consciousness a gonad [*manda*].

11. Nancy Wilson Ross, *Buddhism: A Way of Life and Thought* (New York: Vintage Books, 1981), 16.

conclusion of *Critique of Pure Practical Reason:* "Two things fill the mind with ever new and increasing awe and admiration the more frequently and continuously reflection is occupied with them; the starr[y] heaven above me and the moral law within me."[12] While Petr admires the splendid beauty of the evening sky after a rainstorm, Chapaev looks at the reflection of the sky in a puddle, spits his cigarette butt into the puddle, and remarks ironically: "What has always amazed me...is the starry heaven under my feet and Immanuel Kant within us" (ChP, 181). Here Chapaev—deliberately or not—confuses Kant and Schopenhauer. The reference to the "starry heaven beneath my feet" actually comes from Nietzsche's essay, "Schopenhauer as Educator."[13] Chapaev, as will become increasingly clear, finds no use for fixed time and space, which for him are only a dream.

Chapaev continues the argument about mind, consciousness, and space in a number of ways and with a number of different people. To give the flavor of Pelevin's humor it is well to quote much of the crucial dialogue here. More important for our discussion of identity, this is the only place in the novel in which the word "Russia" appears:

"What do you call your 'I'?"
"I guess, myself."
"Can you tell me who you are?"
"Petr Pustota."
"That is your name. But who is the one who bears that name?"
"Well," I said, "you could say that I is a psychic personage [*lichnost'*]. An amalgam of habits, experience...and whatever else, knowledge, taste."

...

"But if those habits are yours, then it turns out that they are the habits of an amalgam of habits." (ChP, 177–178)

Chapaev reduces Petr's definition of personhood to a useless tautology and then turns his attention to the (post-Soviet) question of the "location" of consciousness:

"OK," said Chapaev, squinting slyly, "we'll get back to the 'who.' But now, my good friend, let's talk about the 'where'.... Where exactly is your consciousness?"
"Right here," I said, knocking myself on the head.

12. C. J. Friedrich, ed., *The Philosophy of Kant* (New York: Modern Library, 1949), 261.

13. Another probable source is the metaphor of heaven both above and below us, used by the Russian symbolist Dmitrii Merezhkovskii to assert the metaphysical value of the corporeal world, "The heaven above, the heaven beneath, Stars above, stars beneath, Everything that is above is also beneath." He repeated this theme frequently throughout his popular turn-of-the-century trilogy, *Christ and Anti-Christ (Khristos i Antikhrist,* 1895–1905), http://lib.ru.russlit/merezhkowskij.

"And where is your head?"
"On my shoulders."
"And where are your shoulders?"
"In this room."
"And the room?"
"In this house."
"And the house?"
"In Russia."
"And Russia is where?"
"In trouble, Vasilii Ivanovich."
"That's enough," he barked. "You can crack jokes when I say you can. So...where is it?"
"Well, what do you mean where? On the Earth."
We clinked glasses and had a sip. "And where is the Earth?"
"In the universe."
"And the universe?"
I thought a moment. "In myself."
"And where is this in myself?"
"In my consciousness."
"So, Petka, you're saying that your consciousness is in your conscious-ness?" (ChP, 178–179; emphasis added)

Chapaev clearly believes that consciousness exists outside the forms of time and space that Kant posits inside the mind. In his dialogue with Petr about the location of consciousness he reduces Kantian consciousness to the tau-tology: my consciousness is in my consciousness.

Meanwhile, the specific national, geographical space that concerns every character, no matter what time they live in, is Russia. Russia is treated as a place conceived in the mind, a place, which is "in trouble," as well as a place in which consciousness resides. Pelevin has changed the conversation about consciousness and identity, extricating it from the geographical-imperial confines of neo-Eurasianist thinking. He further deconstructs the Russian national-imperial psyche in order to answer the implicit question as to why Russia is "in trouble."

Each of the two plots—1919 and approximately 1991—features a leader-type who can be read as embodiments of the Eurasianist view of racial blending and particularly Dugin's view of the cruel "White Tsar" as the only individual worthy of the name. We recall once again Dugin's repeat-edly stated belief that in the new Eurasia only nations, and not individuals, have rights: "the nation is everything, the individual—nothing."[14] In addi-tion, here reigns a form of collective psyche different from, yet rooted in

14. Aleksandr Dugin, *Osnovy geopolitiki* (Moscow: Arktogeia, 2000), 257.

the Soviet collective psyche. The four patients in the psychiatric ward travesty the national-imperial psyche inherent in Dugin's work, divided between the individual ruler (the "White Tsar") and the various national collectives. Here each individual character's psyche participates metonymically in the imperial whole, functioning at one or another level of psychological life—whether the unconscious, the Imaginary, or the Symbolic order. In a more serious vein this psychological approach can help us to answer the question of the nature of Russia's trouble.

Each leader is a spiritual guru, each linked in some way to the Swiss psychologist Carl Gustav Jung, who was centrally interested in Asian religions, especially Buddhism, and the essential forms or archetypes in the psyche. In the 1919 story the spiritual mentor is the Chapaev/Baron Jungern figure, who guides Petr toward nirvana. In the 1990s story it is the psychiatrist Timur Timurovich Kanashnikov, who employs what he calls a "turbo-Jungian" method to cure patients. This method uses drugs, injections, and a strange machine that allows each inmate to experience the fantasies of the other inmates, as well as art therapy, to bring forth archetypal symbols in each patient, to interpret those symbols, and cure the patient (ChP, 120). Each of these leader-characters refers to a cruel, tyrannical historical figure.

Both characters are leaders and, true to Eurasianist notions of ethnicity, combine both European and Asian heritage and habits of mind. Jungern is an asianized European, while Timur Timurovich is a europeanized Central Asian. Jungern is "about forty, with blond hair, a high forehead and cold, colorless eyes," and a "drooping Tartar-style moustache" (ChP, 265), wearing a Mongolian robe and following a Buddhist way of life. He and Chapaev hold virtually the same Buddhist worldview and are closely identified (ChP, 291). Indeed, to judge from the ink bottle episode, the two are doubles. Chapaev smashes the ink bottle to begin with. After Petr discovers Inner Mongolia, 40 pages hence, it is Jungern who is shooting the ink bottle (ChP, 294).

Timur Timurovich, in contrast to Jungern, has a Turkic-Mongolian name, the same name as the great Mongol leader Tamerlane. We never see him, but rather hear him as a voice of authority. A convinced materialist, he is educated in a Western medical discipline, psychiatry, and is seemingly well read in Western philosophy and psychological theory. Social determinism informs Timur Timurovich's psychiatric theories: "the world around us is reflected in our consciousness and becomes the object of thought. And when in the actual world certain established connections fail, then the same thing can happen in the psyche. So that in the closed range of your 'I' a monstrous quantity of psychic energy is released. It's like a small atomic explosion" (ChP, 48). In the world of the psychiatric hospital consciousness is viewed as the product of social and natural forces working directly on the human psyche. The radical changes occurring in Russian life, according to Timur Timurovich's theory, have resulted in "split false identity," or schizophrenia, which the psychiatrist finds in all his patients. For example, Petr Pustota is twenty-six years old and belongs to the "generation that was programmed for life in one socio-cultural paradigm, but has found itself living in a quite different one" (ChP, 48). His problem is caused by some "internal event," triggered by historical changes in his society, presumably perestroika and the end of the Soviet regime, which has dislodged Petr from his "normal socio-psychological niche," so that he seeks meaning in the past and "simply will not accept the new" (ChP, 48).

These leaders, each in one of Petr's two stories, compete with one another, which leads to comic conflicts between the novel's two plots. Each exhorts Petr to give up the other one of his life storylines: Timur Timurovich wants him to destroy his fantasy of Eurasia of 1919, while Baron Jungern wants him to escape the mental hospital. Ultimately, in the Ural River sequence Petr does the first in order to achieve the second.

What interests Pelevin far more than these travesties of Dugin's "White Tsar" is the collective psyche of the imperial nation, embodied in the four inmates of the 1990s psychiatric hospital. Insofar as Pelevin clearly sees each of the four inmates as an individual, he does not subscribe to the Duginesque Eurasianist mentality.[15] Instead, he deconstructs it. Each inmate's fantasy of self fits as a fragmented part of an allegory of the national-imperial psyche. By considering the role of each, we come closer to understanding how Pelevin views Russian identity and why, as Petr jokes, Russia is "in trouble."

Two characters, the ideological bimbo and cross-dressing weightlifter Merely Maria, and the mushroom-eating philosophizing Mafioso Vladimir Volodin, both, in my view, function at the level of the Lacanian Symbolic order. Both offer comic representation of ethical law and the phallic symbols that Freud and Lacan associate with authority. These two characters travesty Soviet-era ethics and metaphysics (if, indeed, the Soviet era can be said to have developed a metaphysics). The only inmate of the hospital who accepts Timur Timurovich's materialist worldview is Merely Maria who pictures

---

15. In his PhD dissertation, "The Post-Soviet Cultural Condition: Cultural Reconfigurations of Russian Identity," University of Pittsburgh, 2006, Gerald McCausland discusses *Chapaev and the Void* as an effort to "reconfigure Russian identity within the realm of possibilities offered by the Symbolic order" (179). He sees each of the four inmates using existing Russian symbolic systems, such as love of the West, the madness of the holy fool, and utopianism (168). In contrast, I interpret *Chapaev and the Void* as an effort to diagnose national-imperial psychosis as Soviet identity disintegrates into fragments and the Symbolic Order gives way to an absurd collage of symbols from a wide variety of cultures, not only Russian.

himself as the heroine of a Mexican soap opera. He sees himself as a simple, kindhearted girl who wants to devote herself to alleviating suffering in the world. He fantasizes about a new leader, a "real man" who will inspire the world with his empathy.

Merely Maria identifies very much with his body and with the corporeal, sensible world around him. For him, body equals sexual body, and his fantasies are filled with phallic images, as we can see from his sketches during art therapy. Petr describes the psychiatric ward's art room with Merely Maria's "almost childish scrawls with various versions of the airplane theme decorated with a powerful phallic head" (ChP, 121–122). Maria fantasizes about flying over Moscow with Arnold Schwarzenegger in his Harrier jet (from *True Lies*), while straddling the jet's fuselage, an act that is sexually exhilarating and that lets Maria escape the squalor of post-Soviet Moscow and see it at an aesthetically pleasing distance. Now Moscow is transformed from a run-down garbage dump to a shining "magnificent panorama" (ChP, 76).

Ideologically narrow, Maria is the only one of the inmates to seek out a this-worldly hero. In his self-image as the modest heroine Maria of the Mexican soap opera he muses: "in this world we need strength, stern and unbending, capable, if necessary, of resisting evil" (ChP, 60). The figure of Maria's hero incongruously conflates the first chief of the Bolshevik secret police Felix Dzerzhinsky (ChP, 73), the bodybuilding star Arnold Schwarzenegger, and the popular image of the post-Soviet "new Russian," who is described as a "young man with a smallish head and broad shoulders, in a double-breasted raspberry-colored jacket, standing, legs apart, by a low-slung automobile" (ChP, 61). Maria particularly admires the robotic body (ChP, 61) and computerized eyes and mind of Schwarzenegger, now in his role as the Terminator:

> His left eye was squinting a bit and expressed a very clear and at the same time limitlessly complex array of feelings, with an admixture of love of life, strength, a healthy love of children, the moral support of the American car industry in its difficult skirmish with Japan, an acknowledgment of the rights of sexual minorities, a light sense of irony with regard to feminism and a calm consciousness of the ultimate victory of democracy and Judaeo-Christian values. His right eye was completely different. It was hard even to call it an eye. A round, glass lens like a big wall eye in a complex metallic holder from the out-turned eye socket with dried rivulets of blood, operated by thin wires under the skin. From the very middle of this lens flashed a ray of blinding red light—right into Maria's eyes. (ChP, 77)

This absurd, automatized body, associated with a list of moral virtues is male, muscle-bound and, to Maria, authoritative. Even though Maria heroizes the secret police in the form of Dzerzhinsky, Dugin would certainly not approve of the hero's Americanized dimension.

The other character who plays with the power structure of the imperial police state, that Dugin so admires, is Volodin the Mafioso. In Volodin's fantasy Pelevin satirizes Kant's wonderment at the moral law within human nature in an ingenious dialogue about moral conscience. Here Volodin and his two thugs, Kolian and Shurik, are in a forest outside Moscow, escaping a crime boss to whom they owe money. They are eating psychedelic mushrooms. Incongruously, the thugs start to philosophize about the grounding for human conscience. Their notion of conscience combines the "I-can-do-what-I-want" attitude of vulgar Nietzscheanism and the brutish inhumanity of the Stalinist secret police (ChP, 311–313). Volodin's thugs visualize Kant's moral law variously as the "inner prosecutor," the "inner OMON" [Black Berets, the Special Police Unit], the "inner GB" [KGB, the Soviet security service] and "inner impeachment" (ChP, 313–314). The afterlife they imagine as physical incarceration is very much like the Stalinist penal system:

> "Tell me, Volodin, do you believe in the end of the world?"
> "That is a strictly individual matter," said Volodin.
> "If some Chechen shoots at you, that will be the end of the world."
> "It depends on who shoots at whom," said Kolian.
> "What do you think, is it true that there will be amnesty for Orthodox believers?"
> "When?"
> "At the Last Judgment," said Kolian quickly and quietly.
> "What's wrong with you, do you believe in all that crap?" asked Shurik suspiciously. (ChP, 318)

An emanation of Volodin's subconscious, the hit man Kolian has started to listen to his "inner cop" (*vnutrennii ment*), his conscience, and is worrying about paying for all his crimes in the torments of hell. In this "religious turn," however, Kolian's understanding of life after death is comically modeled on his understanding of the Stalinist prison system, the "zone." In a moment of doubt following a routine murder, Kolian stops by a shop with Christian literature and icons. Picking up a book entitled *The Afterlife,* he recognizes the similarities of life after death to the Stalinist justice system:

> Dying is like going from prison to the zone. They send the soul to a heavenly transfer, it's called torments [*mytarstva*]. Everything is the way it should be, two convoys, everything, below is the isolation cell and above is OK. And on this transfer they try to nail you on all sorts of counts—both yours and other people's, and you have to win back your losses on each count. The main thing is to know the law code. But if the godfather [*kum*] wants to, he'll put you into

isolation, no matter what. Because in his law code from birth you are already guilty on half of the counts. (ChP, 319)

Although the book appears to suggest that people are responsible for their own actions, Kolian assumes that one can always sneak around the system by currying favor with the boss:

> However much you might tiptoe around, they always find a way to get you. If you have a soul, they'll find a way to try you. But the godfather can get you time off, especially if you accept that you are a piece of shit. He loves that. And he loves it if you are afraid of him.... And he has an enormous radiance, wings spread like a fan, a guard—everything. He looks on from above—yep, you're shit? Did you get it? I read some of it and remembered: a long time ago, when I was training to be a weightlifter and it was perestroika, they printed something like this in *Ogonek*. And I remembered and started sweating. People, it said, lived in Stalin's time like that, the way they live now after death. (ChP, 319)

As a character in Volodin's fantasy, Kolian reflects an important aspect of Volodin's mentality. He sees his welfare depending not on an inner moral law but on the favor of a powerful godfather figure. In these metaphysical musings Volodin shows the continuing impact of the Stalinist police state on his psyche. Fundamentally, although the thugs are interested in killing their inner moral compass, they are terrified of the external sanctions that they have come to expect from living in an authoritarian society. In short, in this vulgar version, the inner moral law that Kant posits is none other than the common practice, ethical or unethical, in one's community, a given that is all but impossible to overcome. It has little to do with what Kant intended as the categorical imperative or a strongly principled individual conscience.

Volodin would like to escape this Stalinist, Mafioso image of the divine. Still, he believes in a strongly phallic image of the leader, and he is a megalomaniac. This mushroom-eating, Castaneda-inspired Mafioso envisions a drug-induced image of his own semi-divine self—he sees himself as a phallic shaft of light from heaven. Because of this mystical vision he has been rejected by his confreres in crime and is committed to the psychiatric hospital.

In the big picture of the late- and post-Soviet polity both Merely Maria and Volodin function at the level of the Lacanian "name of the father." Both are direct, if travestied, descendants of the Stalinist order. Both are compelled by images of the secret police and physical force—aspects of Eurasian rule admired by Aleksandr Dugin. And both admire the leadership of a single strong male ruler. Merely Maria is looking for a leader with a strong body who will save humanity, and Volodin in his fantasy draws attention to the parallels between Stalinist rule and the Christian cosmology.

In distinction to Dugin, who advocates centralized rule by force, Pelevin cleverly discredits it, on the one hand, by comparing the "heroes" of police rule to those of Hollywood and U.S. popular culture and, on the other hand, by drawing parallels between the totalitarian state, crime structures, and religious cosmology.

Neither of these characters can find a path beyond the material, corporeal world and its control by physical force. Although Volodin does not share Maria's complete physical and philosophical materialism, his intellect is still comically bound to the material. As part of their therapy, one of the stranger activities assigned the inmates during art therapy sessions is to sketch the bust of Aristotle, with the presumed goal of imbuing in the inmates a simple, materialist worldview and, with it, psychological health. Although Maria has no problem with sketching Aristotle, Volodin, who seeks a higher truth, objects. Limited to the example of a Mercedes 600 automobile, the very symbol of post-Soviet material success, Maria and Volodin get into a philosophical scrap about the relative "reality" of the material world and the ideal world. It starts when Petr wonders why the inmates have to draw Aristotle. It is worth quoting this passage at length to give a sense of Pelevin's comic attack on both materialism and idealism. Volodin remarks:

And why are we all sitting in the loony bin? They want to restore us to reality. And we are drawing this Aristotle because Aristotle thought up the reality of the Mercedes 600, the reality that you, Maria, want to escape to.

"So that reality didn't exist before Aristotle?" Maria asked.

"Nope," shot back Volodin.

"How could that be?"

"You wouldn't understand," said Volodin.

"Well, just give me a try," said Maria. "Maybe I'll catch on."

"Tell me, why is that Mercedes real," Volodin asked.

Maria wracked his brain for a few seconds.

"Because it's made of iron," he said, "that's why. And you can go up to that iron and touch it."

"You're saying that whatever substance it's made of makes it real?"

Maria thought a bit.

"Generally speaking, yes."

"That's why we're drawing Aristotle. Because before him there was no substance," said Volodin.

"And what was there?"

"There was the basic heavenly automobile," said Volodin, "in comparison to which your Mercedes 600 is nothing but shit. This heavenly automobile was absolutely perfect. And all concepts and images that relate to the essence of automobile were encapsulated in it and it alone. So-called real automobiles that drove on the roads of Ancient Greece were thought to be just its imperfect shadows. Like just its projections. Got it?" (ChP, 140–141)

Volodin continues his incongruous analysis of Aristotelian materialism, using the example of the Mercedes 600:

> Then Aristotle came and said that the basic heavenly automobile, of course, exists. And all earthly cars, it stands to reason, are just its contorted reflections in the dull, crooked mirror of existence. At the time you couldn't argue with that. But Aristotle said that beside the basic form and its reflection, there is something else. The material that takes on the form of the automobile. The substance that possesses its own existence. Iron, as you put it. And that very substance is what made the world real. That's where all this screwed-up market economy started. Because before that everything on earth was just a reflection, and, tell me, what kind of reality can a reflection have? The only thing that is real is what creates the reflection. (ChP, 141)

The blinkered pragmatist Maria wins, showing a certain common sense that will soon win him freedom from the psychiatric hospital. When Volodin quizzes Maria on what exactly he took away from this lecture, Maria catches Volodin on a practical detail, which, of course, is the source of Pelevin's philosophical comedy, "I got that you are a real psycho. How could there be any automobiles in Ancient Greece?" In disgust Volodin predicts Maria's imminent release. Volodin is right to think that Maria is the closest to Timur Timurovich's model of the healthy psyche, precisely because he lacks all higher intellect and cannot conceive of other realities. Even Maria's fantasies reside wholly in Moscow. Meanwhile, Volodin is interesting for his attempts, both philosophical and drug-induced, to see beyond mere materialism. His limitation is his deep attachment to symbols of physical power and force.

In the characters of Volodin and Merely Maria Pelevin has rounded out his comic-philosophical argument against linking identity to time and space. More interesting than Volodin and Merely Maria in terms of revealing Russian identity and its ills are the two remaining inmates, Petr Pustota and Semyon Serdiuk. Structurally, both are important: Petr is the narrator and author of this book, and Serdiuk is the only character *not* to have a double in Petr's 1919 fantasy. The two key chapters for each of these characters make up the structural center of the book, chapters five and six of a ten-chapter book. More important, in his fantasy Petr has managed to capture everyone in the post-Soviet mental hospital in his Civil War story. We have already discussed the parallel leader figures, Baron Jungern and Timur Timurovich. In addition, Anna the machine gunner is the double of Maria; the drug-using officer Kotovsky is the double of Volodin. Even the hospital medics have their doubles in the 1919 sequence. Because only Serdiuk remains outside Petr's construction, we have to ask why. The answer to Petr's question about Russian identity, why Russia is "in trouble," lies submerged in the psyche of Serdiuk.

Before considering Serdiuk, we deal with Petr's piece of the crumbling post-Soviet imperial psyche. In brief, Petr can be said to foreground the national-imperial "mirror stage" and the Imaginary order. Petr focuses on himself and his ambitions couched in the epic defining moment at the birth of the Soviet order. He makes himself into an edgy, irreverent avant-garde poet and, at the same time, a Civil War hero, and, ultimately, the hero of his own compelling book in which he has taken the post-Soviet madhouse and reimagined it and its inhabitants, except Serdiuk, as Civil War figures. As an avant-garde poet he writes poetry that is certainly a "slap in the face of public taste," to cite the title of the 1912 Futurist manifesto. His book of poetry, "Songs of the Kingdom of 'I'," wins accolades from the kingpin of modernist poetry Valery Briusov. At the 1919 café, the Musical Snuffbox, he performs his "Revvoen Sonnet" about the death of the Chekist secret policeman Fanerny, whose "Red" identity Petr has adopted in order to disguise his own monarchist profile.

Ironically, although he is a monarchist resisting the Reds, the Bolshevik organizer Furmanov, and Furmanov's weavers, Petr fights heroically on the Red side in an imagined battle at Lozovaia Station and delights in both his imagined heroic feats and the attention he receives from Anna after being wounded. In his art therapy sessions he paints a detailed picture of this illusory Battle of Lozovaia Station (ChP, 124–126). Performing in his Red persona, Petr identifies strongly with the ebullient spirit of this chaotic beginning of the new Soviet state, as it is conveyed in music. He refers specifically to the boisterous marching song, written in 1920 by Samuil Pokrass and Petr Grigoriev, "White Army, Black Baron" (*Belaia armiia, chernyi baron*).[16] The song attacks the "Black Baron," that is, Ungern, who is "preparing a new tsarist throne." It drives home the assertion that "from the taiga to the British seas" the "Red Army is stronger than all the rest." Its liberating message comes in the last stanza, which proclaims that "we are fanning the flames of worldwide inferno" and "we will raze all the churches and prisons to the ground."

---

16. http://www.marxists.org/history/ussr/sounds/index.htm. It is worth noting that Petr's avant-garde poem, "Revvoensonet" (Revolutionary Military Sonnet), also has its roots in this song—the Russian "Revvoensonet" is a play on "Revvoen-sovet," or "Revolutionary Military Council" from the line "Revvoen-sovet nas v boi zovet" (the *Revvoen-sovet* calls us into battle).

That Petr's well-articulated, highly self-centered embodiment of the early-Soviet imaginary is clearly juxtaposed to the understated late-Soviet unconscious of Semyon Serdiuk is well illustrated by the music with which each character identifies. The driving tempo of "White Army, Black Baron," associated with Petr's fantasy, stands in stark contrast to a more mournful late-Soviet song that will become, as it were, Serdiuk's theme song. Serdiuk, the one potentially tragic figure in this otherwise hilarious novel, is arguably also the novel's most enigmatic character. In the allegorical scheme of the crumbling Russian national-imperial psyche offered here, Serdiuk operates on the level of the unconscious and, thus, comes as close to the Lacanian "Real" as it is possible to come in a verbal text. Lacan famously sees the psyche as being shaped like a language and thus always removed from the disturbing "Real." The "Real" is pre-linguistic and, thus, does not directly lend itself to human cognition. Serdiuk, a taciturn, inarticulate person, has very little relationship to language. He does not participate in philosophical disputes. Of the four inmates his world is the least varnished with his own and others' words. His fantasy, while being lived by him, is ultimately reported by Petr Pustota. His medium of expression is visual art—both sketching and origami, in which he is gifted. In addition, he responds deeply to music, that form of art that philosophers have often linked most directly to the unconscious. In that he responds to his milieu directly and intuitively, rather than intellectually, his story more than the others reveals disturbing aspects of post-Soviet psychological distress.

Serdiuk plays an essential role in Pelevin's travesty of Dugin's neo-imperialism. His name, which suggests the Russian word for heart (*serdtse*), relates to Dugin's geopolitical concept of heartland. Serdiuk represents the psychological Russian heartland (or even Dugin's idea of the inner continent) to which Russians should be paying heed. Visually Serdiuk is a parody of the neo-fascist, militaristic Aryan type, whom Dugin admires in his writings. Resembling a "Slavic knight [*vitiaz'*] of old" (ChP, 115), he is handsome in an ancient, knightly way with long blond hair, blue eyes, and a sparse beard.

Linked in numerous ways to the military theme that runs throughout the novel, Serdiuk is viscerally attracted to military virtues of bravery, honor, loyalty, and sacrifice. In his fantasy he finds an answer in an Asiatic military culture, much as Dugin and the Eurasianists did. Riding the Moscow metro, he notices someone reading a book on Japanese militarism and immediately starts reading over his neighbor's shoulder. He easily immerses himself in the Japanese military ethos:

> For the Japanese the concept of social duty...is interwoven with a sense of natural human duty in a way that generates the emotional energy of high drama. This duty is expressed in the concepts *on* and *giri* (derived from the

hieroglyphs meaning "to prick" and "to weigh down" respectively).... *On* is the "debt of gratitude" owed by a child to its parents, a vassal to his suzerain, a citizen to the state. *Giri* is "obligation and responsibility," and requires that each individual act in accordance with his station and position in society. (ChP, 192–193)

Serdiuk admires the Japanese because of the powerful sense of duty that binds Japanese society together. By comparison, he finds Russian society chaotic.[17]

Serdiuk's symbolic alliance with the unconscious is underscored by the underground spaces and nocturnal time that he inhabits. He comes alive at night and wanders Moscow, riding the metro and sleeping in various basements. Just as ultraconservatives' and ultranationalists' dreams for Russia's future are driven by nostalgia for former power, so Serdiuk's fantasy is filled with nostalgia for the epic illusions of the Stalin era. As he walks nocturnal Moscow, he watches young boys involved in mischief and yearns for the paintings of young people by the famous Soviet-era painter Aleksandr Dejneka (1899–1969) in the Mayakovsky Metro Station. He worries that the future of today's boys is bleak, at best:

> Three schoolboys passed Serdiuk, their breaking teenaged voices energetically repeating the word "scandal" [*bazar*]. Their receding backs moved in the direction of a Japanese amphibious jeep with a large crane on its hood. On the other side of Tverskaia Street, directly over the jeep, hung the sign for McDonalds', like the yellow crenellations of an invisible castle wall. It struck Serdiuk that everything taken together—the backs of the schoolboys, the jeep and the yellow "M" on a red background—reminded him of Dejneka's painting "Future Pilots [*letchiki*]." He could understand why, too—the clarity of the future prospects of the characters in question: the future burglars [*naletchiki*] had already dived into the underground crosswalk. (ChP, 195–196)

Although in Soviet times children might have dreamed of becoming pilots, now they want to become thieves. The lexical link between pilot (*letchik*) and robber (*naletchik*) is clear. Serdiuk, more than any of the characters, suffers from nostalgia for the socialist realist illusion of Soviet life, created by Aleksandr Dejneka's paintings of young people and their dreams (Fig. 8). While Petr looks back fondly to the revolutionary period with its epic verve, Serdiuk pines for the beautiful lie of the Stalinist cult of youth, health, and imperial military power. Contemporary Moscow lacks the order of a productive, meaningful vision. It has lost not just the two national symbols that Petr highlights (the Pushkin Statue and Strastnoi Monastery), but layers of imperial symbols. It now stands empty.

17. See *Kodansha Encyclopedia of Japan* (Tokyo: Kondansha, 1983), vol. 3, 34.

FIG. 8. Aleksandr Dejneka, "Future Pilots" ("Budushchie letchiki," 1937), Art © Estate
of Alexander Deineka/RAO, Moscow/VAGA, New York.

In subtle ways Serdiuk represents the violence and horror of the near past,
repressed in the imperial unconscious. The possible reason for his deep despair becomes clear when Serdiuk remembers the yard of the institute where
he used to study:

> Serdiuk clearly recalled one morning from his youth: a corner of the yard at the
> institute, crowded with boxes, the sun on the yellow leaves and his classmates
> laughing uproariously, sharing a bottle of port.... The port wasn't the main
> thing... the main thing was the endless possibilities and paths that the world
> offered back then, spreading in all directions around that corner of the yard
> surrounded by a wrought-iron fence, that now for a second had flashed in his
> memory, flooding his heart with sadness.
> And after this memory—the unbearable thought that the world as such
> had not changed a bit since then, it was just that one could no longer gaze
> at it from that lost viewpoint: there would be no way to squeeze through the

bars of the fence, and there was no place to squeeze into because *the shred of emptiness behind the fence had long since been filled with zinc-plated coffins full of life's experiences.* (ChP, 194, emphasis added)

The emptiness of that little patch of ground that earlier was filled with young students and the promise of the future is now filled in Serdiuk's imagination with coffins, not just of the euphemistic "life's experiences," but "zinc-plated coffins." Why would Serdiuk focus so concretely on multiple coffins? The trauma of the last Soviet decade was the Soviet Afghan War (1979–1989), and it was this empire-destroying war in which very likely many of Serdiuk's fellow students would have fought and died.

This well-hidden hint at the last surge of Soviet empire-building energy is an important historical subtext that requires our attention if we are to understand Serdiuk as more than just an absurd suicidal alcoholic. He is a martial sort of person in search of a discipline to which he can devote his life meaningfully, and he identifies very much with the figure of the fallen soldier. Just as the institute yard that earlier promised so much has now come to stand for loss, Serdiuk wants not only to die, but to do so in an honorable way, while in the line of duty. He finds an outlet in the Japanese tradition of loyalty and duty and seeks out an imaginary mentor who can lead him to an honorable death. This mentor comes in the form of the fantasy Japanese businessman Kawabata who cynically teaches Serdiuk to commit hara-kiri.

It is significant that Serdiuk is associated with both Japanese and Russian culture and that his crucial symbol is not a leader type but a symbol shared by both cultures, that of the crane. Attracted to the figure of the crane, in the mental ward Serdiuk spends his time folding an absurdly large number of origami cranes. Although this attraction would appear to derive from his feeling of affinity for Japan, where cranes symbolize loyalty, it is actually a key aspect of Russian culture and Serdiuk's own identity. In Russian culture the crane is an important symbol of loss, and in the Soviet era particularly, military loss. The crane represents the military theme central to Serdiuk's character. To underline this connection, early on someone, whom we do not yet know as Serdiuk, asks to listen to a song on the radio:

"Can I turn the radio on?" a quiet voice came from the corner.

Timur Timurovich clicked on a button on the wall...

"Sometimes it seems to me that soldiers," a mournful man's voice sang, "who didn't return from the bloody fields, were not buried in the earth but turned into white cranes..."

Just as the last word "cranes" flew out of the loudspeaker, a hubbub arose in the ward.

"Get a hold of Serdiuk!" a voice shouted right above my ear. "Who put on that stuff about cranes? How could you forget?" (ChP, 82)

The song in question is "Cranes" (*Zhuravli*), a song written in 1969 by Iakov Frenkel to a poem by the Soviet writer Rasul Gamzatov, another Central Asian. In Soviet culture cranes are associated with heroic death on the battlefield. This popular song celebrates fallen soldiers who are heralded as white cranes flying in formation.[18] Here the poet mournfully seeks a place in their flight for himself.

The crane motif pervades Serdiuk's relationship with the imagined Japanese businessman Kawabata. In seeking a job at Kawabata's firm, Serdiuk is looking for an honorable, self-sacrificing way to end his life. Kawabata focuses on leading him toward hara-kiri. Serdiuk receives from Kawabata the blade with which he is to commit hara-kiri, which is decorated with cranes. While he sings a line of the Frenkel song, Kawabata makes the connection between the Japanese meaning of cranes and Serdiuk's desire for self-sacrifice:

> [Serdiuk] stretched out his hands and carefully took the cold instrument of death. On the scabbard was a drawing that he had not noticed earlier. It was three flying cranes—golden wire pressed into the black lacquer of the sheath formed a light, impetuous outline of uncommon beauty.
> "In this scabbard is your soul," said Kawabata.
> "What a beautiful drawing," said Serdiuk. "I even remembered, you know, a certain song, about cranes. How did it go...And in their formation is a small space—maybe that will be a place for me..."
> "Yes, yes," Kawabata rejoined. "And does a person need any bigger space? Buddha Shakyamuni, this whole world with all its problems can easily fit between two cranes, it would even disappear among the feathers of any of them...How poetic this evening is! Shall we have another drink? To the place that you have finally attained in the cranes' flying formation?" (ChP, 231–232)

The difference between Petr's bright epic vision and Serdiuk's nostalgia emerges in the songs that accompany their fantasies. "White Army, Black Baron" is about a young and determined movement to overthrow tyranny, and "Cranes" is about a fervent desire to be honorably released from earthly life through military self-sacrifice, and to join the flock of cranes flying across the sky. The song expresses both despair and rejection. In his despair of ever leading an honorable life and his yearning for an honorable

---

18. http://www.sovmusic.ru. Cranes figure in other war-related works. In a well-known war film, "The Cranes are Flying" (*Letiat zhuravli*, dir. Mikhail Kalatozov, 1957), a young man dies in World War II. His fiancée accepts his death when he does not return home with his comrades. At the end she sees cranes flying overhead.

death, Serdiuk is a symptom of the wasting disease destroying male Russian identity in the post-Soviet moment. He has been betrayed by his imperial country. He is a tragic figure, who becomes absurd with his obsessive folding of origami cranes.

Chapaev and the Void can be called a neo-Baroque allegory of the crumbling national-imperial psyche that Dugin would like to reconstruct. And, as in the Baroque, the fabric of bedazzling colors and busy surface decoration hides some terrible trauma underneath the surface that must be covered with illusion if Russians are to rebuild their lives. In the Baroque period it was the horror of the Counter-Reformation and the Thirty Years' War. Pelevin's neo-Baroque novel is wonderfully decorated—humorously and at times grotesquely. The understated and unhumorous Serdiuk is the single character who perhaps best unlocks the nature of the late imperial horror beneath the lively, amusing surface of Pelevin's novel. While various other characters are flamboyant, Serdiuk's experience is subtle, quiet, and usually hidden in the background. As suggested by his last name, he is actually at the dark, hidden "heart" of this hilarious satire of post-imperial Russian identity disorder. It is sad and revealing that he will eventually be the one inmate who is not allowed to leave the ward. His desire to commit suicide is disturbingly close to the "Real" and to inevitable death. Instead, under the control of his warders, he is fated to spend his days folding origami paper cranes.

In conclusion, we return to the question: What did Petr mean when he quipped that Russia was "in trouble"? First, we see through Dugin's geopolitical imagination, that the Eurasian periphery is a figment of the Muscovite imagination. Pelevin suggests that there is no productive center-periphery dynamic in Russian culture. Second, the collective Russian psyche, insofar as it exists, is in a state of crisis, full of the debris of Soviet ideology, police-state thuggishness, and representations of military grandeur that ended in dead boys coming home from the Afghan War in caskets.

At the end of *Chapaev and the Void* we realize that Pelevin has no intention of openly diagnosing and curing Russia—he refuses to enter this particular literary game beloved by Russian realists. Symptomatic of this irreverence, when Petr leaves the hospital, he gets into a discussion of national identity with a taxi driver recognizable as the moralizing doyen of twentieth-century Russian realism, Aleksandr Solzhenitsyn, "a bearded gentleman who somehow reminded me of Count Tolstoy but with a bit shorter beard" (ChP, 401). Using Solzhenitsyn's terms from his famous 1990 essay, "How Should We Restructure Russia?" ("*Kak nam obustroit' Rossiiu?*"), the driver talks about needing to "restructure Russia." Petr quips that every time a clear concept of Russia comes to mind, he just lets it dissolve in its own amorphous nature, and then it is "restructured" (ChP, 403). The driver castigates

Petr for "doubting the reality of the world" and showing a "lack of courage," and then, deciding Petr is crazy, throws him out of the cab (ChP, 404). The Russian world is left whirling in circles of absurdist repetition—Petr leaves the mental hospital only to reenter his Civil War fantasy, while Serdiuk continues to fold origami cranes.

How does Pelevin's novel respond to the neo-Eurasianist imperial dream? We have seen on many levels how Pelevin challenges the post-Soviet geopolitical linking of identity and geographical space. Ultimately, in Chapaev's pop-Buddhist view, space is an epiphenomenon, something like bubbles on water, and enlightened consciousness exists outside of space. If space is always suspect as a way of defining consciousness and identity, then we are confronted with the question as to why this novel plays so much with seemingly contradictory quantities—national identity and Russian identity, on the one hand, and with "emptiness" and denial of space in its various possibilities, on the other hand. The novel's substance, if there can be said to be "substance" in this neo-baroque novel, is a recurring play with images of the nation, its center Moscow, and the national psyche, embodied by the four inmates of the mental hospital.

In this sense, *Chapaev and the Void* is of a piece with other recognizably postmodernist fiction, in the sense that, by asking about identity, it also crucially asks about ontology, about the nature of the world(s) we inhabit.[19] In contrast to other postmodernist writers, Pelevin may be the first person to have written a novel not about space but about the lack of it, about emptiness, about the "void."[20] The novel is full of empty spaces, and replete with queries about the meaning of emptiness. Finally, although Petr's yearned-for haven of enlightenment is Inner Mongolia, the underlying space that defines identity is always Russia and, in particular, the center of Russia, Moscow. The emptiness of both Russia and Moscow is highlighted through myriad references, songs, memories. Indeed, following Boris Grebenshchikov's popular song "8200 [versts of emptiness]" (1994), Russia is itself is defined as

---

19. Brian McHale in *Postmodernist Fiction* (London: Routledge, 1987) treats ontology as one of the dominants of postmodernist literature. Modernist fiction focuses on the epistemological question, "*How* can we know this world?" and postmodernist fiction deals with the ontological question, "*Which* world is this one?"

20. Pelevin has claimed that, "I am the first writer in world literature whose action takes place in absolute emptiness." Viktor Pelevin, "'Kogda ia pishu, ia dvigaius' na oshchup'" (http://pelevin.nov.ru/interview/o-jap/1.html), cited in M. Sverdlov, "Knigi, o kotorykh sporiat. Tekhnologiia pisatel'skoi vlasti (O dvukh poslednikh romanakh V. Pelevina), *Voprosy literatury*, 4 (August 31, 2003), 35, http://dlib.eastview.com.www2.lib.ku.edu:2048/sources/article.jsp?id=5984068.

emptiness (ChP, 385).[21] Ultimately, Pelevin dismisses not only neo-Eurasianism and neo-imperialism but one of the basic premises of postmodernism: that we define ourselves in terms of the physical space we inhabit. There is no firm, unchanging space.

To return to the preface of *Chapaev and the Void,* what does Pelevin mean by the "peoples of Eurasia"? What does he mean by the "new balance of power on the continent"? All the terms here—peoples, Eurasia, balance of power, continent—make fun of Dugin. Pelevin's novel is dominated by philosophical dialogue that displaces Aristotle and Kant, makes fun of the power of the secret police, of totalitarian rule by brute force, and foregrounds pop-Buddhist concepts. Here the "peoples of Eurasia" are less politically inclined than interested in meditation on the nature of the cosmos as ultimate emptiness—emptiness understood as potential. Judging from the post-imperial psyche represented by Maria, Volodin, Pustota, and Serdiuk, the dominant goals are aesthetic and epic—driven by an interlocking combination of desires, to sacrifice oneself for a noble cause (Maria and Serdiuk) and to aggrandize oneself (Volodin and Pustota). While undermining Dugin's simplistic megalomania, Pelevin highlights the deep contradiction between Dugin's massive bird's-eye view of Eurasia and the inner, psychological view of individual—if allegorical—parts of the Eurasian/Russian psyche, which remains unresolved and provides a useful tension as Pelevin's readers consider who they "actually are."

21. "Vosem' tysiach dvesti verst pustoty—A vse ravno nam s toboi negde nochevat'. Byl by ia vesel, esli by ne ty—Esli by ne ty, moia rodina—mat'...//Byl by ia vesel, da chto teper' v tom; Prosto zdes' krasnyi, gde u vsekh—goluboi; Serebrom po vetru, po serdtsu serpom—I Sirinom moia dusha vzletit nad toboi." http://www.aquarium.ru/discography/kostroma_m235.html#top.

4 RUSSIA'S DECONSTRUCTIONIST WESTERNIZER

Mikhail Ryklin's "Larger Space of Europe" Confronts Holy Rus'

These essays have helped me bear [the last eight years] by placing me in a broader European cultural space. [This space] has not yet been accepted by most of my fellow citizens as an integral part of themselves, [for whom] many aspects of openness are still traumatic, but I am far from being the only one who lives in it.
—*Diagnostic* (*Vremia diagnoza*) (2003)

A cultural iron curtain...is lowering slowly over Russia.
—*Swastika, Star, Cross* (*Svastika, Zvezda, Krest*) (2006)

A spectre is wandering across Russia, the spectre of religious nationalism and intolerance.
—*Swastika, Star, Cross*

RETURNING to Berlin in January 1927 from a two-month stay in Moscow, Walter Benjamin wrote scathingly of his home city: "For someone who has arrived from Moscow, Berlin is a dead city. The people on the street seem desperately isolated, each one at a great distance from the next. All alone in the midst of a broad stretch of street.... What is true of the image of the city and its inhabitants is also applicable to its mentality: the new perspective one gains on this is the most indisputable consequence of a stay in Russia."[1] Almost seventy-five years later, in 2001, the prominent Russian philosopher Mikhail Ryklin felt a similar anomie upon returning to *his* home city, Moscow, after a prolonged stay in Berlin: "Coming back from Berlin, I notice the same things on the streets of Moscow [as Benjamin

---

Citations from works by Ryklin are given in the text with the following notation:
DD: *Dekonstruktsiia i destruktsiia: Besedy s filosofami*. Series Ecce Homo (Moscow: Logos, 2002).
PL: *Prostranstva likovaniia* (Moscow: Logos, 2002).
SZK: *Svastika, Zvezda, Krest* (Moscow: Logos, 2006).
VD: *Vremia diagnoza* (Moscow: Logos, 2003).
1. Walter Benjamin, *Moscow Diary*. trans. R. Sieburth (Cambridge MA: Harvard University Press, 1986), 112–114.

saw in Berlin]: there are more cars than people, it smells of cheap gas, pass-ers-by are alienated from one another, in the metro one sees predominantly gloomy, unsmiling faces. Today's capital of Russia is the city most alienated from itself that I have ever lived in" (PL: 260).

Mikhail Ryklin (1948–) is what we will call a "neo-Westernizer" in a post-Soviet Russian world increasingly surrounded by rightist reinventions: neo-nationalists, neo-Slavophiles, neo-fascists, and neo-Eurasianists.[2] In the atmosphere of bigotry and ultra-nationalism enshrouding Russia since the late 1990s, embattled groups devoted to social, cultural, and religious tol-erance could find a principled, if esoteric, ally in Ryklin. In contrast to his ultraconservative contemporaries, who sometimes view the other formerly imperial, totalitarian European capital—Berlin—as a component of a recon-structed imperial network of cities and states, Ryklin takes it as a model for a post-imperial, post-totalitarian alternatives to empire. Through his concept of post-imperial Berlin Ryklin resists rightist trends toward another iteration of mass conformism and authoritarian rule. In contrast to Dugin, who projects Berlin as the westernmost city in an axis linking major continental world cen-ters, Berlin, Tokyo (*sic*), and Teheran, with Moscow at the hub of power, Ryk-lin views Berlin as a "reality check": "In many ways in my life Berlin corrects the lack of 'reality', which one senses so strongly in Moscow" (PL: 260).[3]

This chapter probes Ryklin's quest for a non-authoritarian Russian iden-tity. Our markers on this quest are the psycho-geographical metaphors he uses to examine the current Russian crisis of identity and to build the psy-chological groundwork for a different identity. Of particular interest are his concepts of "center," "border," and the "West." Ryklin has two main goals. His first concrete goal is to reinvent Moscow as the center after its existence for decades as the Stalinist site of what he calls forced mass "jubilation." Second, Ryklin psychoanalyzes himself, probing his personal identity, exam-ining what in his experience created his sense of personhood, and diagnos-ing the unconscious workings of the Soviet mentality in himself.

Before turning to a discussion of Ryklin's particular imagined geogra-phy, it is helpful to place his thinking in the broader context of Eastern European and Russian philosophizing and theorizing of the past thirty years. Ryklin's public "Westernizing," his project of symbolically opening

---

2. Two books that treat these rightist formations are Wayne Allensworth, *The Russian Question: Nationalism, Modernization, and Post-Communist Russia* (Lanham, MD: Rowman and Littlefield, 1998); Stephen D. Shenfield, *Russian Fascism: Traditions, Tendencies, Move-ments* (Armonk, NY: M.E. Sharpe, 2001).

3. Concerning the image of Berlin among ultraconservatives, see for example, Aleksandr Dugin, *Osnovy geopolitiky* (Moscow: Arktogeia-tsentr, 2000), 228; idem, *Proekt "Evraziia"* (Moscow: Iauza, 2004), 374.

the philosophical and physical Western border and keeping it open, stands in relief against the often underground or exiled Westernizing of philosophy in the late Soviet empire. Since the 1960s a large number of prominent Eastern European philosophers fled the confines of the post-Stalin Soviet bloc and its blinkered ideology. They often adopted French as their critical, philosophical language. Among the losses for the Slavic and Soviet world were such structuralist and deconstructionist luminaries as Algirdas Greimas, Tsvetan Todorov, Julia Kristeva, and Emanuel Levinas.[4] The Slovene Lacanian Slavoj Zizek has returned to his native Ljubljana, although despite this territorial reconciliation he continues to write largely in English.

In contrast, Westernizing Russian philosophers have straddled the western border of Russia, reanimating what had become a moribund Russian philosophical language but often living abroad either permanently or for lengthy periods. The best known among the conceptualist and deconstructionist philosophers are Boris Groys, Valery Podoroga, Elena Petrovskaia, and Ryklin. Although some of these philosophers view the Soviet philosopher Merab Mamardashvili (1930–1990) as their philosophical mentor, and Mikhail Bakhtin as a vital Russian forebear, their thinking developed to an important extent through French post-structuralist thought and through interactions with the group of post-utopian artists, poets, and critics known as the Moscow Conceptualists.[5] In conceptualist art and poetry the philosophers defined a "home base" for their thinking, and for the growth of further dialogue with European and U.S. thinkers. While using Western philosophical models to revive their Russian philosophical idiom, they absorbed German, French, and U.S. philosophical and culturological discourses and disseminated them in Russian translation. As philosophers, however, they typically use Russian, taking as part of their project to revive the Russian philosophical language, often with Westernisms, mainly from English and French.[6] Interestingly, they have revitalized the genres of cultural commentary for which

---

4. An angry riposte to this political-linguistic situation can be found in Julia Kristeva, "The Novel as Polylogue" (1974), *Desire in Language: A Semiotic Approach to Literature and Art*, trans. by T. Gora, A. Jardine, L. S. Roudiez (New York: Columbia University Press, 1980), 160–162. Kristeva blames the 1945 meeting at Yalta of Roosevelt and Churchill with Stalin for the division of Europe, the subsequent submission of East Central and Southeast European cultures to Stalinist ideology and totalitarian rule, and the ensuing evisceration of the region's languages—including her native Bulgarian—as meaningful media in which to philosophize.

5. For a fine volume of articles by and about Moscow Conceptualists, see D. A. Ross, ed., *Between Spring and Summer: Soviet Conceptual Art in the Period of Late Communism* (Cambridge: MIT, 1990).

6. For an excellent introduction to some of the voices in post-Soviet academic philosophy, see Klaus-Dieter Eichler and Ulrich Johannes Schneider, eds., *Russische Philosophie im 20. Jahrhundert*, Leipziger Schriften zur Philosophie, vol. 4 (Leipzig: Leipziger Universitätsverlag, 1996).

some speculative philosophers of the pre-revolutionary period—particularly Vasily Rozanov and Nikolai Berdiaev—were famous, although, it should be noted, their writing is entirely different in tone and theme. Their position is closer to cultural criticism than to academic philosophy, and their emphasis is on philosophical anthropology. All of them belong to a European generation of thinkers that have abandoned the universalist claims of classical or analytical philosophizing and define themselves as thinkers by situating their thought in metaphors of time and space.[7]

Ryklin is the focus of our discussion because, of all these thinkers, he has reinvented himself to the fullest, moving from the position of an academic philosopher and cultural critic into the role of the socially and politically engaged Russian philosopher in post-Soviet life. Drawing usefully on Western psychoanalytical theory, he has examined himself and succeeded in expanding his reach, becoming conscious of the functions of Stalinist terror inside himself and in the artifacts of Stalinist culture. From that base, he has begun to rethink Russian identity in more general terms.[8]

During the 1990s Ryklin launched a rather idealistic mission to link intellectuals in Russia and Europe and, through philosophical discourse, to change Russian thinking. He did an enormous amount of translating, editing, and publishing work to introduce the educated Russian reading public to contemporary European philosophy—Derrida, Baudrillard, Deleuze, Guattari, Habermas, Rorty, Buck-Morss, among others. In the early 1990s after the fall of the Soviet Union, he started a "Westernizing" trend in philosophy and the study of culture. With other philosophers and conceptualist poets he helped to start the publishing house Ad Marginem to translate and disseminate European philosophy that had been banned during the Soviet era, for example, Zimmel, Weber, Cassirer, Benjamin, Jaspers, and Heidegger. In addition, Ad Marginem published works of deconstructionist French philosophers, for example, Deleuze, Derrida, and Baudrillard, as well as works of German phenomenology and social thought by Jürgen Habermas and U.S. pragmatism, for example, by Rorty and Buck-Morss. The venture of Ad Marginem

7. See, for example, Groys's books on Stalinist culture, *The Total Art of Stalinism* (Princeton: Princeton University Press, 1992), *Tyrannei des Schönen* (*The Tyranny of the Beautiful* [New York and Munich: Prestel, 1995]), and his philosophical diary *Filosofskii dnevnik* (Paris: Sintaksis, 1989); Podoroga's books on landscape in European philosophy and on the body (*Fenomenologiia tela: vvedenie v filosofskuiu antropologiiu* [Moscow: Ad Marginem, 1995]); Elena Petrovskaia, ed. and intro., *Dialogi: 1990–1994* (Moscow: Ad Marginem, 1999).

8. Mikhail Ryklin, "Bodies of Terror: Theses toward a Logic of Violence," *New Literary History*, 24 (1993), 51–74, esp. 58. Ryklin started the process of rethinking himself in the post-Stalinist context in "Bodies of Terror," written in 1990, in which he called the critical act of turning artifacts in the Moscow metro into the "objects of contemplation," a transformation that he called "an extremely aggressive act."

enjoyed strong support from the Soros Foundation's Center for Contemporary Art, which in the 1990s was dedicated to helping Russian intellectuals permanently change their country's authoritarian social and political culture. The result, in Ryklin's view, was that in the 1990s the "local culture" of Moscow actually intensified and became "internationalized" (VD, 45).

Ryklin exported his efforts to draw Europeans and Russians into a closer understanding in a series of essays on post-Soviet Moscow that he wrote for the Eurozine *Lettre Internationale,* published in Berlin and elsewhere in a broad array of languages. Ryklin sees himself as a philosopher with an academic background and increasingly as a public voice attempting to "translate" between a Russian consciousness of being "different" and "particular" and a secular European universalism: "As a philosopher I participate in the process of overcoming muteness, and for me it is important *not just to be a Russian writer,* although other forms of writing are not foreign to me. I try to speak German and—here is the real point—I strive to make my experience of thinking translatable, to demonstrate the participation and collaboration of the Other in this experience" (PL, 260). As this self-definition suggests, Ryklin is a strong advocate of inclusive, tolerant thinking and social action. His thought fearlessly engages the racial and religious prejudices of Russian neo-nationalism. An important aspect of Ryklin's project has to do with language: although he is rarely simple to read, he is very concerned to write in a critical, philosophical idiom that is easily "transferable" and accessible to educated Russians and Europeans alike. What emerges sometimes sounds strange, with a large number of Latin-based Russian words or direct translations of English idioms.[9]

Ryklin's cultural-psychological project starts with a reconsideration of the meanings that the word border can have—whether territorial, psychological, or philosophical. He asks what it means to cross various borders. Among them the psychological border between the conscious and the unconscious—the Imaginary and the Real; the temporal borders separating the old Soviet utopian cultural space from the more amorphous post-Soviet cultural space; and the spatial borders between a mass, collective sensibility and a "Western" person-centered social and cultural sensibility. He asks how focusing on the physical border can lead to a process of rethinking oneself no longer as a cell in the collective body but as a self-conscious, ethical person and a citizen with legal rights, while still inhabiting Russian territory. Finally,

---

9. For example, *politicheskaia stsena* (the political scene), *reprezentirovat'* (to represent politically), *konspiratsiia* (conspiracy), *konsensus* (consensus) (VD, 112, 159, 162, 163); *rigidnost'* (rigidity), *blefovat'* (to bluff), *piarit'* (to engage in PR), *inkorporirovat'* (incorporate) (SZK, 12, 67, 94, 168).

through thinking about the relationship of border to center, Ryklin reconceives Moscow itself.

For almost seventy-five years Moscow was the center of a massive country with closed borders, for the second half of that time buffered and protected by "friendly" republics and states. Now when there are open borders instead of buffer countries, Ryklin envisions Moscow potentially as a center like Berlin, with lots of ethnic, linguistic, and ideological "borders" running through it. In other words, a space enlivened with debate and tolerant of many views and ways of life. Ultimately, Ryklin wants Moscow to become part of what he calls the "broader space of Europe" (VD, 8).

The border, understood by Ryklin as a threshold space that differentiates self from other, functions complexly across three different stages of Moscow's twentieth-century existence: 1) the Stalinist era, leaving its imprint throughout the Soviet decades; 2) the specific moment of World War II, when the border was suddenly and traumatically transgressed; and 3) the post-Soviet geographical reconfiguration of Russia.

Ryklin's *Spaces of Jubilation* (*Prostranstva likovaniia*, 2002), a remarkable study of Stalinist spaces and their psychological and symbolic import, develops the notion of the western border of Russia as the significant border for defining modern Russian identity. By 1930 Stalin had sealed off the homeland of world communism from all interaction with the West with a tightly controlled border that became the line that separated Soviets from the cultural Other (PL, 65, 76). During the Stalin era that border was physically blocked, with the exception of one crucial interval of four years, and then subsequently blocked and buffered. The goal was to create and enforce the notion of a utopian "we," a jubilant mass society, and to defend it against the capitalist Moloch of the West.[10]

When in 1941 the western border opened as the Nazis invaded Soviet territory, the border became the pretext for renewed consciousness of ethnic difference. For Ryklin, born after the war, and listening as a young child to stories of the survival of his Jewish mother during the Nazi occupation of western Russia, the brief opening of this border was a moment that changed the family's identity forever. Not only did it become clear that to be a Jew meant to be different from the mass of Soviet citizens, but the word Jew reasserted itself as a floating signifier, designating otherness in general.

---

10. Ryklin points out that the border was always a little porous, when convenient, permitting the import of crucial technology from that same Western Moloch. For example, the Moscow metro was built in part with the help of imported technology for the escalators, among other things. All the same, the metro embodied an anti-Western Stalinist spirit of "powerful mass enthusiasm, overturning all reckoning and sketches, realizing allegedly significantly more than what the reason can" (PL, 85).

A crucial aspect of Ryklin's diagnosis of Stalinism and the role of the border in creating identity is the examination of his own and his family's experiences of crossing the border. He finds that the western border played a crucial
role as a metaphor, reinstating a traumatized sense of otherness, which leads
eventually to a search for personhood. Metaphorically speaking, the western
border marked the difference between the Soviet utopia—the purportedly
perfect place outside of time—and history. In a number of ways the Nazi
invasion of June 1941, reintroduced Russians to "history," to the notion of
difference and change. In Ryklin's personal life, stories of the western front
and the Nazis were his first window into self-consciousness and living history (PL, 43). Ryklin begins *Spaces of Jubilation* by recounting his mother's
experience of visiting her grandmother in Vitebsk and suddenly finding herself on contested territory. Through sheer happenstance, as well as a series
of interactions with ordinary German soldiers and help from non-Jewish
friends and strangers, she survived and found her way back to Moscow.

When Ryklin hears this story, the western border of the Soviet Union
now becomes the site of his first consciousness of being different from the
Soviet collective, of being the Other. Through a bewildering series of events
it became clear that people of Jewish heritage, self-consciously or not, were
a threat to the jubilating totalitarian collective body that Stalin had forced
into existence to mask the terror he continued to perpetrate (PL, 31). First,
Ryklin's mother was called Stalina by Soviet true-believer parents who wanted
to honor the "Great Leader." Subsequently, as a young girl Stalina was nearly
destroyed by the Nazis, and later by the person and institution her name
honored. Meanwhile, Stalina's true-believer father died in the camps for
protesting inhuman working conditions.

Stalina Sergeevna's story of survival led to Ryklin's own sense of alienation from both sides. Stalina's name contained an irremediable irony that
lies at the basis of Ryklin's sense of otherness—the gap between the Stalinist collective and stereotypical ethnic appearance. The name Stalina bears
with it further gaps and slips in understanding beyond the ones mentioned
above. It symbolically commits to a merger with the Soviet Stalinist collective body, only then to become a signal of rejection and alienation from
that body, when Stalin denied that Jews were deliberately singled out for
destruction by the Nazis, refused to publish the appalling *Black Book,* and
subsequently planned and partially executed his own liquidation of the
Jewish intelligentsia.[11] The symbol of the complexity of the metaphorical

---

11. *The Black Book: The Nazi Crime against the Jewish People,* edited by The Jewish Black
Book Committee (New York: Duell, Sloan and Pearce, 1946).

relationship between acknowledged Nazi murders and taboo Stalinist murders is his mother's name. In June 1941, just after the German invasion, Stalina's grandmother tore up her granddaughter's identification card, ironically not because it showed Stalina as Jewish, but because she believed that her granddaughter's name—with its clear statement of devotion to communism—would be enough for her to be killed by the Nazis (PL, 31). She mistook genocidal ethnic hatred for class warfare. The issue of being Jewish—or, at least, looking Jewish—immediately became the other side of this catch-22. Ryklin understood that "Jew" was a floating signifier, meant to designate *anyone* who is Other, "enemy," "not us": for example, the girl Stalina remembered German soldiers looking at a calendar with portraits of Stalin, Voroshilov, and Molotov, each of whom they called a "Jew" (PL, 36).

The border as lived space and as psychological metaphor thus opens up Ryklin's own creative path to critical thinking. Both genocides—Nazi and Stalinist: "this death passing through the bodies of my relatives"—gave rise to a sense of his own personhood [*lichnost'*] that he knew could not be taken away from him (PL, 45). His mother's story led Ryklin, as he puts it, "along an ascending line of individuation" (PL, 46). He realized that the chance event of his birth was connected with the issue of Jewish ethnicity, his mother's survival, and the double whammy of his mother's given name, which might have brought immediate death and which also marked the taboo on discussion of the Stalinist terror, masked by the "concept of communism as higher good [*blago*]" (PL, 46). As a child, he worried over the logical connection between being the victim of the Nazi genocide and then after the war becoming the victims of a planned Stalinist massacre (PL, 52). It is this problem that made Ryklin a self-conscious person.

Ryklin emphasizes that the various waves of Stalinist terror were taboo—they were unmentionable even in family circles. Because this trauma had no outlet, it became even more fully anchored in the Soviet subconscious and, now, is all the harder to bring to light, to confront, and, ultimately, to change. In contrast, the openly acknowledged and reviled Nazi crimes served a good purpose, becoming an Aesopian way of mentioning Stalinist crimes. "Although they had in part 'lost their charm,' the crimes of Nazism, which my mother witnessed when she was a girl, now openly discussed, served for me as a model for explaining other crimes that could not be named, which at that time we had to hide from ourselves" (PL, 21). Because they could be discussed, even if in a historically distorted way, in some ways, the acknowledged Nazi atrocities, stylized and shaped in post-war literature and film, became a metaphor for the unspeakable Stalinist ones and, in that way, provided some level of psychological relief.[12]

Ryklin sees the post-Stalinist experience as being much more disadvantageous to a healthy identity than the post-Nazi experience in Germany. The secret police, the perpetrators of Stalinist crimes, have never been tried in court; thus, Ryklin argues, they will not be isolated, brought into the open, and even possibly made into an object of public moral scrutiny: "Soviet guilt is reworked exclusively in such a way that it is repressed from consciousness; it has no subject onto which to lay responsibility. There is no juridical procedure by which to localize this freely hovering substance, to fasten it to a particular social group" (PL, 21).

In 1991 with the collapse of the Soviet Union the same western border that had stimulated Ryklin's childhood self-consciousness opened physically, revealing the extent to which it had been the load-bearing symbol for Western myths about Soviet Russia and Soviet Russians' myths about themselves. The shock of recognition on both eastern and western sides of the border was palpable. Russians worried that they had lost their status as the imperial Third Rome. On the other side of the border, Europeans panicked at the influx of Russians into the West:

> Even the gigantic dimensions of this plane of projection are unique. Even with the expansion of virtual reality, after January 1, 1992, the post-industrial world became more fully immanent to itself, it was deprived of the enjoyment of the border, which left in its stead a gaping hole. Post-Soviet Russia will long be gathering the harvest of disappointment and mourning over the end of its great and terrible precursor... beyond issues of domestic politics the nostalgia for the Soviet Union is fed by the vexed reaction of the rest of the world at the erosion of that all-important defining border. (PL: 18)

The border had created clear political and cultural identities, the "we" versus "them" of the Cold War. Opening the border, against all expectation, actually operated in negative, anxiety-arousing ways in both directions. The Western world suddenly saw the social and cultural realities beneath the boastful façade of Soviet ideology and panicked, and the Russian world was

---

12. For more on the censorship of efforts to draw parallels between Nazism and Stalinism, see Gary Rosenshield, "Socialist Realism and the Holocaust: Jewish Life and Death in Rybakov's *Heavy Sand*," *PMLA*, 111, no. 2 (1996), 240–255; Edith W. Clowes, "Remembering the Holocaust: The Ambiguous Figure of Babi Yar in Soviet Literature," *Partial Answers*, 3, no. 2 (2005), 154–182; Frank Grüner, "Die Tragödie von Babij Jar im sowjetischen Gedächtnis: Künstlerische Erinnerung versus offizielles Schweigen," in *Zerstörer des Schweigens: Formen künstlerischer Erinnerung an die nationalsozialistische Rassen- und Vernichtungspolitik in Osteuropa*, ed. F. Grüner, U. Heftrich, and H-D. Löwe (Köln: Böhlau Verlag, 2006), 57–96.

forced to confront its economic condition as a "banana republic" (by which Ryklin means a gross exporter of raw materials and gross importer of manufactured goods). Russians faced the historical horrors long concealed behind the Soviet ideological screen, and almost immediately they lamented the loss of that grandeur that the ideology machine had projected onto that screen. On the positive side, Ryklin welcomed the possibility that Russia and Moscow might function not in terms of the unitary nation-state or an imperial network but as part of a global interaction of peoples and cultures.

Juxtaposing Benjamin's and Ryklin's responses to Berlin and Moscow, we see that at the bookends of the totalitarian experience, these cities became the mirror images of one another, and in crucial ways alien to each other. As Ryklin pictures them, during their respective totalitarian phases they shared parallel historical events, while remaining culturally distinctive. Even despite all the contrasts, the intertwined history of Moscow and Berlin gives Ryklin in the 1990s hope for Moscow's future. He sees Berlin as a particular version of the "West," which could become a workable model for post-Soviet Moscow. Berlin, in Ryklin's view, shares important aspects of a totalitarian history and the role of center of a totalitarian empire. First it was the capital of the modern German state, then the Nazi empire, and after World War II the westernmost reach of the Soviet empire. Since 1989, Ryklin notes, Berlin has moved in a new direction, integrating and building beyond its Nazi and Soviet history.

In Berlin Ryklin finds a significant geographical other to a Moscow still struggling to confront its past: "Berlin is the only city in which the forces of democracy that participated in the war against Nazism coexisted for decades side by side with totalitarianism of another type, largely imported from the USSR" (PL, 137, 255). For decades Berlin was split between east and west, with two architectural styles and two centers, and it is, perhaps for that reason, the home of readers who are real, serious interlocutors for post-Soviet Russians looking to break the mold of their authoritarian mentality (PL, 254). Unlike other Europeans, Germans are deeply concerned with Russia and the renewed reality of Russian authoritarianism (PL, 256).

In contrasting the two cities, Ryklin takes as his point of departure Hannah Arendt's *The Origins of Totalitarianism*. Although Ryklin agrees that the two capitals of totalitarian states share some crucial characteristics and historical experiences, he also argues that the deep differences between the two cities and the two totalitarianisms must be grasped if Moscow is to overcome its authoritarian past. For example, the impact of communal thinking and behavior is much stronger in Russia than in Germany. Ryklin makes much of Benjamin's early observation, still in the relatively "free" year, 1926, of the widespread anxiety and fear of speaking one's mind and the attitude among the public of waiting for the next directive from above, both of which helped to make Stalinism and full totalitarianism possible.[13] In this overwhelming social conformism, even in a time of relative freedom and peace, Ryklin sees a totalitarianism that, despite Arendt's comparisons, differs significantly from Nazi totalitarianism—the difference is the strength of a collective insistence on conformity of thought that became the basis for Stalin's transformation of Moscow and the whole Soviet Union.

The reconstructed Moscow of the 1930s and following decades became a metaphor for what Ryklin calls the specifically Soviet "collective uncon-scious." It featured nodal "spaces of jubilation," public architectural and sculp-tural ensembles that projected ideological statements which, in turn, shaped a Soviet mass consciousness and gave the collectivized, newly urbanized masses a self-image and a reason to exist. Primary examples are the Stalin "wedding cake" skyscrapers, the Exhibition of the Achievements of the Na-tional Economy (Vystavka Dostizhenii Narodnogo Khoziaistva, VDNKh), and the never-realized Palace of Soviets, to be built on the site of the nine-teenth-century Cathedral of Christ the Savior. Of all these spaces of jubila-tion, the Moscow metro, in Ryklin's view, is the most important because, although obviously a remarkable network of glistening underground pal-aces celebrating the Soviet masses and their achievements, it most clearly preserves in its statuary, its frescoes, and its stained glass images not just of celebration but of the subconscious repression of terror.[14] In this country and this city that historically had never fully developed a bourgeoisie based on private capital, Stalinist architecture created a public mask of ecstatic jubilation. It was a crime to scowl on the street. Arendt's "atomized self," a keystone of her definition of totalitarianism, had no firm historical roots and no social basis for survival. In this new Soviet society the atomized self was blown away—removed into exile, sent to the camps, or shot.

Another major difference between the two modes of totalitarianism, Stalinism and Nazism, is in the metaphorical status of their capitals as cen-ters and the concomitant defining significance of their borders. Moscow developed a great deal stronger cache than Berlin ever did. The Bolshevik

13. PL, 128, 130; see also *Moscow Diary*, 33.

14. Ryklin, "Bodies of Terror," 59. As examples of such hidden signs of terror, Ryklin dis-cusses the mosaics at Novoslobodskaia as a document of the "Party's seizure of the energy of artistic creation." He writes further: "Such faces appear in Russian culture only after the trauma of violent urbanization" (59). He later links the artist's sense of terror to " 'etatization,' the governmentalization of the creative act as the property of the client" (62). He also discusses the mosaic of steelworkers with female technician observing them at Avtozavodskaia as one example of hidden terror (65). For a fuller discussion, see chapter 1 in this volume.

Revolution turned Moscow into the beacon of world communism and the hope of left-leaning Western intellectuals in a way that mutatis mutandis Hitler's Berlin could not become. The geographical metaphor of the border dividing the new Soviet utopia from the decadent bourgeois West—and a decade later Stalinism from the Nazi world—was a powerful defining image for this new sacred ground, an effect that one could only perceive fully in 1992, when it no longer existed. Ryklin writes in *Spaces of Jubilation:*

> Independently of whether it was accepted or rejected, the Soviet phenomenon set the intellectual horizon of Europe for three generations. In a deeper sense, those who claimed to ignore it still had to have a relationship to it. Therefore, the disappearance of the USSR could not but bring on an intellectual crisis: the enormous theatricalized space, onto which the boldest high hopes, the most radical rejection of bourgeois values had been projected, had now disappeared. (PL, 18)

The Soviet space generally became a symbolic homeland of radical change for the better for all peoples, a fantasy that was then smashed to pieces when the border opened in 1992.

These differences between these two totalitarianisms, Ryklin argues, must be fully appreciated if post-Soviet Moscow is ever to gain the will to move beyond the oppressive mass conformism that characterized it for much of the twentieth century. In the early twenty-first century the conformist face of the Russian masses that Benjamin described has reemerged—now angry, old, and ignorant, rather than young and jubilant; now around an ultra-rightist form of Russian Orthodoxy, rather than the communist ideal. In 2003 the signal event of the vandalizing of the postmodern art exhibit "Caution, Religion!" (*Ostorozhno, religiia!*) showed that this mass mentality is very much alive though now supporting a different ideology. Ryklin's response in *Swastika, Star, Cross* was to warn Russians of their tendency to isolate themselves, paraphrasing Winston Churchill: "A cultural iron curtain…is lowering slowly over Russia," and Karl Marx: "A specter is wandering across Russia, the specter of religious nationalism and intolerance." The Russian tendency toward dogmatism has changed its stripes, exchanging one orthodoxy for another.[15]

Ryklin's next step after diagnosing the psychological structures of Stalinist Moscow is to diagnose himself in order to become conscious of the "Stalin-in-myself" (PL, 265). Ryklin finishes *Spaces of Jubilation* by recounting five

---

15. This phenomenon is not new. Nikolai Berdiaev considers the dogmatism of the radicals of the late nineteenth and early twentieth century in his classical work, *The Origin of Russian Communism*, trans. R. M. French (Ann Arbor: University of Michigan Press, 1960), 9.

dreams noted between June 2000 and March 2001—in which he finds himself at once in the old USSR and in contemporary post-Soviet spaces with leaders and celebrities who at once represent and contradict Soviet ideals. It is worth noting here that the former secret police officer, Vladimir Putin, became acting president in January 2000 and was formally elected in March 2000, just before the start of Ryklin's dreams. Ryklin probes how various Soviet spaces and personages figure in his own subconscious. In these dreams Ryklin experiences complex and bewildering feelings of terror, nostalgia, and complicity with regard to the Soviet past and the post-Soviet present, and confusion as to the "revaluation of values" that has taken place since the end of the Soviet Union. The dreams occur in the following chronological sequence:

> Dream 1 (16 June 2000). Ryklin is returning by train to Leningrad. Waking up after a deep sleep he finds himself in an unknown place. He checks whether his wallet has been stolen. It has not. He exits the train and finds that he is not in Leningrad, as he intended, but in Baku. He reasons that he had taken the Moscow-Baku train and slept through the Leningrad stop. He goes to the airport to buy a plane ticket and notes that the airport is built in the pompous Stalin style. He is allowed in by the security guards [okhrana] but cannot find the right gate. At one gate he finds a rehearsal of a large women's choir, at another girls from a kindergarten are arranged in geometric figures. Ryklin finds a door to the open air, forgets about his tickets, and loses interest in the future. He is overcome by a feeling of relief.
>
> Dream 2 (8 August 2000). Ryklin has a book on the privatization of launching pads belonging to the former Soviet space program, for which he is being paid to write a review. He sees the Soviet astronaut Leonov in "some hotel near Moscow University," it is not clear where (PL, 267). He wants to compliment Leonov, but sees that Leonov is indifferent and irritated that he has been excluded from the sell-off.
>
> Dream 3 (25 August 2000). In Moscow it is Mayor Luzhkov's birthday. Ryklin shows a film about Luzhkov's achievements. Ryklin makes a decorated general happy by telling him that younger generation never criticizes Soviet times but fails to tell him that the young are totally indifferent. Ryklin ends up in a post-Soviet sauna with the TV personality Evgeny Kiselev, who gives him a hanger and tells him not to talk about what an elite place they are in. Ryklin feels alienated.
>
> Dream 4 (15 February 2001). On the bank of a river, which reminds Ryklin of Bremen, Germany, Ryklin and his wife, the artist Anna Alchuk [pseudonym of Anna Mikhalchuk, 1955–2008], are collecting pretty

stones. They come upon old Stalin-era medals and red Communist Party membership books. Ryklin is not sure about their value, whether they are treasure or trash.

Dream 5 (27 March 2001). In the Kremlin Stalin watches his retinue, which includes Ryklin, as they consume enormous amounts of sweets. Stalin hardly participates, but tests Ryklin, asking him to list his, Stalin's, favorite sweets. Ryklin does so, but also confuses Stalin's favorite for a popular Jewish sweet, which Stalin-in-the-dream says he likes.

Significantly, these five dreams are presented and analyzed out of chronological order. In the text the first of the five occurs in March 2001, the second is eight months earlier, and the third is the earliest—June, 2000. The fourth and fifth then proceed chronologically forward from August 2000 to February 2001. Thus, the textual order of the dreams is: 5–2–1–3–4. Possible goals here might have been to foreground the figure of Stalin hovering over the rest of the dreams and to create symmetry, by putting the theme of power (Stalin, his retinue) and its reward systems (food, membership, decoration) in the marked positions at the beginning and end, and the dreams with post-Soviet socio-economic themes (privatization, elite clubs) in the second and fourth positions. The first dream, which is directly about Ryklin's identity and his geographical sense of home, chronologically the first dream about the train trip, is here placed in the center of the sequence, the third of the five dreams. In my view, this strange chronological order serves to emphasize the only dream not in a thematic pair, the first dream about identity, the anxiety regarding the concept of home and returning to a quite coercive home, and the impossibility of reconciling Soviet and post-Soviet spaces.

What does Ryklin learn about himself in the process of this self-analysis? Each brief dream is followed by a discussion, which brings to light a number of absorbing themes. Among the first that Ryklin notes are his mixed feelings of nostalgia (trying to return to his home city, Leningrad), anxiety about returning to his police-state "home" (presence of security guards at the Baku airport), relief at not returning (coming out of the airport into the fresh air). In other dreams he feels shame about his role in the new elite (the book review, the elite club), anxiety at the devaluation of ruling institutions of the Soviet era (pride in the stupendous space program, military pride, party loyalty), and confusion over Soviet-era symbols of status (and complicity), such as party membership books and military medals, that appear to have become post-Soviet trash.

In terms of his goals of apprehending the Stalin-in-myself, perhaps most interesting is his repeatedly probed sense of complicity with the old Soviet and the venal post-Soviet order. In the Stalin dream Stalin appears as a benevolent man. Ryklin is part of Stalin's inner circle and is trying at once to please Stalin and to bring him closer to himself, which in this case means "judaizing" him through a discussion of sweets. In answer to Stalin's request that Ryklin list the tyrant's favorite desserts, Ryklin mentions one of the historical Stalin's favorites, churchkhela, which he describes as nut cake in honey. In fact, Ryklin-in-the-dream has conflated churchkhela, which is actually made of nuts in grape syrup, with the Jewish teiglakh, which is a honey-nut cake (PL, 266). In this way the subconscious mends a deep rift between Stalin, the benevolent image of the authoritative "Name-of-the-Father" in Lacanian terms, and the heinous crimes of Stalin against Ryklin's immediate family and the Jews. Another moment of complicity arises in the third dream, during Luzhkov's birthday party, when Ryklin participates in a lie—he comforts a Soviet-era marshal by telling him that the younger generation never criticizes Soviet times, which the marshal is glad to hear (PL, 272). He does not explain to the marshal, however, that young people are completely indifferent to the Soviet era and never even talk about it.

The most interesting dream in terms of ambivalent national identity and national space is the "nostalgic" train trip to Leningrad that ends in Baku. Here the disjunction and incongruity between Soviet and post-Soviet space, the desire to return home (Leningrad is the city of Ryklin's birth, but does not exist as such any more, having in 1991 reverted to its original name, St. Petersburg) and the anxiety at the possibility of returning, the sense of confusion and not belonging—all become palpable. Ryklin immediately identifies Baku with Stalin and the spaces of monumental Stalinist architecture. In the logic of the dream the airport is conflated with Stalinist "spaces of jubilation," the pavilions of the Exhibit of the Achievements of the National Economy and Soviet-era "houses of culture": what look like exit gates leading to airplanes are actually spaces of collective culture, for example, women singing in a choir and gymnasts forming in geometric patterns. As we now know, Ryklin sees these spaces of jubilation as masks for Stalinist terror and coercion—thus his trepidation. That the airport is guarded by security police, who permit him entry, adds to his anxiety. This dream Baku is not home but is in the same geographical territory of his home, Leningrad—both of which, USSR and Leningrad—no longer exist. Associating home with a locus of terror is uncanny, or *unheimlich*, to use Freud's term. Ryklin uses Lacanian vocabulary to say something similar: "The Imaginary preserves the pulsating point of the Real, which never stops both attracting and frightening off" (PL, 271); the Imaginary is that anxious point at which the child realizes that he is a being apart from his environment and the people in it. In his dream Ryklin has reenacted the horror of home as

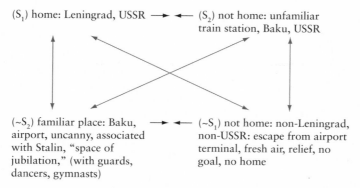

(S_1) home: Leningrad, USSR ⟶ ◂— (S_2) not home: unfamiliar train station, Baku, USSR

$(\sim S_2)$ familiar place: Baku, ⟶ ◂— $(\sim S_1)$ not home: non-Leningrad, airport, uncanny, associated with Stalin, "space of jubilation," (with guards, dancers, gymnasts) / non-USSR: escape from airport terminal, fresh air, relief, no goal, no home

FIG. 9. Semiotic square charting spaces in Ryklin's Dream No. 1.

"space of jubilation," realizing that more than anything he does not want to be there.

It would be instructive to apply to these dream spaces a Greimasian semiotic square, which helps to see the complex relationship between "home" and "non-home" and seek out what is significantly unarticulated (Fig. 9). This dream has a great deal to say about identity, space, and territory. In the Greimasian square the two top items are binary opposites—home and not-home, that are stated at the start of the dream. The bottom items are extrapolated from the first two terms, as their unstated "absences" and as their respective contradictions and complements: the items diagonal to one another are in contradiction—Leningrad is home and not-Leningrad is not-home, a situation that produces relief; and Baku is both an unfamiliar place and an uncannily familiar place associated with Stalinist culture. The items in vertical relation to one another are complementary or, at least, do not conflict with one another: thus, S_2 and $\sim S_1$ agree that neither of them is "home" and are associated with limbo and release from anxiety. S_1 and $\sim S_2$ are two familiar places, one of which is a goal, "home," and the other of which is "familiar" but anxiety arousing. By combining both horizontal concepts, one arrives at meta-concepts of home and unknown place on the top line and, on the bottom line, which is more interesting—familiar, anxiety-arousing place and escape from the familiar, which releases anxiety but provides no clear goal. This last meta-concept can be said to express the aimless dynamic of the post-Soviet era, an absence that drives people back to familiar, if anxiety-producing, forms of behavior and social interaction.

Ryklin claims that these post-Soviet dreams fit a psychotic rather than neurotic model—that is, they express direct acts of violence rather than frustrations mediated through metaphors of desire. I would argue that all five dreams fit neither mold. In Dream 1, Ryklin is left with a sense of relief at not being able to do what he desires to do: to go home. As Ryklin puts it, "I do not want to return and act out a return in order to bring forth the point of trauma that would exclude return. What I consciously desire [to go home], in fact, calls forth horror: more than anything precisely that is what I do not want" (PL, 271). Thus, this particular post-Soviet unconscious expresses a deep sense of ambivalence and lack of direction and identity, while also expressing deep relief he cannot "go back" (*vspiat'*). Here Ryklin's expression of personal relief echoes a frequently heard refrain among older Russian intellectuals in the 1990s.[16] At most, we find here a negative identity of "not being" what was previously expected that one should be—what is lacking is a productive identity that provides a context, a goal, and a direction.

What then have we learned from Ryklin's self-diagnosis? Although trauma, anxiety, disjunction, and desire are apparent everywhere, there are relatively few signs of frustration and no acts of violence. The future seems to be wholly lacking, just as there is a lack of clarity with relationship to the space in which Ryklin feels himself to belong, Ryklin-in-his-dreams is able to come to clear realizations, even judgments and decisions. He observes his and others' duplicity and, in the Luzhkov birthday dream, is able to reject the fraternity of the new elite. At the end of the Stalin gourmandizing dream, while still asleep, he observes the circularity of the events of the dream as they repeat and comes to the judgment that they are boring and he awakens. Although there appears to be no space or time to which Ryklin feels he belongs, his judgment is intact. In a real sense, what his dreams show is that he has become what might be called a "free agent." He has reinvented himself as a psychologically reflective individual who has reclaimed personal agency and, thus, has achieved a major goal of his "Westernizing" philosophical project.

This self-empowerment has been more than useful, giving Ryklin the sense of public agency and the courage to speak out against the repressive tactics of the Putin regime. In the early twenty-first century Ryklin's project of rethinking Moscow as a tolerant place with borders running through it has suffered enormous, even debilitating, setbacks. Instead of embracing

16. Ryklin's temporary sense of relief in his dream, of course, is belied by a deep-lying fear that, by electing as president Vladimir Putin, a spy and influential servitor of the former totalitarian state, Russia is indeed "going back." For a recent documentary that shows the trauma associated with the realization that post-Soviet Russia is indeed returning to its repressive ways, see http://halldor2.wordpress.com/2008/07/26/seven-years-on-the-front-line/. Thanks to Ray Finch for this information.

the other within oneself, however one might define that other, the ultra-conservatives have erected verbal, legal, and coercive barricades against all possible others. Ryklin's initial project has now become a rearguard action of unswerving confrontation with growing contemporary chauvinism and authoritarianism. Post-Soviet Moscow is no longer the cohesive center of Soviet times but rather a place with a number of hostile peripheries and borders running through it. The borders are on the street, in bookstores, in museums and theaters, and in the courtroom. They represent a struggle between at least two ideals, if not more—that of secular civil society and that of Holy Rus', the ultraconservative Russian Orthodox community supported by the Putin government (SZK 11, 24). Ryklin declares war on what he calls the "conservative revolution" (VD, 21). He sees a Russia that is just starting to shed its imperial, ideologically benighted habits, but now is re-embracing them (VD, 320).

The first personally hurtful shift that bespeaks the return of authoritarianism of a sort is the story concerning the change of direction of Ad Marginem, which Ryklin helped to found. Beyond disseminating contemporary Western and Russian philosophy, Ad Marginem started to publish neo-fascist trash novels purportedly to make money and stay afloat. Among the most famous works was Prokhanov's anti-liberal novel, *Mr. Hexogen* (2002), which we consider in chapter 6. Repeatedly venting his anger at this ideological flip-flop in one of Russia's leading westernizing presses, Ryklin sees here a significant shift toward fascism and away from contemporary Europe, away from critical discourses toward an advocacy of race-oriented violence.[17] The worrisome message that one takes from this incident is that the toxic combination of chauvinism and anti-Western hatred and ethnic violence sells books.

A much more wide-ranging and publicly significant event showing a shift toward protecting violent acts on the part of the Russian religious right and "Russian patriots" is the vandalizing of the conceptualist art exhibit, "Caution, Religion!" at the Sakharov Center in Moscow. To put it in perspective for American readers, we compare this exhibit with the anti-dogmatic exhibit of summer 1999, "Sensation: Young British Artists from the Saatchi Collection," at the Brooklyn Museum of Art. Then New York mayor Rudolf Giuliani sued the museum, arguing that the city no longer was obligated to fund the museum. Significantly, Giuliani lost in court.[18]

17. VD, 13–14, 17, 181, 308; SZK, 94.
18. Dan Barry and Carol Voge, "Giuliani Vows To Cut Subsidy Over 'Sick' Art," *New York Times* (September 23, 1999), A1 (http://www.nytimes.com, accessed 050108).

In *Swastika, Cross, Star,* Ryklin sees a dangerous precedent in the "Caution, Religion!" affair. In his view, it is the first "cleansing" (*zachistka*) in post-Soviet Moscow cultural life, one that brings the earlier cleansings of Chechnya and Chechens chillingly close to home (SZK, 13). He details the progression of the exhibit affair, which in many ways brings back memories of the trial in 1966 of two young writers, Andrei Siniavsky and Iuly Daniel, that signaled the end of the relative permissiveness of the Thaw Era (1956–1965). In Ryklin's view, the treatment of civil liberties in this instance proves that rights have no legal protection in Russia and that indeed the concept of the rule of law is regressing toward Soviet standards (SZK, 20, 107, 136).

The exhibit opened on 14 January 2003, and was vandalized just three days after the opening, by thuggish parishioners from a local church, who became humorously known as the "altar boys." Works by both minor artists, such as Ryklin's wife, and well-known conceptualist artists, including Aleksandr Kosolapov, Elena Elagina, and Oleg Kulik, were destroyed. On 11 August 2003, the trial of the vandals ended with the victory of the defendants. By December the two exhibit organizers and one of the artists, Anna Alchuk, were accused. The goal was to punish the organizers allegedly for "instigating ethnic discord" (*razzhiganie rozni*) and for insensitivity toward viewers' religious feelings, and Alchuk for daring publicly to protest the widespread threats and hate messages against the artists and even their children after the attack (SZK, 19–20). At the second trial, the organizers and Alchuk were represented by well-known Soviet-era civil-rights defenders, who unsuccessfully defended the celebrated oil magnate Mikhail Khodorkovsky, also in 2003. The lawyers noted the similarities of this trial to the 1966 Siniavsky-Daniel trial, in which the two writers were accused of spreading anti-Soviet propaganda. The defense argued that making fun of Orthodoxy by no means causes people to hate that religion. The judge generally ignored their arguments and, according to Ryklin's account, conducted his courtroom in an "inquisitorial" manner (SZK, 32). In March 2004, the sentences were read: the two organizers had to pay a small fine of 100,000 rubles (about US$3,000). Alchuk was found innocent. Only two of the pictures were ruled to be "anti-orthodox." Still, the damage had been done—clearly the right to non-violent public protest and speak one's mind had suffered a serious setback.

Ryklin argues that the vandals were the tools of a deliberate, well-planned attack on free speech and freedom of social and political criticism, which the Sakharov Center stands for, and that it had strong support among well-known rightist cultural figures and many parts of the Russian government (SZK, 17, 22). This view was supported by a number of public statements from the right issued soon after the attack, largely by people who had not even bothered to visit the exhibit. On 21 January 2003, a document was posted on www.credo.ru, titled "Letter from Academics and Artists on the Blasphemous Exhibit at the Sakharov Center" (*Obrashchenie deiatelei nauki i kul'tury v sviazi s provedeniem koshchunstvennoi vystavki v tsentre Sakharova*). Signatories included prominent Orthodox nationalists—for example, the film celebrity Nikita Mikhalkov, the artist Ilia Glazunov, the sculptor Viacheslav Klykov, writers Valentin Rasputin, Vasily Belov, as well as the famous mathematician and member of the Russian Academy of Sciences Igor Shafarevich. Although they had typically not seen the exhibit, they described the affair as the work of "marginal blasphemers and Satanists publicly gloat[ing] in the center of Moscow over Orthodox sacred objects." Once again the Russian Orthodox faithful were cast as the victims of persecution: "our people are functionally deprived of the ability to defend their faith and their sacred objects from mockery. Nothing of the sort is imaginable in relation to Islam, Buddhism, or any other traditional religion, let alone Judaism. And this is happening in Russia, where statistically around 70 percent of the population consider themselves Orthodox" (SZK, 44–45). Harking back to the Holy Rus' concept of Russian identity, Russia, in this view, continues to be a "holy object."

On 12 February 2003, members of the State Duma sent their "Appeal" to the office of the General Prosecutor Ustinov. In Ryklin's view, this letter demonstrated that the main player in the "Caution, Religion!" affair was not the Russian Orthodox Church but the Russian State, which is destroying the public political sphere (SZK, 18). The Duma address supported the idea that the exhibit was meant to instigate religious hatred, to humiliate the faithful and to insult the Russian Orthodox Church (SZK, 52). Increasingly, in Ryklin's view, contemporary Russia can be compared to Italy in the 1920s and Germany in the 1930s.

In his description of the trial Ryklin gives a particular picture of Russians that seems reminiscent of pre-revolutionary images of the peasant masses: "Mostly aged, badly dressed people filled the corridors, stairwells, and meeting rooms. In their hands they held icons, crosses, and religious books, they continually crossed themselves and sang prayers, sometimes dropping to their knees right in the corridor of the court.... They walked in a procession around the courthouse building" (SZK, 24). The protesters from the religious right, as Ryklin describes them, were undereducated (they were unaware, for example, that the Russian state is secular), poor, ritualistic, loud, aggressive, bigoted, and racist (SZK, 145). Filled with malice, these people spewed anti-Semitic epithets and defended the "pogrom" as an "act pleasing to God" (*bogougodnoe deianie,* SZK, 25). Anna Alchuk and Ryklin were blindsided by this attack, believing naively that Muscovites had finally outgrown this kind of behavior (SZK, 7). Ryklin claims that "after living and working in western countries over the last 15 years my wife's and my instincts of the unquestioningly loyal citizen (*vernopoddannicheskii*) had atrophied" and now it turns out that they needed those instincts as citizens "started to turn into the subjects of the next Russian autocrat" (SZK, 7). Ryklin feels confounded as he tries to address people of a fundamentalist Orthodox frame of mind, groping for a language in which to negotiate with such people, who live in an entirely different mental and discursive sphere (SZK, 36).

Ryklin hears in this affair a resurgence of rhetoric he calls "pogrom discourse" that, we note, in most respects resembles Aleksandr Dugin's vocabulary (SZK, 161, 171), suggesting perhaps that Dugin is much closer than Ryklin to ordinary people's thinking. These people are intent on reestablishing the "Moscow-as-third-Rome-and-Holy-Rus'" identity (SZK, 25, 31). Ryklin describes the vocabulary of this identity. For example, the Sakharov Center artists were accused of "russophobia [*russofobiia*]" and "blasphemy [*koshchunstvo*]," of violating "sacredness and spiritual community [*sakral'nost' i sobornost'*]," of expressing their "sacrilegious idea [*sviatotatstvennaia ideia*]." The exhibit seemed to the frenzied faithful to foretell "the death of Christianity [*gibel' khristianstva*]," "the destruction of the church [*unichtozhenie tserkvi*]," and "propagation of another religion [*nasazhdenie inoi religii*]" (SZK, 31).

Perhaps not unexpectedly, the results of the court trial of the artists resonate with a Soviet-era tendency, still very much alive in the post-Soviet public subconscious, to attack the thinking person—artist, intellectual, or private citizen—who dares to question dominant values and mindsets (SZK, 16). The note from members of the State Duma, who supported the "pogrom" (SZK, 18) and the trial, Ryklin calls an official challenge to the civil rights of free speech of the artists (SZK, 7, 112). The sentence, in his view, asserted a Russian identity not based on language or a shared culture and history, but the idea of one ethnic group and one religion (SZK, 83, 158) that is above criticism and that "creates the state" in which only people defined as Russians will live (SZK, 136). The sentence is another statement of a bigoted national identity: "'Russian culture developed on an Orthodox foundation, and ethnic Russians make up the main part of the flock of the Russian Orthodox Church'" (SZK, 83). To be Russian means to be Russian Orthodox.

As a Westernizer, Ryklin does everything within his power to repudiate the imperial geography of Russia's neo-fascists, the concept of the Russian center as Holy Rus' and the Third Rome (SZK, 162–163). In *Swastika, Star, Cross*, he mocks Dugin's rhetoric of the new imperial-ecclesiastical "Byzantine symphony," when he suggests ironically that the trial against the curators of the "Caution, Religion!" exhibit was scripted to the last note to show that the "Byzantine 'symphony' of church and state performed impeccably" (SZK, 161). He openly condemns Dugin's ally, the ideologue and director of the rightist Center for Effective Politics Gleb Pavlovsky, for calling for nothing less than the "project of the Most Recent Middle Ages" and the transformation of the Russian state into a theocracy (SZK, 172).[19]

Among the current ruling elite Ryklin notes a serious poverty of ideas: in his words, " 'Domostroi,' the Most Recent Middle Ages, Project Eurasia, Orthodox Rus'—the choice of topics is not great" (SZK, 173). These labels are linked to the goals of the new secret police in power, the "strong men" in Putin's Kremlin—to destabilize the Russian citizenry and destroy voluntary organizations, making full use of what Ryklin terms "our own anxiety [and] insecurity with regard to our legal rights" (SZK, 173). Most worrisome is the tendency that Ryklin sees in the increasing domination of force over discourse. And it comes as a shock to see how easily this turn backward is happening.

In the early twenty-first century, although Moscow may be a wealthy city, it has become spiritually, and even politically, what might be called a "center on the periphery" of Europe. Ryklin points out Moscow's marginality in a number of ways: the "colossal power vacuum" that allowed someone like Putin to come to power (VD, 136), as well as Putin's own lack of values and his manipulation of anti-U.S. feelings and Russian dreams of empire (VD, 135). Instead of following the Berlin model, Moscow has become a vacuous ruling center without a moral compass, without the firm, consistent rule of law, and possessed of a disturbing tendency to normalize what should be "marginal" or peripheral, for example, rightist politics, criminality, hard drug use, and crime bosses. These are the fare of popular TV and book culture, and they have become the rule for political life and the ideal for young people (VD, 8). With a nod to Arendt's theory of totalitarianism partly defined by the atomization of individual citizens, the hollowing out of voluntary organizations and social institutions, and the creation of front organizations of the state, Ryklin sees in Russia a "growing space of loneliness" (VD, 18). Since the onset of the Putin regime in 2000, Ryklin has been pointing to the reality of growing authoritarian, neo-fascist sentiment on all levels of Russian society. The universalist-minded "Westernizers," people who, like Ryklin, speak in defense of citizens' rights and the rule of an independent judiciary, find themselves under increasing threat. Putin's Russia is a place of waning sensitivity and empathy for the social other, whether that

19. It is yet another Moscow Conceptualist, the bad boy of contemporary literature Vladimir Sorokin, who satirized this mentality in his 2006 novella *The Day of the Oprichnik* (*Den' oprichnika*).

person is a rich or poor person, an artist, a journalist, a Chechen, a Jew, or anyone of a different race, age, or gender (SZK, 91).

What worries Ryklin most is the effort on the part of the Putin regime to disguise state-orchestrated terror—even if, so far, that effort is much more limited than in the 1930s. The Second Chechen War is the new "that-which-must-not-be-mentioned," the new taboo, the open discussion of which Putin is guilty of repressing. Ryklin rightly sees this repression of open debate as a slippery slope leading to other repressions of public debate. One must also mention the radical step of murdering the outspoken journalist Anna Politkovskaia, in October 2006, and the 2007 verdict of defamation against Mikhail Kashulinsky, the Russian editor of *Forbes Magazine*, specifically for speaking openly about misconduct by the real estate company owned by Yelena Baturina, the wife of Mayor Luzhkov.[20] Another incident in this tragic process of literally killing free speech is the disappearance and possible murder of Ryklin's wife in Berlin in March 2008.[21]

Ryklin advocates social behavior defined by tolerance, dialogue, and the free press instead of the totalitarian idea embraced by religious-fascist extremists like Dugin, Pavlovsky, and Prokhanov. His point of view is inclusive, exposing the exclusive mentality at the heart of nationalist religious and racial extremism (SZK, 146). Ryklin embraces the Other, both in himself and in his social surroundings.

Border, in Ryklin's thought, serves as metaphor for security, on the one hand, and for psycho-cultural ban or repression, on the other hand. The open border with all its risks represents open thinking. During the 1990s, while living both in Moscow and abroad, and crossing borders frequently, Ryklin developed arguments against the encroachments of narrow nationalism and for a new universalism based on a faith in tolerance. Writing in 2001, he observed, "In the open world in which we live, where various forms of migration and emigration are the rule and not the exception, the problem of national identity has become more complex than ever. The simple exteriorization of the Other in the sense of the 'good old days' seems increasingly false" (PL, 262). Ryklin's Berlin—and the Moscow Ryklin hoped he would return to in the late 1990s—is characterized by tolerance, correspondence, dialogue, the freely exploring feuilleton, and the free press.

20. See "Editor of Russian Edition of Forbes Guilty of Defamation," *New York Times,* 22 March 2007, section C, page 4.

21. Official news media report that the Berlin police ruled out foul play, http://www.newsru.com/world/18apr2008/mikhalchuk.html.

Ryklin's Berlin is politically, socially, and culturally inclusive and shines a bright light on ethnic and religious exclusivism in Russia (SZK, 146). The Berlin of 2001 seemed to Ryklin a symbol of a reconfigured Europe that includes east and west, and that could also embrace Moscow:

> Inside Berlin in a soft, mediated form there exists a contradiction, which in Moscow takes on a dramatic, only minimally mediated form. I have in mind the contradiction between post-industrialism and socialism, which although pronounced dead, still is very much alive in cultural life. For that reason for a long time yet Muscovites visiting Berlin will certainly sense something familiar. Berlin is not just a city turned toward the east of Europe, but the east is an essential part of its character. For that reason it is precisely Berlin that has the best chance to become the center of a Greater Europe, which will include Russia; Europe, whose existence has only been declared but whose groundwork has been being laid over the last twelve years. (PL: 255–256)

Returning to Moscow, Ryklin could see clearly and unavoidably that the "broader European cultural space" is indeed an increasingly hostile space for most of his Russian compatriots. As he put it in his collection of short essays, *Diagnostic* (*Vremia diagnoza*): "[This broader space] has not yet been accepted by most of my fellow citizens as an integral part of themselves, [for whom] many aspects of openness are still traumatic." Nonetheless, he added optimistically, "I am far from being the only one who lives in it [this space]" (VD: 8).

The ensuing decade has made a huge difference. In a 1998 interview with the U.S. philosopher Susan Buck-Morss, Ryklin brightly suggested that his Westernizing project was having some good effect, at least among the educated reading public:

> The local intellectual marketplace has experienced quite broad changes: many key texts of contemporary philosophy, sociology, psychology, anthropology have been translated into Russian. One could talk about the end of the domination of Russian literature, which now has become one of many writing practices and has lost its totalizing function. As a result, the Western experience has become significantly more accessible and transferable than it was 10 years ago. (DD, 202)

Since 2000, in contrast, expressions of identity under the Putin regime have turned resolutely in the direction of defining Russianness by drawing thick ideological borders between itself and all the "others" out there—Chechens, Jews, new, politically engaged Russian entrepreneurs, artists, freemasons, freethinkers. And Ryklin, in turn, has returned to a role familiar from Soviet times, the role of the dissident.

5 THE PERIPHERY AND ITS NARRATIVES

Liudmila Ulitskaia's Imagined South

He loved looking at this land, with its weathered mountains and its rounded foothills. It had been Scythian, Greek, Tatar, and although now it was part of the Soviet farming system and had long been languishing, unloved and slowly dying from the ineptitude of its masters, history had not forsaken it but was hovering in this blissful springtime, every stone, every tree reminding him of its presence.

—LIUDMILA ULITSKAIA, *Medea and Her Children*

The right to signify from the periphery of authorized power and privilege does not depend on the persistence of tradition; it is resourced by the power of tradition to be reinscribed through the conditions of contingency and contradictoriness that attend upon the lives of those who are 'in the minority'. The recognition that tradition bestows is a partial form of identification. In restaging the past it introduces other, incommensurable cultural temporalities into the invention of tradition.

—HOMI BHABHA, *The Location of Culture (2004)*

IN the critical discourse about national identity since the mid-1980s the figure of the north-south geo-cultural axis has begun to compete with the east-west axis of modern Russian consciousness and of traditional "orientalism."[1] The post-Soviet debate about the definition of "Russian" and "outsider" refers to both, although certainly more than before to the north-south axis. The issue of the stature of post-Soviet Russia is couched solidly in north-south terms. For example, the worry in the 1990s of Russia turning into a "banana republic" draws on a decidedly southern image from

---

In this chapter citations from Ulitskaia's work are given in the text, using the following notation and page number:

B: *Bednye, zlye, liubimye* (Moscow: Eksmo, 2006).

KK: *Kazus Kukotskogo* (Moscow: Eksmo, 2002).

L: *Liudi nashego tsaria* (Moscow: Eksmo, 2006).

M: *Medea i ee deti* (Moscow: Eksmo, 2003). I use the Tait translation, which is excellent.

1. Benedict Anderson, *Imagined Communities: Reflections on the Origin and Spread of Nationalism* (London: Verso, 1983), 157–158. The book as a whole deals largely with Southeast Asia, stressing the imagined south perhaps more than the east in colonialism and the rise of nationalism.

the post-colonial world.[2] In his novel *The Life of Insects* Pelevin imagined the exploitative U.S. businessman, Sam Sucker, arriving in the Crimea—the formerly Soviet south—transforming into a mosquito and both really and metaphorically sucking the blood of various southern natives. In another context, one has sometimes heard northern Russians' scabrous designation of southern Russian citizens, particularly Chechens, as "treacherous southerners" (*verolomnye iuzhane*), suggesting that "real" Russians are northern and honest. What used to be the exotic "orient"—the Caucasus and the Crimea, for example—is now just as often designated as the south. In the post-Soviet period it is possible to argue that the north-south axis of identity has become as important as the traditional east-west axis of identity so familiar in the modern era for two reasons. This axis points to the fear of being perceived as or becoming a colony, and it points to the worrisome problems of being a multiethnic society as being a *southern* problem.[3]

This chapter introduces one aspect of Russia's "southern problem" through a broader discussion of peripheries in the work of Liudmila Ulitskaia.[4] Of particular interest here is the Black Sea region. The next chapter deals with the Muslim Caucasus, an aspect of the "southern problem" that has had a disastrous effect on the post-Soviet public dialogue about identity. If Pelevin in *Chapaev and the Void* interrogates the reality of "Eurasia" and the neo-imperial mentality embedded in Dugin's thought—reconfirming the centripetal, even solipsistic focus of Moscow on itself, then Ulitskaia importantly focuses on the life of all kinds of peripheries and their crucial, if ignored,

2. In 1999 Marina Rozanova, the publisher of the Paris Russian-language journal *Sintaksis* (and wife of Andrei Siniavskii), commented: "We aren't even a banana republic since we have neither bananas nor a republic. We're a parody of autocracy plus Orthodoxy plus national consciousness [*narodnost'*]. I don't even know what to call our system [*stroi*]" (quoted in *Novye izvestiia* 137 (8 August 2002), http://dlib.eastview.com.www2.lib.ku.edu:2048/sources/article.jsp?id=4263719. See, for example, a quote from President Dmitry Medvedev in "Slova," *Vedomosti*, 132 (18 July 2008): "We aren't a banana republic, after all, that other people have to offer us ways to join civilization. We have our own options," http://dlib.eastview.com.www2.lib.ku.edu:2048/sources/article.jsp?id=18663483.

3. Major works predicated on this assumption are Edward Said's *Orientalism* (New York: Vintage Books, 1979) and Larry Wolff's *Inventing Eastern Europe* (Stanford: Stanford University Press, 1994). The shift can be seen in the autobiography of the populist-fascit politician Vladimir Zhirinovskii *The Drive to the South* (1993). Zhirinovskii sees peace between east and west in the new world order and the south as an area for Russian expansion and enrichment. See Wayne Allensworth, *The Russian Question: Nationalism, Modernization, and Post-Communist Russia* (Lanham, MD: Rowman and Littlefield, 1998), 194–200.

4. A number of critics confirm that Ulitskaia is "really recognized and loved by essentially the whole reading public—both readers looking for intellectually taxing fiction and simpler readers" (Elena Plakhova, "Proza. Velikolepnyi ochevidets," *Moskovskaia pravda*, 177 (17 August 2005), 4, http://dlib.eastview.com.www2.lib.ku.edu:2048/sources/article.jsp?id=8106716.

role for the vitality of the country.[5] Two striking aspects of Ulitskaia's "universalist" literary project are her respect for a broad array of approaches to being human, for disparate ethnic voices and points of view, as well as her sustained argument against Russian chauvinism. Russian ultraconservatives, such as journalist Aleksandr Prokhanov, typically imagine their homeland space as being the north and east, while Ulitskaia's imagination embraces the multicultural diversity, particularly of the Black Sea south. This chapter examines the theme of the periphery—and particularly the Black Sea and its symbolic meanings—in a number of stories and two major novels, *Medea and Her Children* (*Medeia i ee deti*, 1996) and *The Kukotsky Case* (*Kazus Kukotskogo*, 2001).

Until now our discussion has treated the hypertrophy of the center in relation to its peripheries. This overdevelopment only stresses the isolation of the center and its, at times, xenophobic mood. In the post-Soviet Russian situation there is nothing like the productive interplay of center and periphery that Homi Bhabha hopes for. There is no revivifying "hybridity."[6] Ulitskaia is the first major post-Soviet author actually to listen to cultural voices on the periphery and take seriously their articulation of tradition and identity. According to Bhabha's optimistic argument, tradition is never set in stone, but evolves through engagement. Ulitskaia "restages the past," and "introduces other, incommensurable cultural temporalities into the invention of tradition" in the hope of moving Russians and non-Russian readers beyond the straightjacket of a narrow Russophile, xenophobic mentality.[7] Ulitskaia's project casts doubt on the "originary" Russian and Soviet myths and the fixed mentalities, value systems, and rituals that attend to them. She would certainly agree with Bhabha that it is on the "borderline engagements of cultural difference" that the culture of the center is renewed and rekindled, and the cultures of the periphery gain traction.[8]

The contrasting geographical spaces of center and periphery loom large in Ulitskaia's novels and stories. The center—Moscow—is a place of ideological and social dysfunction, leading always to cultural homogenization and occasionally to threats of violence and even suicide. The act of going to the center is frequently an act of surrendering one's originary identity to buy into the relatively comfortable life and career opportunities in the capital of the Soviet empire. In contrast, the act of leaving the center is frequently a

5. The fullest English-language treatment of Ulitskaia to date is Benjamin Sutcliffe, *The Prose of Life: Russian Women Writers from Khrushchev to Putin* (Madison: University of Wisconsin Press, 2009).
6. Bhabha, *Location of Culture* (London: Routledge, 2004), 55.
7. Ibid., 3.
8. Ibid.

way for a character to discover her or his identity and to see the center in a new light. To counter the gravitational pull of Moscow, Ulitskaia narrates from an "eccentric" standpoint, both focusing on disenfranchised characters and setting her characters in a number of peripheries, some close to or even in Moscow, some far away.

The search for identity and authenticity happens when protagonists leave the capital and discover their inner voice in a different cultural landscape. There are at least four ways of leaving Moscow. The first is to leave the official Moscow for Moscow's underground and the nocturnal, backstreet spaces of the capital. The second possibility is to leave Moscow for the near periphery of villages and private dachas around Moscow, and their typical Russianness. Another way of resisting Moscow is simply to leave the country, to emigrate. Finally, and most trenchantly, characters resist Moscow by exploring the geographical edges of the empire and experiencing their palpably different cultures and historical narratives. This discussion focuses on the near periphery and the southern peripheries of the empire, because they directly address Ulitskaia's approach to the question of national identity.

Ulitskaia's near periphery is Podmoskov'e or the Greater Moscow Region. Here we will find penetrating insight into the Russianness that the ultraconservatives hope to resurrect. The move to this periphery is a classic Russian ritual of the weekend or holiday visit to the dacha, which provides Ulitskaia with darkly humorous scenarios for examining identity. In two stories, "Moscow-Podrezkovo. 1992" and "Open Seating" ("*Obshchii vagon*"), she addresses Venedikt Erofeev, who first made this symbolic railroad journey to national self-discovery in his inebriated travelogue *Moscow-Petushki*. With a nod to the socialist realist requirement that art should reflect national consciousness or *narodnost'*, Venichka sings, among other ironic paeans, a hymn in "praise" of the Russian people:

I like that the people of my country have such vacant and protruding eyes. That fills me with a justifiable feeling of pride. You can imagine what eyes in other countries are like. In a place where everything can be bought and sold...hidden deep, secretive, predatory, and frightened eyes....But my people, what eyes! They are always bulging, but—they show no stress whatsoever. Complete absence of meaning—but for all that, what power! (What spiritual power!)....in times of doubt, in times of painful hesitation, in a time of trial and tribulation—those eyes won't blink....I like my people. I'm happy that I was born and came into manhood under the gaze of those eyes. The only bad thing is: what if they noticed what I just did out on the back platform.[9]

9. Venedikt Erofeev, "Moskva-Petushki," in *Ostav'te moiu dushu v pokoe* (Moscow: Kh. G. S., 1995), 46.

The title "Moscow-Podrezkovo. 1992" immediately signals the story's debt to *Moscow-Petushki* (L, 280–286). It describes a train trip from Moscow to an outlying town, like Erofeev's Petushki, also starting with the letter "P." While Erofeev's drunken narrator pictures Petushki as an idyllic spot, the name of Ulitskaia's Podrezkovo suggests "clipping" or "cutting in front" of someone. This village is a place where all sorts of bad and untoward things happen, including children abusing alcohol and getting into petty crime. The story describes the rundown, filthy train and the "typical" Russians (*dachnyi narod*) traveling to their dachas—as an allegory of the state of Russia itself in 1992: "Devastation was palpable but not final. Like a small rehearsal. After all, there was still a train schedule, and a familiar hoarse voice announced, 'Next station...'" (L, 282). Ulitskaia sets the tone for the question we are about to hear: the narrator asks why one is always touched by the filthy poverty of Russia, with its littered byways, ugly suburbs, and young people gone astray (L, 282).

Central to her response to Erofeev, who celebrated his own—alcoholic's—moral honesty and rhetorical verve, is a debate between two drunks about what it means to be a "real" Russian. The first drunk is quite handsome but barbaric, a hard-line nationalist whose angry eyes, as the narrator wryly notes, convey an "honest Pugachev-like sparkle" (L, 283). The other drunk is bald, milder, and more nuanced in his thinking. The first drunk raises a toast to Russia, only to expound on the idea that "Russia [ought to be] for the Russians!" He ends with an appalling expression of anti-black racism: "This isn't America. It's not for black assholes [*ne dlia chernozhopykh*]" (L:283). It should be noted that black here also includes any people of color, or even people with black hair, including Chechens and other peoples from the Caucasus Mountain region. This first drunk conveys a familiar sense of wounded national pride, because Russia "carried the war [World War II] on its shoulders" (L, 283), by implication, Russians deserve to have more authority and respect. Being Russian here implies having the pronounced passive-aggressive consciousness of the victim, of having been manipulated and abused—and, thus, having the right to ruin one's own life and sour the lives of the people around one. The bald, rather less visually appealing, but certainly wiser and more circumspect "drunk-number-two" joins the argument, wondering "which Russia" we are talking about (L, 284). When drunk-number-one proposes a pogrom, slicing down non-Russians [*rezat' poidem*], the second drunk refuses, upon which the first accuses him of Russian passivity: "There it is...that Russian laziness...no pain, no gain" (L, 285).

As the narrator leaves the train, she passes a young couple having sex near the entryway, again with a nod to Venechka's passion for his beautiful "white she-devil" waiting for him in Petushki. Near the train platform she notices children hidden in some bushes, dividing up stolen money. The narrator challenges Erofeev's romanticized, if ironic, picture of Petushki and the Russian periphery. In her experience it is nothing if not barbaric and lawless:

> [Those boys] won't be folding their bedraggled wings under the old fence, they won't be shedding a dejected tear of repentance and resignation, rather, with drunken bloodshot eyes, they will take up an ax or a BTR armored transport vehicle. And there'll be no Petushki, sticky candies, smooth, honeyed ginger cookies…those nice drunks with their bottle of Salkhino sweet wine will set our poor land afire. "And what will happen to the little guys?" I asked the deceased Venichka Erofeev without any hope of an intelligible answer. (L, 286)

In the "real" Russia, adults have no moral compass, and it is far from clear what will happen to these children who have no positive role model.

Ulitskaia's second dacha story, "Open Seating" undermines the good-hearted, generous stereotype of ordinary Russians. Russian families taking the suburban train to their dachas for the New Year's celebration stand in contrast to their despised cultural Other, a somewhat swarthy Russian nicknamed the Chechen. The Russian family is comprised of a bossy mother—a saleswoman in a food store—with her plastic bag of food for the family; the father, a telephone mechanic, who sits self-importantly "like a Chinese mandarin," and lets people serve him; a son, daughter-in-law, and their fearful German shepherd. The narrator focuses on the dog, who, frightened by the women's squabbling, pees on the floor of the train. The narrator sympathizes: "its eyes show despair and madness—people with those eyes end up committing suicide" (L, 341). As the whole train gets drunk, the narrator and her two friends notice one other sober person, a handsome dark-haired man known as the Chechen. Again referring to Erofeev, the narrator comments, this person "did not get drunk and merge with our people" (L, 342). In conversation they find out that he is from a Mennonite German-Dutch family, who came to Russia in the eighteenth century. Even after his family's recent emigration, this man made a conscious decision to stay in Russia and embrace it as his home (L, 343). He is proud of his Russian nationality, freely chosen. Here Ulitskaia clearly prefers the Chechen's Russianness based on sober, conscious choice, to the shrill ethnically based nationalism of the drunk in "Moscow-Podrezkovo. 1992" or the loud nastiness of the Russian family.

The distant peripheries of the Soviet empire offer opportunities to define one's identity. Being Russian gains a particular meaning, whether positive or negative. For example, in "Carpathians: Uzhgorod" (L, 253–255), set on the westernmost edge of the Soviet empire in August 1968, a young graduate student on a biology field trip sees bombers flying west and realizes that they are probably headed to Czechoslovakia to halt the political liberalization of the Prague Spring. On returning to Moscow, she learns of her friends' arrests for protesting the invasion. In a flash, the periphery reveals the poverty and oppressiveness of the center.

The periphery can also offer greater economic and personal liberty. In *The Kukotsky Case*, the protagonist Tania, who has shed her identification with the Soviet scientific elite, finds a new, successful, if quite illegal, life on the northwest edge of the Soviet empire, in Leningrad, where she finds life less constrained. She enters the underground business world as a jeweler, making beautiful jewelry that one could not find in any official state store. Soon other artists are imitating her work. On the periphery, she is supporting herself and her family wholly outside the official economy.

In Ulitskaia's work Moscow is closely aligned with the north and is the ideological counterpoise to the south, which challenges the claim of the center to ideological authority, civilization, and culture. The "meta-periphery," which allows us to define Ulitskaia's concept of periphery is the south of the Black Sea coast and, particularly, Crimea. Before turning to the south, we need to consider the mentality that Ulitskaia sees informing the center of Russian power, Moscow, and the north.

In Ulitskaia's novels no imagined geographical space is so strongly associated with ethnic Russian selfhood and contemporary Russian chauvinism as the North, nor any so associated with the ethnic Other" as the South. Ulitskaia pictures the North as the area between Moscow, Lake Onega, and the White Sea, for example, Vologda in *Medea and Her Children* or Kargopol in *The Kukotsky Case*. The characters from this North are of ethnically Russian peasant stock, generally mystically inclined, dogmatically minded, dour of character, and, in the Stalin era, turned paranoid by suffering and hunger. In *Medea and Her Children* the quintessentially northern character is Vera Ivanovna, the grandmother of the gifted young Greek-Russian poet Masha. It is through Vera Ivanovna and her family that Moscow becomes associated with the Russian North. This delusional woman is a horrifying echo of the pure Russianness that contemporary ultranationalists find in northern character and speech. Born to a Vologda peasant family, Vera Ivanovna grew up in the early 1930s during the worst of the famine but now enjoys a life of privilege as the wife of a high-ranking army officer. Having become well-to-do, she cannot help herself and becomes an obsessive collector of material possessions (M, 150). After the tragic death of her daughter (Masha's mother), she focuses her fears on Masha. Sure that her granddaughter is conspiring to deprive her of her possessions, she starts to wrap them in towels. Vera's distant relative Motya, who lives with the family in their large apartment, is the comical double to Vera's terrible suffering: "having twice experienced famine in Russia, [she] had long been slightly deranged herself. She lived in order to eat" (M, 151). These unbalanced northern peasants, who after a horrible childhood have unexpectedly come into wealth, are at once cruel and pitiable. They surely do not merit idealization as pure Russians.

In *The Kukotsky Case,* the peasant housekeeper of the Kukotsky family Vasilisa comes from Kargopol. Fervently religious but physically clumsy and mentally slow, she is a modern-day holy fool and wanderer. As a child she lost one eye, pecked out by a rooster (KK, 78). Despite all her shortcomings Vasilisa is a handsome woman with an iconic, "Byzantine" face and has a grateful, goodhearted character (KK, 81, 85). As a young girl, Vasilisa was sheltered in a convent by a progressively minded abbess, to whom she remains devoted her whole life. From time to time she disappears from the Kukotsky apartment and sets off for a long pilgrimage to the north to visit her abbess's grave. Vasilisa is by nature fateful, passive, and suspicious of all non-Russian people and non-Orthodox ways of thinking. These attitudes translate into anti-Semitism (KK, 128–129) and a distrust of modern scientific thought and particularly Pavel Kukotsky's medical specialty, gynecology.

For such people as the simple northern peasant Vasilisa, the south is Greek, an extension of the Russian Orthodox north, and the destination for a religious pilgrimage. In contrast, Ulitskaia's imagined south is by far more complex, multicultural, and life affirming. At the outset we note that in her literary art there are two souths, the "black" one of the Caucasus and the multiethnic one of the Black Sea coast. As in "Moscow-Podrezkovo. 1992," the "black" Caucasus is a hostile mental geography, one that Russians flee, taking refuge in the center. In "A Terrifying Travel Tale" ("Strashnaia dorozhnaia istoriia," L, 261–268), the narrator has to take an overnight train trip in a compartment filled with Georgian men. To avoid rape and theft, she—like Scheherazade—tells amusing tales throughout the night. Ulitskaia has relatively little to say about this South, except to make it a figure of the Russian chauvinist imagination.

⌐⌐

The periphery that functions significantly as a site of liberation for some of Ulitskaia's protagonists is the Black Sea south. Ulitskaia's imagined south is complex and multicultural, the soil of many civilizations and empires. In this vibrant place ethnic groups interact and co-exist, sometimes peacefully, sometimes not. Brutal and uncivilized as it may be, even the contours of the land breathe a deep sense of the past and a richness of overlapping cultures. As Ulitskaia puts it in *Medea and Her Children*, the Black Sea coast is a "minor area of world history" (M, 4), the borderland of many empires, where many peoples at many different times met, traded, and fought over territory. Although this coast epitomizes the periphery, it is also a site of historical significance and cultural complexity. And as such, it has an authenticity of its own.

Beneath its semi-glitzy veneer as a Russian summer resort area, which is so familiar from Vasily Aksenov's prose, for example, "A Change of Life Style" (Peremena obraza zhizni, 1961) and *The Island of Crimea* (Ostrov Krym, 1981), Ulitskaia captures the South as a potential site of cultural hybridity, a place where various cultures can find themselves in productive dialogue. Indeed, in *Medea and Her Children* Ulitskaia calls the Crimea an "*oikumene*" (M, 202), a Greek word for "inhabited world."[10] It is the civilized realm of the novel's title character Medea. An elderly Greek woman, whose life spans much of the twentieth century, Medea lives her entire life in the Crimea and never sets foot in Moscow. All her family and non-Slavic neighbors congregate around her. In fact, she has no children of her own but welcomes all her nieces and nephews and their children who visit her during summer holidays. It is this extended clan that becomes her children.

Because of its complex history as a colony of multiple empires, the Black Sea south became a crucial symbol of modern Russian identity. In ancient times, the Black Sea coast was dotted with Greek trading settlements and later settled by Scythians and Khazars, and much later by Tatars and Turks. Peter the Great tried unsuccessfully to annex a part of the coast to the growing Russian empire. Successfully conquered and colonized in the 1780s by Catherine II, the Black Sea was the centerpiece of her empire-building and represented an important step toward realizing her greatest ambition, to liberate Orthodox Christian Constantinople from the Ottoman Turks. Interestingly, the Black Sea figured in Catherine's plans for her park in Tsarskoe Selo, in which one end of the Big Lake featured various exotic structures, for example, the Chesmen Column, the Turkish Bath, a pyramid, and a Red or Turkish Cascade.[11] The goal of defending Orthodox Christians in the Ottoman empire led to the last great war on this cusp of empires, the Crimean

10. Note that Dugin uses the word *oikumene* to talk about the Orthodox world. See *Proekt Evraziia* (Moscow: Iauza, 2004), 25.
11. See Priscilla Roosevelt, *Life on the Country Estate* (New Haven: Yale University Press, 1995), 37.

War (1853–1856). Although he ultimately lost the war and lost claims to defend the rights of Orthodox Christians, Emperor Nicholas I defended the Russian coast from Turks, English, and French.

A story rarely told is the deportation of Crimean Tatars throughout the nineteenth century, but much more thoroughly and brutally under Stalin's regime. Suspecting the Crimean Tatars of collaborating with the Nazis, in May and June 1944, Stalin ordered the deportation of about 200,000 Tatar Soviet citizens.[12] Following World War II and Stalin's death, the Crimea became the site of an intra-Soviet conquest. In 1954 Nikita Khrushchev bestowed Crimea on his native Ukraine, and proceeded to colonize it with Ukrainians.[13] After the collapse of the Soviet Union in 1991, Crimea became the site of further disagreement. The Soviet Black Sea Fleet was moored partly in Crimea, and Russia and Ukraine squabbled about its future ownership. In addition, Crimea proclaimed its autonomy on 5 May 1992, but subsequently agreed to remain an autonomous part of Ukraine.

The Black Sea Coast is an important imagined geography in Russian literature. In the Romantic period it served as an exotic, "oriental" literary setting. We think of Pushkin's long poem, "The Fountain at Bakhchisarai" ("*Bakhchisaraiskii fontan*," 1823) and Lermontov's disconcerting tale of contraband traders, "Taman," as something of a representation of hell and of the transgressive nature of life on this edge of the empire. By the beginning of the twentieth century Crimea would be considered a watering hole, made world-famous by Chekhov's story of extramarital love, "The Lady with the Small Dog" ("*Dama s sobachkoi*," 1899). In addition, the Romanovs built their summer palace at Livadia in the 1860s, and the Russian literary beau monde sojourned in Koktebel, building fanciful residences.

It is important to note that after World War II Crimea was a favorite Russian and Ukrainian tourist destination. In a way it can be said to have become its own kind of Potemkin Village: Crimea with its Mediterranean beauty was packaged as a resort, even as the terrible social dislocations of the nineteenth and twentieth centuries were swept under the rug. During the 1960s Thaw the vacation settings of Abkhazia, Crimea, especially Yalta and Koktebel, and the Russian Black Sea coast, particularly Sochi, became significant literary settings. Among the most important are Vasily Aksenov's 1961 story, "A Change of Life Style," emphasizes the irreality and inauthenticity

12. See, for example, Amy Knight, *Beria: Stalin's First Lieutenant* (Princeton: Princeton University Press, 1993), 127.

13. William Taubman, *Khrushchev: The Man and His Era* (New York: Norton, 2003), 186. See also *http://dictionary.laborlawtalk.com/Crimea#Post-Soviet_Crimea*. This site suggests that Khrushchev gave Crimea to his homeland as part of a celebration of the 300th anniversary of the reunion of Ukraine and Russia.

of the Black Sea resort of Gagri with its palm trees and southern warmth. In his fantasy novel, *The Island of Crimea*, Aksenov imagines what might have happened had Crimea remained independent, ruled by Russian aristocracy after 1920. He imagines a wealthy, Mediterranean resort, something like Lebanon of the 1960s.

The first post-Soviet decade saw the appearance, along with Ulitskaia's *Medea and Her Children*, of a number of striking works, in which the Black Sea littoral appears as an empty place into which characters from elsewhere inject their aspirations. Two works follow Aksenov in foregrounding the inauthentic, touristy aspects of this region. Both Nina Sadur's fantasy, "The South" ("*Iug*," 1992), and Pelevin's novel, *The Life of Insects*, take place on a dilapidated and unkempt Black Sea coast. Sadur stresses the fantasy of a northerner Olia, who visits Sochi to restore her health. The experience is alienating; Olia is jarred by the trash and filth, the rumors of irradiation, the strange languages she hears around her, other people's savage children, the "cavaliers" who harass her. Olia herself becomes fiercely aggressive, eventually tipping the balance into madness.

Ulitskaia's imagined Black Sea south symbolizes two different identities. The one pictured in *Medea and Her Children* is the ancient and idyllic Crimean peninsula, whereas the seacoast in *The Kukotsky Case* is the northwest coast near Kherson, a desolate backwater. In both cases Ulitskaia makes the coast a problematic, colonized place, from which to react to and re-evaluate the official version of Soviet history. Introducing non-conformist voices of a variety of ethnicities, genders, and generations, her goal is to celebrate the peripheral world with its multitude of cultures and its potential for alternative points of view.

In *The Location of Culture* Bhabha argues that one of the structural axes according to which colonizers justify colonization is the opposition between those dominant, colonizing cultures that claim to have a history and those, which the very same dominant cultures claim do not have a history. The colonizer makes the claim that the culture being colonized is static.[14] We have noted the complexity of the Russian colonizing experience in this regard. Ulitskaia successfully draws attention in her novel to the living memory of the ancient peoples in Crimea. The icon of this memory is the title character of *Medea and Her Children*, Medea, whose ancient Greek dialect bears within itself layers upon layers of history. Medea is the "last remaining pure-blooded Greek of a family settled since time immemorial on the Tauride coast, a land still mindful of its ties with Ancient Greece" (M, 3). In

---

14. Bhabha, *Location of Culture*, 54.

her spoken tongue words are still bound simply to things and actions and have very few abstract or metaphorical overtones. Indeed, in Medea's dialect the very noun for metaphor, "metaphorisis," we are told, "retained to this day a pristine literalness" and "meant 'transportation'" (M, 3).

This ancient language also bears meaning for Medea's family name, Sinoply, which contains two Greek roots. The prefix "sin-" or "syn-," meaning with or together, combines with the "p-l" root of polis, or city, community. These roots bring to mind a larger human community that is together—despite the depredations of war and persecution. The family history of the Sinoply family reaches much farther into the past and promises to reach much further into the future than either Stalin or the Soviet Union itself. Although most of Medea's generation of the family has died, descendants are spread all over the Soviet Union—Central Asia, the Baltics, Moscow, and the Black Sea. And by the end of the novel, Medea's family is spread across three or four continents—Europe, Asia, and the Americas.

In *Medea and Her Children* Ulitskaia adds layers of mythic structure to complicate and deepen the historical picture: she overlays events of the twentieth century with the Greek myth of Medea, producing the sense that Stalinist history is at most an epiphenomenon. Here "originary" myth is on the side of the assimilated Greek minority. The mythic Medea came from the eastern Black Sea, much as the modern Medea's grandmother did. The mythic forebear would seem to have very little to do with her modern namesake. The ancient Medea is a wise woman and sorceress from Colchis. She helps Jason to win the golden fleece and escape from her father. She then marries Jason and has two children. When Jason abandons her for a younger woman, she murders her children, so that they would not suffer as the children of an abandoned mother, and then she murders Jason's young wife. There is no such tragedy in *Medea and Her Children*. Medea herself has no children of her own, but is motherly toward everyone around her and is the heart and soul of the family. She is indeed an icon and the keeper of the mythic family home.

Even with the clear difference between the two Medeas, the presence of the Medea myth in the title invites the reader to approach the novel through the ancient themes of treachery and murder. Seen from this point of view, the novel does re-enact the Medea myth, though in a quite unexpected way. Medea is certainly "upstaged" in her marriage to the Jewish dentist, Samuel Mendez, by a younger contender, her own beloved younger sister, the "fun-loving" Alexandra. With him Alexandra has a daughter Nike. Eventually the oldest of Aleksandra's four children, Sergei, marries Tania Gladysheva (Vera Ivanovna's daughter) and they have Masha. These two children—Nike and Masha—are quite close in age, even though they belong to two different generations, and they think of themselves as "sisters," even though they are actually aunt and niece.

It is with this foursome of characters, two pairs of sisters, that the Medean themes of betrayal, treachery, and murder develop. First, Aleksandra betrays her older sister. Then she betrays her granddaughter Masha by leaving her with her crazy maternal grandmother. Subsequently Nike, who is endowed with her mother's fun-loving seductiveness, betrays Masha by seducing Masha's lover Valery Butonov. In this complex of relationships Masha is the victim. A gifted poet and brilliant literary-philosophical mind and a delicately strung psyche, she has long considered suicide as an option, indeed, ever since the tormenting nights at Vera Ivanovna's apartment. It is now, midst the complex ménage à trois with Nike and Valery, that she finally commits the act. Perhaps the crucial difference between the ancient Greek tragedy about Medea and this post-Soviet epic about Medea's family is that none of the characters is a true villain. Certainly Alexandra and Nike make an illegitimate mother-daughter pair who share much the same robust, sensuous personality. Both are seductive but also caring, though their overly high libido leads them into thoughtless sexual liaisons. Although Masha's death is tragic in all senses of the word, neither Alexandra nor Nike should be labeled a murderer. By ignoring Masha's fragile personality, mother and daughter on separate occasions help to push her toward taking her own life.

Against the vivacity and depth of this ancient Greek culture, in the case of many characters, the figure of Stalin takes on a different meaning. For a very few Stalin's Moscow is a theatrical backdrop of sumptuous apartments and a privileged life. Stalin exerts a strong psychological influence on the hunger-crazed madness of Vera Ivanovna and on Medea's husband who realizes toward the end of his life that he has lived for decades "in a state of profound fear" (M, 190). Although Samuel had fought in the Civil War, performing raids on recalcitrant peasants, he soon discovered that he did not have the stomach for shooting people and instead became a "jolly Jewish dentist" (M, 3). Falsely ringing Stalinist rhetoric about "everyone's wonderful tomorrow" penetrates Medea's Greek world through Samuel, who has absorbed its poison and repeats it with a good dose of anxiety and irony (M, 60). He proposes to Medea, almost imploring her to marry him, ironically paraphrasing Stalin's famous phrase: "Of course, life is just getting better all the time, but I think we shall find it easier to get through this wonderful life together, if you see what I mean" (M, 69). It is only when Samuel holds Medea's hand that he stops jittering and calms down. Samuel dies at the time of the infamous Doctor's Plot in the early 1950s, which but for Stalin's death would probably have become a new pogrom against the Jews (M, 190).

Alexandra is associated tangentially with Stalin. She has a suitor who lives in a "splendid Stalinist apartment" (M, 140). Because she moved to

Stalinist Moscow (by inference abandoning her homeland and "selling out" to the people who destroyed the rich culture of the Crimea), the narrator in the very first sentence of the novel suggests that "we disqualify" her from being a "pure-blooded Greek" (M, 3).[15]

There is one crucial link between Medea's personal life, the thread of treachery in the Sinoply clan carried through Alexandra, and the Stalinist story of treachery, destruction, and suffering. Medea makes the intuitive connection in a dream on the very day of Stalin's death, about a year after Samuel's death in March 1952. Waiting for some "news from beyond the grave" from Samuel, she dreams of Samuel in his white dentist's coat:

> That was good. His hands were covered in plaster or chalk, and his face was very pale. He was sitting at his worktable tapping with a little hammer at some unpleasant jagged metal object, but it was not a set of dentures. Then he turned to her and stood up, and he was holding a portrait of Stalin, which for some reason was upside down. He took the hammer, tapped it on the edge of the glass, and removed him neatly; but while he was fiddling with the glass, Stalin disappeared, to be replaced by a large photograph of the young Alexandra. (M, 197–198)

Although she does not understand the dream, Medea has intuitively linked Samuel with Alexandra and possibly, in some sense, associating the treachery of her sister with that of the treacherous tyrant Stalin. It is important to note, in contrast, that Medea remains "completely unmoved" during the actual mourning of Stalin's death. Stalin, the historical figure, is all but irrelevant to her life.

The point of this reframing of the history of the twentieth century—now with Stalin relegated to the sidelines—becomes clear: it is to remind us of the story of one marginalized, voiceless minority and its story. The narration of *Medea and Her Children* focuses most obviously on Greek and Jewish experience, though with a strong, if ironic, consciousness of the Russian peasantry and its horrific suffering. The untold story that hovers significantly in the background of this novel and that keeps Medea's Crimean oikumene from being a simple Crimean idyll, is that of the Crimean Tatars. Tatar characters, who appear early in the novel, have no written legacy and have been relegated to historical silence and suffering. Their history gains a voice through Medea and her nephew Georgy. Ravil Yusupov, the grandson of a

---

15. It is interesting to note that with Alexandra, the Greek history that elsewhere appears to lend such depth and meaning to this novel, and to its central character Medea, becomes superficial, on the order of a lightly fatuous anecdote that one might tell at a cocktail party: "from the Pontic seafarers she [Alexandra] had probably inherited a drop of royal blood and honorary kinship with those queens who always had their profile toward the spectator as they spun wool, wove tunics, and made cheese for their husbands, the kings of Ithaca and Mycenae" (M, 143–144).

carter whom Medea had known even in pre-revolutionary times, appears at her doorstep in the spring of 1976, with a car full of Soviet police operatives not far behind. Sitting in Medea's kitchen, Ravil records on tape his family's wanderings since their deportation in the 1940s. He is now active in a movement to reclaim Crimean Tatar lands that had been so carefully cultivated for centuries only to be destroyed by Soviet collective farmers. When the police come to arrest Ravil, he throws the tape into the stove to protect Medea. Medea, in turn, relays this history in a personal letter to her life-long friend, Elena Stepanian, thus becoming the bearer of memory of the old Crimea (M, 10–11). Medea writes:

> He eagerly asked me in great detail about the old Tatar Crimea. He even produced a tape recorder and recorded me so that his Uzbek and Kazakh Tatars could hear what I had to relate. I told him what I could remember about my old neighbors...Galya and Mustapha, and grandfather Akhmet the ditcher who cleaned the irrigation aryks here from dawn to dusk, pulling out every speck of rubbish like a mote from someone's eye....I told him too about how in 1947, in the middle of August, the order came to cut down the nut groves here, which the Tatars had planted. No matter how we begged them, the dimwits came and cut down those wonderful trees, not even waiting for us to gather the harvest. So there the murdered trees lay all along the road, their branches laden with unripened nuts, and then the order came to burn them. (M, 10–11)

Despite Soviet depredations, Medea bravely preserves a part of Tatar history in this letter. More important, the fabric of Tatar culture is woven into the very landscape of the Crimea: Ulitskaia remarks on the orchards and vineyards cultivated by Tatars and the deep stone reservoir dug by Tatars. In addition, we are reminded of Tatar culture on a daily basis—the copper pots in Medea's kitchen, Tatar clothes and Tatar jewelry, and the sturdy house in which Medea lives.

The aging matriarch manquée of a large extended family, Medea serves as the bearer of this repressed history. She re-empowers Ravil by willing to him his family's old homestead where she and her extended family have lived for half a century (M, 72). Although this man from a different religious, racial, and cultural world may not speak with his own voice, his history is mediated through layers of narration. In this technique Ulitskaia resembles Yevgeny Evtushenko's poem "Babii Iar" (1961), or Adrienne Rich's "An Atlas of the Difficult World" (1991).[16] All three authors come from privileged backgrounds but are painfully aware of the experience of oppressed and

16. Rich's poem is cited in Bhabha, *Location of Culture*, xix. For a discussion of Evtushenko's effort to speak for the Jews murdered on 19 September 1941, see chapter 4, note 13.

marginalized social groups who have been deprived of their political voices. All three speak for those voices, with a greater or lesser sense of authenticity. Of the three, Ulitskaia would appear to be most sensitive to the question of authenticity, as the character who speaks for the Tatar would genuinely know, understand, and be sympathetic to the Tatar's plight.

The south in Ulitskaia's second novel, *The Kukotsky Case,* is the area around Kherson, which is described as a wasteland of beaches and dunes and cheap tourist hangouts. Nonetheless, young Russians of the Thaw Era, such as the protagonish Tania Kukotskaia, could flee the center and find here on the beaches a space of their own in order to breathe relatively freely, to escape the current ideological regime, and to discover their own emotional and creative resources. While at a Soviet spa unimaginatively named "Spa" (Kurortnoe), Tania discovers a homegrown band playing jazz. She and one of the musicians fall in love, after which she moves with him to Leningrad and, for a brief time, becomes a successful underground jeweler. For the first time in her life Tania has found something and someone she genuinely loves. She discovers a measure of inner freedom, dreams an idyllic dream of a life with lots of children, a house with a garden, and lots of music, but eventually dies in the south of hepatitis in a substandard hospital run by corrupt medical personnel.[17]

Although it is more barbaric, the south of Tania's liberation bears some resemblance to the south described in *Medea and Her Children.* These beaches and dunes are also the ancient periphery of several empires:

> The sand spit, covered in places with reeds and wormwood, stretched on for kilometers, washed on one side by the listless sea and on the other by the brackish water of the estuary, or rather, one of its long, former riverbeds that in the spring floods connected to the main channel but for most of the year was cut off. Remarkably this whole area resembled this small sand spit: abandoned, almost nameless, cut off from its own history and alien to the present time. This was the hinterland of the Bessarabian steppes, a quarter of the ancient world trodden by the Scythians, Hets, Sarmatians, and other nameless tribes. It had once been the hinterland of the Roman Empire, now it was the wasteland of another, modern empire. Abandoned by all the gods, it was the unlucky homeland of colorless feather grass and fine, stifling dust. (KK, 359)

In contrast to the picture of the Crimea given in *Medea and Her Children,* here we find a much higher level of cultural and environmental degradation;

---

17. See Julia Kristeva, who offers a warning against utopian thinking that forgets the awful actuality from which it springs, see *Strangers to Ourselves,* trans. L. S. Roudiez (New York: Columbia, 1991), 117.

in contrast to the Tatars who cared for the Crimea, no one has taken stewardship of this land. Marking "nature" as the theme of this trip to the south, Tania's friend and traveling companion Koza chooses for her vacation reading Lev Tolstoy's novelistic meditation on the "natural man," *The Cossacks.* Conversely, Tania sees barbarity in the Moldavian and Ukrainian tourists who nomadically arrive, camp, leave litter, and move on. These people, we are told, "whatever they called themselves,... were the true descendants of the barbaric world long since disappeared" (KK, 362). The ill-bred tourists, cultural underdevelopment, political corruption are just a few of the kinds of barbarism within the gates of the Soviet empire.

The Russian and Soviet relationship between center and periphery, as Ulitskaia depicts it, differs on two counts from and promises less than the situation that Bhabha describes in *The Location of Culture.* First, the periphery and its cultures are repeatedly being ravaged and the land returned to wasteland. Second, the power center, Moscow, is focused only on itself. In the case of Medea the Soviet Muscovite civilization is upstaged by other civilizations and their histories. Given these fundamental differences, how can Bhabha's paradigm help us understand Russia's and later the Soviet Union's relationship to its peripheries? Here we have a colonizing center that has constructed its modern history, largely motivated by a suspicion of its own cultural and historical inferiority, by the anxiety that, by comparison to other centers ancient and modern, it has a poor history. In the case of the Black Sea coast, Russia is only one country to have conquered this territory. This region is an ancient periphery to many empires. Indeed, it is a "meta-periphery," a periphery that can tell us a great deal about the nature of peripheries. It is a border zone and the site of numerous historical events, participating in multiple histories, which makes it productive and rich in its own way. Though impoverished and without a single unbroken story all its own, it has a braid of histories, stories, legends, and myths that give it a rich multiethnic identity.

Temporal stasis is a more complex issue in this Russian realm than it is in Bhabha's postcolonial world. Here the peoples from the perimeter of the ancient world conquered that world, and subsequently those peoples, whether Greek or Tatar, Turk or Slav, transformed themselves—each in their own time—from peripheral ethnic groups to power-wielding centers. The difference between this experience and Bhabha's model is that this time the new center remains perhaps without the same ideological authority as the ancient conquered empire and without the credible claim to history. It is unclear, which is ultimately static—the center or the periphery. It is not by chance that Ulitskaia refers to Medea's realm as an oikumene, a civilized place, a kind of center in its own right.

Similarly, the contrast of the center with the periphery in Bhabha's model is a contrast in the minds of the colonizers between respective "civilization" and "barbarism." In Ulitskaia's work this opposition is reversed in a number of ways. On the one hand, the southerners on the periphery of the Soviet empire are relatively civilized; for example, they have cultivated and developed the land. On the other hand, the "colonizers" to the north, the Russians and Ukrainians, are brutal. They are the Stalinist collectivizers, who ripped down the old trees and destroyed a functional farming culture, and the post-Stalinist enforcers, who make it impossible for the descendants of ancient ethnic groups to return to the land.[18]

The issue of truth and authenticity in the Soviet and post-Soviet instance is more fragmented than in Bhabha's model. In Ulitskaia's view, authenticity lies with the older cultures of the peripheral area, and much less so with the center. Furthermore, there is no hybrid model that brings center and periphery into dialogue with one another. All the hybridity and multicultural interaction emerges on the periphery, if at all, and, at least in Ulitskaia's works, does not really penetrate to the center, which enforces gray, ethnically prejudiced conformity.

Finally, in Ulitskaia's work we see relatively little of the racial and ethnic fetishes of colonial prejudice brought out in English postcolonial literature. Active sexuality is certainly a part of the south, both in the very description of the Crimean landscape and as a particular quality of Greek female character. The land itself is described through the admiring eyes of a northern visitor to the Village with the sensuality of a Georgia O'Keefe painting. "Nora gazed over enchanted to where the gorge met a hill and there seemed to be a long, meandering fold in the earth, and a house with a tiled roof nestled there in its groin, its clean windows sparkling to welcome three graceful figures, one black, one white, and one red" (M, 15). The Greek women in *Medea and Her Children,* with the exception of Medea, are sensuous and sexually active, conforming to the stereotypical labels imposed on people in southern peripheries. This innate sensuality, however, is treated not as a fetish but as the source of betrayal in the Sinoply family. Interestingly, we find transplanted into Ulitskaia's ideal multiethnic world the stereotypical Russian and Slavophile iconic figure of the elderly woman who holds together the clan or the village (M, 49).[19] Despite the central theme of betrayal, we find the reaffirmation of not just family, but "clan."

---

18. In addition, it is unclear to what extent the Slavic colonizers are themselves being forced to repress their own ancient traditions and be colonized by the Stalinist center.

19. This figure is a fixture of village prose. Certainly the most famous is Turgenev's story "A Living Relic," in which she is more a figure of spiritual stamina and strength, and Solzhenitsyn's

In conclusion, we repeat Bhabha's question from *The Location of Culture:* "How [should] our own intimate, indigenous landscapes...be remapped to include those who are its new citizens; or those whose citizenly presence has been annihilated or marginalized?"[20] Unlike Dugin, Ulitskaia thinks toward and embraces the global world without having to control it or assert an exclusive national identity built on a notion of the imperial state or a state religion. She conveys a strong desire to show the connectedness of all people, certainly even too much so, as at the end of *Medea and Her Children,* when Medea's extended family grows to include East Asians and someone of African heritage from the Caribbean. Indeed, it is the metaphor of the extended, multicultural family that dominates Ulitskaia's writing.[21]

Although Ulitskaia's fiction with its strong multicultural outlook and critical thoughts about the poor state of Russian identity has enjoyed an enormous audience, it is still hard to gauge the impact of her meta-discourse on identity and the Others who populate her stories and novels. Her books are extremely popular, even to the extent that some critics snappishly suggest that she provides "ideal reading for the dacha and the beach," but really did not deserve the 2001 Booker Prize.[22] A recent interview sheds light on Ulitskaia's strong social consciousness and her determination to find an alternative to the poverty of the contemporary Russian self-image that currently informs acts of juvenile brutality toward non-Russians. Ulitskaia expresses horror at all-too-frequent racial attacks against darker-skinned non-Russians and at the new generation of girls dreaming of becoming hard-currency prostitutes.[23]

---

novella "Matryona's House." She has been a focus of late- and post-Soviet parody in such stories as Liudmila Petrushevskaia's "The New Robinsons: A Chronicle of the Twentieth Century" or Dmitry Prigov's poem, "When Once I Happened to be in Kaluga." For further discussion, see Kathleen Parthé, *Russian Village Prose: The Radiant Past* (Princeton: Princeton University Press, 1992), 86; Edith W. Clowes, *Russian Experimental Fiction: Resisting Ideology after Utopia* (Princeton: Princeton University Press, 1993), 198–207.

20. Bhabha, *The Location of Culture*, xxii.

21. In a number of ways, Ulitskaia's thematics and style bear a resemblance to magical realism, which also deals with the eccentric and the marginalized. Ulitskaia sometimes incorporates the near-fantastic with the naturalist and hyper-realist in her plausible descriptions of familiar Moscow people and settings. Although in good realist tradition her three main novels—*Medea and Her Children* (1997), *The Kukotsky Case* (2002), and *Sincerely Yours, Shurik* (2004)—chronicle the life of a family over several generations, the concept of family and its strange and often treacherous relations are always interrogated. Beyond the family theme, calling to mind Gabriel Garcia Marquez's *One Hundred Years of Solitude,* Ulitskaia's novels often juxtapose conflicting scientific, intuitive, and mystical modes of seeing and observing.

22. Andrei Nemzer, "Pervaia ledi," *Vremia novostei* (7 December 2001), http://dlib.east view.com.www2.lib.ku.edu:2048/sources/article.jsp?id=2462405.

23. *Izvestiia*, 19 June 2006.

Ulitskaia's answer is to edit a new series of children's and young people's novels, "Liudmila Ulitskaia's Children's Project: The Other, Others, about Others," designed to reach the politically apathetic, socially callous young adults of the post-Soviet era.[24] To date twelve short novels by a number of different authors have appeared. The books entertain but also sensitize pre-teen readers to the many cultures of the world.

It is well to remember Julia Kristeva's *Strangers to Ourselves,* a book written by a Bulgarian from the "borderlands" among the Soviet empire, Europe, and the Muslim world on the eve of the Velvet Revolution, which brought peaceful change to Central Europe and spread to the Soviet empire.[25] She sees a—perhaps overly utopian—chance for peace and for a richer, more productive life if we can tap into and work with the "stranger" within each one of us. Her words carry weight in this conflicted, war-torn "post" time of coming after empires and after enlightenment values. As Nikolai Berdiaev put it in 1923, we are confronting a new "middle ages"; only now in the early twenty-first century a crusading religious fervor and global capitalist greed have overtaken all sense of reason and moral measure and are creating still greater rifts in the fabric of human existence. Ulitskaia is engaged in finding what all people,—the disenfranchised, the outsider, as well as the "typical"—have in common, and this is a quality that makes her art crucial to the contemporary dialogue about Russian national identity.

---

24. The series "Other, Others, about Others," edited by Ulitskaia, is published by a prominent Moscow press, Eksmo, http://lib.1september.ru/articlef.php?ID=200602103.

25. Julia Kristeva, "Might Not Universality Be...Our Own Foreignness?" in *Strangers to Ourselves,* 169–192.

6 DEMONIZING THE POST-SOVIET OTHER

The Chechens and the Muslim South

You can't go to the south. Chechens are there. First come steppes and more steppes—your eyes drop out from looking,—and beyond the steppes are the Chechens.
—TATIANA TOLSTAIA, *Slynx* (2001)

IN the Russian geographical imagination the Caucasus Mountains have long been the site of exotic nature and untamed humanity, the Other, resistant to the perceived civilizing forces of Russian empire. The Caucasus embody life force. They are a place where the Russian protagonist feels both reinvigorated and threatened, discovering himself through confronting alien people. We think of Mikhail Lermontov's letters from the Caucasus. While climbing Krestovaia Mountain in 1837, he wrote: "really I can't explain or describe this amazing feeling: for me the mountain air is balsam; away with melancholy, my heart is beating, my chest breathes high—at this minute I don't need anything: I could just sit and look for the rest of my life."[1] Somewhat later Lermontov recorded that he was headed into Chechnya to "take that scoundrel," the north Caucasus rebel leader Imam Shamil.[2] These two responses lie at the heart of a richly suggestive imagined geography that emerged in the course of the nineteenth and twentieth centuries: the exhilaration of coming alive in a landscape of dangerous beauty and the excitement of challenge from a wily native opponent. Both of these sensations became important to Russians' efforts to define themselves. And in Putin's Russia, as nationalist mythmaking has replaced factual reportage, this "other south"—particularly Chechnya—has become an important touchstone for defining who is Russian.

The following discussion probes the polarization of positions in the debate about identity and the central role that both the imagined Caucasus and that most intransigent of Caucasus ethnic groups, the Chechens, have

---

1. M. Iu. Lermontov, *Polnoe sobranie sochinenii* (Leningrad: GIKhL, 1948), vol. 4, 432.
2. Ibid., 445.

played in sharpening the hostility between competing variants of post-Soviet Russian identity. I argue that the Russian government has used the issue of Chechnya to restrict free speech and to enhance the image of the state. Ultraconservatives see in the Chechen conflict a chance to strengthen some combination of ethnic and statist Russian identity, and those supporting a broad notion of Russian citizenship and universal civil rights have fought to keep abuses in the public eye. What emerges is a dialectical counterpoint of discreditation of the old Soviet universalism of "friendship of peoples," assertion of something like a "blood and soil" nationalism, and argument for a new universalism.

Many Russian writers, most famous among them Pushkin, Lermontov, Aleksandr Bestuzhev-Marlinsky, and Lev Tolstoy, have used the Caucasus and its peoples as that alien setting against which Russian characters discover and define themselves. Pushkin's "Prisoner of the Caucasus" (Kavkazskii plennik, 1821–1822) initiated the enormously popular literary theme of the Caucasus, making him what Susan Layton has called the "most highly influential propagator of imaginative geography," at least of the imagined Caucasus.[3] What is more, Pushkin created a narrative of the Caucasus, characterized by a plot that foregrounds a Russian soldier fighting for the empire. Although he is taken prisoner and strives to escape, he comes to appreciate the beauty and the mores of the Muslim other. A number of works by the same title followed Pushkin's "Prisoner," for example, by Lermontov (1828) and Tolstoy (1872).

Throughout the last two centuries the north Caucasus peoples, and particularly the Chechens, as probably the most independent-minded of all the north Caucasus peoples, have been a thorn in the side of the Russian state. In December 1994, the Russian Federation started what many believed to be an unnecessary war in Chechnya—mainly to protect oil lines and to quell Chechen secessionism.[4] The television was crucial to reporting the depredations of war and turning public sentiment against the war. It showed the Russian Soldiers' Mothers' Committee and independent mothers of federal soldiers protesting the war and physically appearing in the arena of war to take their sons from the battlefield. Being able to air disagreements in the open and seeing the contest between the state and its citizens was one of

3. See Susan Layton, "The Creation of an Imaginative Caucasian Geography," *Slavic Review* 45, no. 3 (1986), 470–485; esp. 471.
4. A fine general treatment of the first Chechen war can be found in David Remnick, *Resurrection: The Struggle for the New Russia* (New York: Random House, 1997), 260–291. For a fascinating radio feature on the aftermath of the Chechen wars, see Gisela Erbsloeh, "Unter den Füßen wächst die Wüste. Gänge durch Grosny," Deutschlandradio, 2007, http://www.bosch-stiftung.de/content/language2/html/8797.asp.

the great benefits of the newly granted freedom of speech and freedom of the press since the glasnost years of the mid-1980s. In September 1999, in violation of the terms of the treaty that ended the First Chechen War, Putin mired Russia in a second Chechen conflict, during which Chechens had their constitutional rights suspended, and Chechnya was all but destroyed. Since 1999 the military has assumed the right to control all information concerning the campaign and the battlefield, and the newly centralized state has once again taken control of the mass media.

The resurgence of the Chechen conflict in the post-Soviet period prompted still more literary and film "prisoners of the Caucasus." The first were Vladimir Makanin's novella *Captive of the Caucasus* (*Kavkazskii plennyi*, 1995), and the 1996 film by Sergei Bodrov *Prisoner of the Mountains* (*Kavkazskii plennik*), based in large measure on Tolstoy's novella transposed to the 1990s.[5] If in Makanin's story and Bodrov's film we find a nuanced treatment of a complex interaction between federal forces, Chechen militants and Chechen civilian voices, then after 2000 in such works as Aleksandr Prokhanov's novel *Mr. Hexogen* (*Gospodin Geksogen*, 2002) and Aleksei Balabanov's film *The War* (*Voina*, 2002), we find a precipitous shift toward demonization in the artistic treatment of Chechens. Interjected among these fictional treatments of Chechnya is the documentary reportage of Anna Politkovskaia and cultural commentary of Mikhail Ryklin. In their work the Chechen issue gains greater urgency as the fulcrum on which the future of Russian society turns—either toward a multiethnic civil society that guarantees the rights of all citizens or toward an authoritarian state ruled by ethnic Russians. In brief, through the Chechen theme we see in Russian writing and film culture a recognition of the failure of the old Soviet-era universalism and the articulation of a new, civic universalism that is of a piece with thinking we have already seen in Ryklin and Ulitskaia. Pushing against this new universalism from the ultraconservative side is the demonization of the Chechens as the insidious other and a justification for the extension of state power through the military and the secret police.

During the First Chechen War one could hear the futile remnants of a Soviet-era egalitarianism and consideration of the reasons for its decline. In Makanin's and Bodrov's works universalist ideology rings hollow and

---

5. See Susan Layton, *Russian Literature and Empire: Conquest of the Caucasus from Pushkin to Tolstoy* (New York: Cambridge University Press, 1994). See also Harsha Ram, *The Imperial Sublime: A Russian Poetics of Empire* (Madison: University of Wisconsin Press, 2003); and Margaret Ziolkowski, "Russian Orientalism: Inventing the Evil Chechen," in *The Chechens and the Navajos in Russian and American Literature* (Newark: University of Delaware Press, 2005). Ziolkowski juxtaposes the shifting image of the Navajo from savage to psychically gifted and the stagnant, demonized Russian image of the Chechen.

is being undermined by more basic psychological drives, subliminal sexual desire, and tribalist sentiment. Feelings slip toward a zero-sum attitude of "either you will kill me or I will kill you." Through their nuanced treatment of Chechens and Chechen culture, however, these works still offer a middle ground in which words and negotiation could win over arms, fighting, and torture. So far we find none of the demonization of Chechens that will characterize works of the Putin era.

In Makanin's novella, which appeared during the First Chechen War in April 1995, the narrator describes this conflict as a "limp war" (*vialaia voina*, KP, 45).[6] Although conditions are relatively lax, each side gradually starts to tighten its hold on the other. In this quite ambiguous narrative it is never entirely clear who is the captive of whom—the Russians of the Chechens or the Chechens of the Russians. Although in the mountainous terrain each side snipes at the other, there is more negotiating and trading than there is bloodshed. The Chechen side needs arms, while the federal side needs food. Thus, Russians make raids on Chechen guerillas, steal their weapons, and then trade the weapons for food.

Attitudes start to shift as one of these raids turns deadly when two soldiers on patrol, Rubakhin and Vovka the Sharpshooter, find one of their comrades shot dead and then by mistake kill a Chechen soldier. A simple, well-meaning soldier, Rubakhin takes a young Chechen prisoner in order to take his weapon; he genuinely means to turn him loose again. On their way to the village they encounter a Chechen band that has blockaded a supply truck. Fearing that the young Chechen will cry out for help, Rubakhin strangles him.

The surface of Soviet-era ideology proclaiming "friendship of peoples" is clearly wearing thin in this situation. The commanding officers on each side are used to each other and know the rules of the game. The situation is more fluid and murderous among ordinary soldiers and guerillas. When he takes the young Chechen hostage, Rubakhin still thinks in Soviet formulas: "if you really think about it, what sort of enemies are we—we are close [*svoi liudi*]. We used to be friends! Isn't that the way it was?" (KP, 33). In response Vovka ironically paraphrases the Soviet anthem: "Long live the inviolable friendship of peoples" (*Da zdravstvuet nerushimaia druzhba narodov*, KP, 33). Rubakhin persists in his earnest statements of good will: "I'm the same sort of person as you are. And you're the same as I am. Why should

---

6. Vladimir Makanin, "Kavkazskii plennyi," *Novyi mir*, no. 4 (1995). This novella is also available in English translation as: "Captive of the Caucasus," trans. by B. Lindsey, *The Loss* (Evanston: Northwestern University Press, 1998). Further references to this work will appear in the text with the notation "KP" and the appropriate page number.

we be at war?" (KP, 33). Rubakhin's words prove to be empty, evoking no response from the captive and upstaged by Rubakhin's own sudden and powerful feelings of sexual attraction toward this young man.

Much more powerful, as Makanin pictures the situation, is the dominance of repressed homoerotic desire over the belief in equality of all humans inculcated since childhood. What marks Makanin's treatment of the Russian-Chechen conflict is a process of "feminization"—and victimization—of the Chechens, a process of imagining the Chechens as vulnerable. First, one of the Russian officers talks about the young guerilla as one whom the Chechens themselves would "love like a woman" (KP, 28). Rubakhin is indeed struck by the Chechen's "beauty" (*byl ochen' krasiv,* KP, 28). Between taking the young Chechen hostage and releasing him again, Rubakhin, Vovka, and their prisoner spend the night in the mountains. Rubakhin cares for and protects the young Chechen, wondering how he is doing and giving him his own warm wool socks to wear. Huddling together for warmth, Rubakhin is shocked to discover himself sexually aroused when he touches the younger man. The ordinary soldiers' sexual banter and the non-sexual sharing of warmth contrasts with Rubakhin's painful discovery. The young Chechen's injured, weakened body with its swollen ankle and twisted shoulder, his beautiful young face, his hair—which he combs slowly and carefully, as if proud of its beauty—all call forth a medley of compassion and desire in Rubakhin (KP, 39).

Rubakhin feminizes the young militant further as he carries him across a stream—because the Chechen cannot walk well on his own. He unties his hands and huddles with him for warmth. Finally, just before he strangles him, in order to keep him from crying out to his Chechen comrades, Rubakhin holds him in a tight embrace, that is at the same time powerfully sensual (KP, 42). Remembering the young Chechen later, Rubakhin again becomes sexually aroused. Ironically, through his complex of feelings and by killing the young guerrilla, Rubakhin has tipped the fragile balance of his commanding officer's game, the game of taking hostages' weapons and releasing the hostage in order to trade for produce. Through the two deaths—of the Russian scout at the start and the young Chechen at the end—the Russian state has moved a little further toward out-and-out hostility.

In Makanin's novella a complex aestheticization of the Caucasus parallels the process of undermining Soviet universalism. The sublime magnificence of the mountains captivates Rubakhin and keeps him from returning to his home on the Don steppes. Ironically citing Dostoevsky's thought that "beauty will save the world" (KP, 7, 43), Makanin finds a more problematic beauty in the simultaneous attraction and alienation between Rubakhin and the young Chechen. In short, beauty captivates. Neither the majesty of the mountains nor the exotic beauty of the young man saves anyone.

In Makanin's work there are no stereotypes—everyone is a person in his own right. Although we know the young Chechen through the optic of Rubakhin's conflicting ethical consciousness and sexual desires, we can still say that the two Chechen characters here, the Chechen commander Alibekov and the nameless young Chechen, are people in and of themselves, not a simple projection of Russian fears and ambitions onto Chechen stereotypes. The Chechens are not yet the mythical Other or the utter challenge to Russian civilization and to Russianness that they will become after the turn of the century.

Sergei Bodrov's film balances attraction and otherness, respect and contempt even more finely.[7] Bodrov's film deals with the process of negotiating the mutual release of three hostages—two Russians, the sergeant Sasha and the soldier Vania Zhilin (who has the same last name as Tolstoy's hero in "Prisoner of the Caucasus"), and the son of a Chechen leader Abdul Murat. Mismanaged, the process ends with Sasha murdering one of Abdul's Chechen guards, Sasha then having his throat cut, and a Russian officer ordering the shooting of the young Chechen, as he attempts an escape from prison. In the final scene, Russian helicopters laden with bombs fly toward the Chechen village. Zhilin, who has been released by Abdul, runs across the field, waving his hands wildly, hoping to attract the pilots' attention and stop them from deepening the conflict.

The chief ideological goal of Bodrov's film is to celebrate the middle ground where negotiation and even respect is possible and to mark the moment when it was finally lost. The middle ground opens when Abdul refuses to kill the two Russians despite considerable pressure from his comrades—because he sees an opportunity for a hostage trade. This slim strip of negotiating space is held open by Zhilin, his mother, and Abdul's young daughter Dina. Each resists the general attitude that the opposite side is nothing but evil and seeks a medium through which cherished lives can be spared. Fundamental tensions arise here not just between Chechens and Russians but within each camp. On the Russian side, federal and grassroots approaches to treating the hostage situation conflict and among Chechens radicalism and family loyalties lead to disagreement.

To a greater degree than Makanin's novella, Bodrov's film offers a respectful, even sympathetic display of Chechen village culture and personal

7. Tolstoy's "Kavkazskii plennik" is available at http://orel2.rsl.ru/rgb-sh/tolstoi/kavkaz. htm. According to Irina Shtefanova, Bodrov apparently started working on the film before the First Chechen war, http://www.ruskino.ru/review/19. His film is the first of a number of Caucasus films—Vadim Abdrashitov's "Vremia tantsora" (1997), Aleksandr Rogozhkin's "Blokpost" (1998), Fedor Popov's "Kavkazskaia ruletka" (2002).

relationships. The two Russian hostages receive decent treatment, billeted in the barn with the donkey. Zhilin and Dina are the first to open the door to tonalities and registers of interaction other than hatred and violence. Dina brings Vania and Sasha bread and water. Like Tolstoy's character, whose name he bears, Vania has golden hands. He fixes a broken watch belonging to Abdul, which makes Dina happy, and then carves Dina a rough marionette in the shape of a bird.

The camera work adds a strong spatial, geographical dimension to the concept of the middle ground, supporting the idea that life is much more than guns, bombs, knives, soldiers, and killing. The film plays out amid stunning scenes of the arid mountains, the river, sheep grazing in meadows. Village women gather hay and have donkeys pound it down to soften it. Young women dance. Abdul's house is carefully whitewashed and covered with rugs. We are even offered insight into private family relations, when one of the village women advises Abdul to remarry because Dina needs a mother. This brief conversation brings Abdul to pay more attention to his young daughter and, because he sees and values the friendship between Dina and Vania, he spares Vania's life.

Importantly, the Russian side is the first to escalate tension. The first hostage trade fails because of bad faith on the Russian side: the commanding officer brings the wrong prisoner to the meeting place. Even when this first attempt fails, Abdul does not give up hope of success. He orders Sasha and Vania to write to their parents to pressure the federal authorities into working out the hostage trade. Eventually Vania's mother appears and meets with both the federal commandant and Abdul. When the commanding officer starts to push the usual line that Chechens are no good and will only deceive (we remember that *he* was the deceiver during the first hostage trade), Vania's mother starts to pummel him with her handbag. Abdul's and her basis for understanding is their love for their children, something the Russian authorities ignore.

Russian self and the Chechen Other are strongly bound: the commandant is corrupt and deceptive, worse than many Chechens who are fiercely loyal to family and the Chechen community. The problem of Russian identity deepens in the character of the sergeant Sasha. Vania and his mother are both decent, friendly, loyal people, but Sasha is a matryoshka doll of lies, deceptions, disguised with madcap humor, but covering an empty space at the center. His prominence in the film raises serious questions about who Russians are. To begin with, Sasha appears as a witty, swashbuckling, hard-playing, and hard-drinking soldier who is afraid of nothing and makes light of everything. When Abdul tells Sasha and Vania to write letters, Sasha, it turns out can barely write and writes a letter full of mistakes and blotches.

When asked about his parents, he says that his mother is an actress and his father—a general, and that they live in the far north (appealing to the "pure Russian" geographic space of the ultraconservatives). As his character peals open layer by layer this story turns out to be a lie. Vania sees through Sasha, calling him a "psycho." Eventually Sasha says that he grew up in an orphanage, suggesting that he had no one to whom he could write a letter. Sasha has served in three wars and is a survivor who happens to be fighting on the Russian side. He feels no loyalty to anything except himself and his freedom. Ultimately, it is Vania who survives, though he is caught in between in the Russian-Chechen conflict and the Russian conflict between federal and family interests. He survives not because of a strong national identity but because he, like his mother, is a decent human being who treats everyone with genuine respect. Here is authentic universalism put into practice. The issue of Russian national identity seems less important than the human virtues of honesty and trustworthiness.

The First Chechen War clearly belied the old Soviet universalism, and the Second Chechen War badly undermined civil liberties in post-Soviet Russia and the hope for a tolerant, multicultural Russian identity. In his volume of social and political commentary *Diagnostic* (Vremia diagnoza, 2003), Ryklin called the gaining of civil freedoms, particularly freedom of speech and freedom of the press, the "only real achievement of the Yeltsin period" (VD, 120). He defined a "Chechnya syndrome" in the general waning of civil rights, particularly freedom of speech, during the Second Chechen War.[8] Because the army assumed a monopoly on war information and the war became "virtually invisible," Chechens lost their civil freedoms. In addition, because most journalists were afraid to go to Chechnya, very little information appeared in the print media (VD, 120). Writing in the first years of the twenty-first century, Ryklin saw the disappearance of free speech and social action around the Chechen conflict as one of the pressure points at which a nascent Russian civil society and civic consciousness founded. In place of the free public expression of a range of social values, Ryklin diagnosed the psychological repression of frustration, the process of open frustration becoming taboo in the broad social "subconscious." He argued that this repression is directly connected to unacceptable expressions of social rage, including ethnic and other violent outbreaks (VD, 186).

Ryklin's remarks proved true in shocking fashion through state-supported provocation and murder. The entire post-Soviet era is remarkable for violence against independent journalists and liberal politicians, the vanguard

---

8. Mikhail Ryklin, *Vremia diagnoza* (Moscow: Logos, 2003), 118, 127, 176, 201. Further references to this work are given in the text with the notation "VD" and page number.

practitioners of free speech and multicultural tolerance. In 2005 Russia counted among the five most dangerous countries to be a journalist.[9] In 2006, appalling murders took the lives of people who were challenging the regime's rosy lies about Chechnya. Anna Politkovskaia, one of Russia's most outspoken critics of the excesses of the Putin regime and the Chechen wars, was murdered on 7 October 2006. The November 2006 poisoning and death in London of former security agent Aleksandr Litvinenko added evidence that social-psychological repression is being supported by political repression. Litvinenko's *Blowing up Russia: Terror from within* (2003) claimed that the bombings of some Moscow apartment houses in September 1999, were not the work of Chechens, as the Putin regime claimed, but rather of the secret police, an allegation that is supported by pro-Kremlin writers, such as Aleksandr Prokhanov. These bombings were among the events that precipitated the Second Chechen War.

The balanced complexity of depictions of the "other south" in the mid-1990s was replaced after the start of the Second Chechen War by much more polarized articulations of national identity. There have been two basic responses to the Second Chechen War. One approach has used the Chechen conflict to argue for stronger civic identity. We find the best example in Politkovskaia's documentary journalism, which refuses to paint all Chechens as treacherous. The second approach has been to demonize Chechens, using fiction and film to reassert simple, "blood and soil" nationalist myth, as in the art of Aleksandr Prokhanov and Aleksei Balabanov. The two views are in direct conflict with one another, which has resulted in severe, though completely unnecessary, consequences.

Since the beginning of the twenty-first century, when the mass media were largely gathered under the control of the Putin regime, the defense of civil rights fell to a small group of newspapers, journals, and activist intellectuals, foremost among them the brave Anna Politkovskaia. Politkovskaia started her *Novaia gazeta* column in 1999 to draw attention to the civil rights abuses of the newly authoritarian government, centering on the mistreatment of ordinary Chechens during the Second Chechen War. Under the conditions of increasingly centralized management of the media Politkovskaia developed a clear approach to the war in Chechnya meant to disprove the official media's lacquered picture of the Russian military and its war, which Politkovskaia described as: "Machine-guns, bullet-proof jackets, mud, and helicopters boastfully zooming overhead" (DW, 115).[10] She challenged the

---

9. The website http://www.cpj.org/Briefings/2005/murderous_05/murderous_05.html shows deaths of journalists 2000–2004.

10. Anna Politkovskaia, *A Dirty War: A Russian Reporter in Chechnya*, trans. J. Crowfoot (London: Harvill, 2001), 115. Citations from this work are given in the text with the notation

incursions of the Russian state against its own citizens and tried to embarrass an increasingly passive intelligentsia and public into action. Her focus was always on relatively innocent, helpless people caught between the federal authorities and the Chechen militants, primarily children, educators, and old people, both Russians and Chechens.

Among Politkovskaia's chief themes are the lawlessness of the state and its enforcers in the armed forces and secret police. Politkovskaia never shies from naming names of public officials and their henchmen and letting her readers know exactly where those people are and what crimes they have committed. In this way she leaves for the future a number of profiles of secret police and military functionaries, people who have abused their positions of authority (DW, 136). Two examples illustrate Politkovskaia's mode of operation, one against a well-known public figure and one against a seemingly anonymous threat. She carried out a sustained attack on Colonel General Valery Manilov, the first deputy of the Russian General Staff and frequent public voice for the military. Manilov was the military's media spokesperson in the Second Chechen War, asserting the low number of losses to the army and the effectiveness of the well-oiled military machine.[11] He frequently asserted that the military was committed to "preserve the lives of military personnel." Politkovskaia points a finger at Manilov, accusing him of lying and hypocrisy, much like his Gogolian forebear.[12]

Politkovskaia has a great deal to say about recruiting abuses and poor treatment of soldiers.[13] Her purpose was to re-establish some sense of reality against the state-controlled mass media that merely parrot the lies of the central administration and the military: "As before, ordinary soldiers remain no better than dirt beneath the officer's boot. No one regards them as 'sacred'.... Though the TV constantly tries to persuade us it is so: it shows us leading government officials, press spokesmen, and the army's professional political advisers—like Manilov, who will not rest until he can equal the

---

"DW" and page number. Politkovskaia's articles appearing in *Novaia gazeta* are available at http://politkovskaya.novayagazeta.ru/pub/pub.shtml.

11. Anna Politkovskaia, "Za chto?" (Moscow: Novaia gazeta, 2007), 28. Further references to this work are given in the text with the notation "ZCh" and page number.

12. Nikolai Gogol's novel, *Dead Souls,* features a feckless, seemingly cultivated landowner Manilov, who has become a stereotype in Russian culture.

13. Among Politkovskaia's most poignant cases for the regime's contempt for its own citizens were her descriptions of the treatment of ordinary Russian soldiers, who, she argued, were paid miserable wages and given rotten food to eat. As one soldier put it, "that's the condition we fight in" (DW, 35). Even more outrageously, in an article from October 1999, Politkovskaia related the lies and deceptions told to new recruits. As the war was starting in August and September, parents called the regiment in question, worried that their sons would be fighting in Dagestan. Although they were always reassured, officers often got new recruits drunk and then shipped them south in the middle of the night (DW, 44).

achievements of Movladi Udugov, the man who brainwashed so many during the first Chechen war" (DW, 129). In ensuing years, Politkovskaia found repeated instances of bad treatment of ordinary soldiers: "The army is not being reborn, it is collapsing. Ordinary soldiers are fleeing ever more brutal mistreatment from their officers—even 'battle bonuses,' now handed out each time they fight, are not enough to hold them" (DW, 244).

Politkovskaia confronted the shadowy terrorists of the Federal Security Service (FSB), who regularly denied the practice of free speech, and she highlighted numerous cases of the Putin regime's support for illicit secret police behavior. Between 2001 and 2005 she documented the efforts to silence the journalists of *Novaia gazeta* on the part of an OMON Special Forces agent Sergei Lapin, operating under the code name "Kadet" (ZCh, 373, 388). In September 2001, *Novaia gazeta* received an email about a person named Kadet who served in the special camps of the secret police. The author claimed that Kadet was armed and coming to Moscow. A second email from Kadet threatened to harm *Novaia gazeta* and its journalists for Politkovskaia's article about "People Who Disappear" (ZCh, 373). Politkovskaia enjoyed the success of seeing Lapin called into court in Piatigorsk for harassing her (ZCh, 388). Two years later, in February 2004, Lapin returned to the police force in Nizhnevartovsk and was shockingly awarded a presidential medal (ZCh, 397). Clearly, the Putin regime was supporting the secret police, not the independent media. Lapin was tried in Groznyi in November 2004 for torturing Chechens, and in March 2005 sentenced to eleven years in prison (ZCh, 398, 402). Politkovskaia's bold reportage not only challenged the secret police but helped to put one of them behind bars, for however short a time.[14]

Beyond bearing witness to abuse and terror tactics of the Putin regime, Politkovskaia's central goal was to record the innocent sufferings of ordinary Chechens, caught between Chechen terrorists and federal forces, and thereby to show the weakening of Russian society as a whole. She made a special point of asserting Chechens' status as Russian citizens, and she humanized Chechens by bringing to her readers specific voices and personalities. Her main goal was to show that the Russian authorities confused law-abiding Chechens and the bandits, assuming all Chechens were lawless.

14. Amnesty International reports other cases of crimes against Russians attempting to build bridges with Chechens, for example, the September 2005 threat against Stanislav Dmitrievskii, the executive director of the Russian-Chechen Friendship Society (www.amnestyusa.org/document.php?id=ENGEUR460362005&lang=e). The year 2009 saw the deaths of civil rights lawyer Stanislav Markelov, *Novaia gazeta* journalist Anastasia Baburova, and Natalia Estemirova—all of them involved in fighting for Chechen human rights (www.amnestyusa.org/document.php?id=ENGUSA20091005003).

Her point extended to the entire Russian polity: "By allowing such a war to be fought in our own country, without any rules, not against terrorists but against those who hate their own bandits perhaps even more strongly than we do, we are the losers and the loss is irreversible" (DW, 85).

In her effort to humanize Chechens Politkovskaia discredited the tactics the Russian military use to demonize them, for example, the military's practice of thinking of Chechens as rodents. As one soldier put it: "They [the Chechens] aren't people, they are vermin [*zver'ki*]. And like vermin they multiply fast" (ZCh, 36). Politkovskaia also showed Russian military behavior from a Chechen point of view, particularly drawing on experiences of Chechen children (DW, 85). A column from June 2004 tells about an incident in Chechnya during which a federal helicopter suddenly appeared and dropped four bombs on the central part of Ordzhonikidze Station, killing one boy and badly wounding two others. In Politkovskaia's experience, Chechen children often hate and fear anyone who looks like a Slav (DW, 85). Politkovskaia described graffiti left by federal soldiers in a local school. Walls were covered from floor to ceiling with "obscenities, outlining in graphic terms what should be done to finish off the Chechens.... a vivid textbook of ethnic hatred" (DW, 234).

Politkovskaia argued that the abuse of Chechens posed a severe threat to civil freedoms of all Russian citizens by relating the federal treatment of Chechen civilians on the periphery to federal treatment of politically active Russian civilians in the center. She saw differences between these cases as a matter of degree rather than of kind, showing convincingly that the Russian state is indifferent to the welfare of its citizens, regardless of their ethnic group (DW, 52–56). Politkovskaia highlighted a case from February 2006 of a Dagestani civil rights organizer Osman Boliev, who was serving time in prison for helping people write to the European Court in Strasbourg (ZCh, 466).

Politkovskaia also reported on Muscovites expressing their political opinions legally in a non-violent way. In January 2005, she wrote about young National Bolsheviks who in December 2004 had walked into the reception area of the president's administration in Bol'shoi Cherkasskii pereulok 13/14 and demanded that Putin resign. Forty of this group received prison terms from twelve to twenty years for allegedly trying to "usurp power by force" (ZCh, 734). Politkovskaia argued that, just as in Chechnya, young adults in Moscow and Central Russia, and often the "best young people," are being radicalized because of clumsy, coercive government handling of the political opposition. "The reason for this radicalizing is much the same, with allowance being made for the war—there is no legal release for...oppositionist feelings, there aren't and there cannot be, the powers that be will leave only illegal options. The remaining alternatives are brute physical re-sistance for those with the means or inner emigration for those who 'cannot occupy a public reception area or head for the mountains' " (ZCh, 740).

Ryklin's view of a multicultural, tolerant Moscow as a center with borders running through it has no traction in the world of the Russian police. As Politkovskaia shows, the police infringe regularly on the rights of southern-ers legally residing in the capital. Politkovskaia related several cases of police harassment of Chechen Russian citizens, for example, "A Tale of Love and Fascism," published in October 1999, shortly after the Moscow apartment bombings. Here a young couple of mixed ethnicity, Chechen and Russian, had to deal with police provocation and detainment in order to renew a residence permit. Politkovskaia compared being a Chechen in contemporary Moscow with "being a Jew in Germany sometime after 1933 or in German-occupied Minsk or Kiev after 1941" (DW, 52). Referring to tsarist practices she argued that, "encouraged from above, a pogrom against anyone from the Caucasus is under way in Moscow" (DW, 52). Politkovskaia showed here that before the outset of the Second Chechen War the police were busy "labeling the Chechens as a nation of criminals" (DW, 56).

Politkovskaia successfully punctured the state's mythmaking balloon. Her articles drove home truths that the Russian administration wanted least of all to be heard—that the Chechens are humans, that the state cares very little for the rights of ordinary citizens, and that the military cares even less for the welfare of its recruits. Indeed, it is often the authorities who behave more like the stereotypical Chechen—deceptive, corrupt, and murderous, in a word, treacherous.[15] Implicit in Politkovskaia's reporting is the assump-tion that, when we treat Chechens as less than human, we are also treating ourselves the same way. Everyone deserves respect and legal treatment, and it is not just the Chechens whose rights are being abrogated.

The Second Chechen War was part of what Politkovskaia called a larger "anti-constitutional putsch" (DW, 136). As she put it, "We are moving toward the creation of some anti-constitutional territory [in Chechnya], a reserva-tion jointly controlled by the harsh military rule of the federal authorities and the so-called police force of the Gantamirov band. This reservation has been set aside for people of inferior status, Russia's Red Indians of the late twentieth century, who are guilty of having been born in the Chechen Republic. Russia, it seems, cannot live without a Pale of Settlement" (DW, 137). By excommunicating certain people from the community, by fencing them off in a place where all is permitted to the state, in Politkovskaia's

---

15. In 1999 Politkovskaia pointed out the corruption of the Russian Interior Ministry that allowed the slave trade of Chechen girls and women directly in Moscow (ZCh, 428).

view, Russians are creating the conditions for future rebellion. Such, in her view, is the case for Russia in general.

As Politkovskaia exposed civil rights and military abuses on the part of the Russian state, nationalist mythmaking was growing ever more visible. Two popular Putin-era works, Aleksei Balabanov's film *The War* and Aleksandr Prokhanov's novel *Mr. Hexogen,* create myth through the twin processes of sanctifying the Russian homeland and demonizing the Other. The stages in the process of gaining an identity are seen in terms of masculine coming-of-age. The storyline typically includes the following plot elements: the protagonist/the homeland is taken captive; the ethnic Other rhetorically challenges Russian identity; the protagonist hears the call to save the homeland; the Other is demonized, painted as inhumane and duplicitous, giving the protagonist justification to fight him and defend the homeland; the protagonist retreats to his mythic Russian home in the north, receives strength, and possibly a blessing; the protagonist returns to the fight and wins.

The War takes place in a Chechen mountain village occupied by the commander Aslan and his militants.[16] In an underground cavern Aslan is holding a number of captives, among them two British actors John and Margaret, a Russian soldier Ivan, and his wounded captain. In need of money, Aslan releases John and Ivan to raise a two–million dollar ransom. If they do not return with the money, Aslan threatens Margaret with gang rape and execution.[17]

Aslan represents a powerful challenge to Russianness. He is cruel, as well as enviably strong, having survived the "zone"—the Soviet prison camps. He has a strong clannish identity and takes pride in being able to name his ancestors going back seven generations. His identity is based firmly on a symbolic geography of homeland. The setting for the conversation between Aslan and Ivan is filled with metaphors of Chechen power. Outside the window Chechen men are praying, and a soldier leads a beautiful dapple gray

16. Aslan may well be a reference to the militant leader of the late 1990s, Aslan Maskhadov.

17. Mark Lipovetsky, "Post-Sots: Transformations of Socialist Realism in the Popular Culture of the Recent Period," *Slavic and East European Journal,* 48, no. 3 (Fall 2004), 356–377, esp. 369. Lipovetsky sees Aslan as a "new Russian" who has used terror to hijack "real power." John is the old "stereotypical Soviet…intelligent." Ivan is an "archetypal figure of Russian/Soviet cultural mythology," the "simple man" and the "ultimate victim" of the post-Soviet redistribution of power (369). Aslan, in Lipovetsky's view, represents the East, John—the West, and Ivan—Russia. While Lipovetsky places Russia on the modern-era east-west axis, I argue here that it is more productive to place it on the colonial and post-colonial north-south axis.

horse, underscoring the strength and beauty of this primitive identity. Aslan believes that because Russians are "white," they should stay in the north, by the White Sea. Conversely, Chechens are "black," which in Russian discourse means having swarthy skin and black hair, and to them belongs the south. Russians, in Aslan's view, cannot fight because they are typically weak and stupid, and as he puts it to Ivan, "you are not fighting for your homeland."

After his release Ivan returns to his home in Tobolsk, Siberia. In contrast to the southern fringe with its "treacherous" peoples, Tobolsk marks the north, the true Russian heartland. Importantly, the imagined geography of the homeland in *The War* corresponds closely to the northern imagined geography one encounters in Dugin's and other ultraconservative and ultranationalist writings. The organization of scenes and settings speaks to the life-giving rituals of this heartland. The northern home has all the iconic features: a father figure with a simple, war-like notion of manhood, a devoted mother, a submissive girlfriend, and the Orthodox Church. Here Ivan receives a blessing from both his mother and his father, who says it is good that he fought in the war and that he has now become a man.

On the other hand, Aslan's challenge to Russians is justified. *The War* honors the Russian homeland in the breach. Balabanov supports the view of many ultraconservatives that the contemporary Russian family, like society in general, is dysfunctional.[18] Ivan's parents have divorced. His father's grand words filled with proud militaristic patriotism are undermined by his physical condition; he lies incapacitated in a hospital bed. Although abstractly devoted to her, Ivan has nothing to say to his mother. He himself has trouble settling into the civilian world of work and family. He is indifferent to his girlfriend who wants to marry him. Ivan lacks a sense of community in a world where various school friends have died in gang killings. This homeland lacks the visceral wholeness and the immediate sense of belonging that Aslan claims Chechnya has for Chechens and that Balabanov's camera confirms.

Because of the weakness of the iconic northern homeland and the protagonist's identity (he has become a man merely because he has become emotionally calloused and has learned to kill), Balabanov's film seems particularly defensive of Russian national identity. National identity is defined weakly and negatively, by demonizing Chechens. There are two parts to the process of demonization. The first is to show a strong Chechen (Aslan)

---

18. See, for example, Eduard Limonov, *Drugaia Rossiia: ochertaniia budushchego* (Moscow: Ultra. Kul'tura, 2003). A focus on the weakness and lack of will of one's own national group and the vitality and cohesiveness of the ethnic other is typical of ultraconservative thinking.

delivering what is meant as an accurate critique of Russian national identity. The second is to show the dishonesty and duplicity of the Chechen character. The film makes it abundantly clear that there is no such thing as a good Chechen. Early on in the film, video images show Chechen militants cutting the throat of a federal soldier. Ivan himself does not distinguish between good and bad Chechens and is willing and able to beat and kill any Chechen. Unlike the proud, fatherly Abdul Murat in *Prisoner of the Mountains,* Balabanov stresses the nastiness of the Chechen treatment of prisoners. Beyond imprisoning captives in a hole in the ground, the Chechen militants train the younger generation to abuse prisoners. Chechen boys are allowed to practice karate kicks on prisoners bound and lying helpless on the ground.

Still worse is the Chechen militants' appalling treatment of women. It should be noted in passing that Balabanov makes his women characters into either victims or mental midgets. The militants torture the hostage Margaret through a form of simulated drowning—they strip her naked, tie her up, taunt her, and throw her in a stream, pulling her out only when she is about to drown.

Cameo female characters articulate the two main positions in the debate about identity embedded in the film. The film takes a rhetorical stand against the neo-universalist view, being supported by liberal journalists—implicitly the likes of Politkovskaia—who speak in defense of the humanity of Chechens. We encounter the journalist interviewing a Russian soldier, who asserts that: "all Chechens are bandits." Instead of making a real argument to the contrary, the journalist comments fatuously that the soldier is just embittered.

Secondary female characters also demonize Chechens. Russian prejudice against Chechens is most pointedly articulated when Ivan visits his commanding officer's—Captain Medvedev's—mother in St. Petersburg. Medvedev's mother makes clear that she has always boycotted Chechen fruit and vegetable sellers and "never bought clementines from Chechens." The point is underscored when Medvedev's little daughter says that her father is fighting in Chechnya to "defend our homeland from bandits."

Demonization of the "southern Other" moves from leitmotiv to center stage toward the end of the film in Ivan's encounter with the Chechen sniper Ruslan. When Ivan and the Englishman John return to Chechnya to save Margaret and the captain, Balabanov seems to soften his efforts at demonization, only to redouble them by the end of the movie. Chechens seem not to be fully the Other that they become in some ultraconservative writing. In this final segment of the film Balabanov appears to differentiate between evil Chechens and good Chechens. Ivan, however, does not make that distinction—all Chechens are ultimately contemptible. After capturing Ruslan, Ivan beats him mercilessly at every chance, calling him his "slave." John, who is more peaceable, prevails on Ivan to treat Ruslan well. Soon Ivan and Ruslan start to talk; Ruslan talks about his dreams for his children who want to study at a university in Moscow. Ivan accepts him as a good Chechen, perhaps because Ruslan wants to russify his children. Ruslan says he hates Aslan, and proves himself loyal to Ivan, cutting off Aslan's ear once John has shot him. However, in the film's final scene the demonization is complete. Ruslan proves to be a liar: after the incident he informs on Ivan, claiming Ivan beat him, which is true, but that Ivan also raped women and abused children, which is untrue. Ivan ends up in prison, while Ruslan returns to Moscow a free man.

The imagined geography in *The War* is more refined than that of a Dugin or a Prokhanov. The non-Christian south is not all evil—rather a place where the protagonist is tested and attains manhood. The West, a foe of the ultranationalists, is depicted as unconcerned with the war in Chechnya, self-absorbed, and unheroic. Still, in the persons of John, who has a moral consciousness—asking Ivan why he beats Ruslan all the time, and Margaret, who, despite being the victim, is caring, brave, and resourceful, the West gains a feckless, but certainly not a hateful character. John, who represents a rather indecisive Western type, is fearful of war, violence, and death.[19] Upon finding Ivan in Tobolsk and returning to Chechnya, John learns to stand up and fight. When he learns that Margaret has been raped, John—who had been afraid to shoot a gun—shoots Aslan, thus symbolically becoming a man.

A point that *The War* shares with ultraconservative thinking is the generally positive treatment of the Russian state and the military. It should be said that the FSB receive their share of criticism, depicted as being self-serving and untrustworthy. Ivan considers asking an FSB agent to guide them into Chechnya and help with disabling Aslan and his unit, deciding not to, when he sees that his FSB contact is just as much a bandit as Aslan is. Although both *Prisoner of the Mountains* and *The War* end with the metaphor of the Russian military as helicopters flying to the rescue, the image has a quite different meaning here. The helicopters in Bodrov's film ignore Vania's pleas to spare the Chechen village, but here they make a relatively welcome intervention, appearing just in time to save Ivan's little band, which is hiding in a stone tower surrounded by Chechen militants. The military sweeps in, kills

19. In "Post-Sots" Lipovetsky argues that John hurts the Russian cause by killing Aslan. He has ruined any chance of gaining intelligence about Chechen organizations and plans. From a nationalist point of view, however, John can be seen as having accepted mentorship from Ivan and having thus reached manhood.

the mountaineers, and transports the group back to base. The state is clearly the savior, even though it will imprison Ivan.

If viewed as an archetypal young Russian, Ivan bears little promise for the future: he is indifferent to his family and he lacks higher goals for his life. He has gained an identity only through fighting in the Chechen war. Although he has learned to think, to consider before acting, to shoot to kill, he has no deeper goals and nothing to live for. Like Bodrov's Sasha, he is an adventurer and a survivor, but without the latter's wit and humor. He has been defined only in contrast to the Other and has absorbed the violence of the Other in himself. He lacks a strong identity based on anything other than the story of the war, which throughout the film he narrates to his interrogator in prison. In contrast to Bodrov's treatment, in Balabanov's film Chechens prove to be the stronger of the two nationalities, demonized partly because of their callousness and dishonesty, but mainly because Russian characters have no positive identity of their own and need an enemy to hate.

Aleksandr Prokhanov's novel *Mr. Hexogen* demonizes the Chechens much more decisively. In order to delineate a Russian sense of self, Prokhanov endows the ideal of the strong Russian state, controlled by the secret police, with much greater emotional power. In addition, he dismisses the ideal of civil society and civil rights and much more pointedly vilifies various ethnic and racial groups, particularly Jews and Chechens. The novel is set in Moscow in the months preceding the September 1999 bombings of the apartment buildings that became a justification for launching the Second Chechen War.[20] Prokhanov actually agrees with Aleksandr Litvinenko's analysis that the Chechens were not to blame for the bombings, although he does imply that they might have provided the explosives (GG, 196).[21] Indeed, Prokhanov dramatizes a scenario in which the secret police use provocation to place the blame on Chechen militants and to discredit the relatively liberal Yeltsin administration, making it look ignorant and ineffectual. Although his secret police characters are prone to horrifying excesses, these excesses—the attitude that persecution, blackmail, and murder are fine for the purpose of defending their own power—are implicitly condoned because of the characters' loyal nationalism and their goal of replacing a West-leaning administration with their own man, a Putin type. *Mr. Hexogen* is a rightist allegory of the late Yeltsin period. Many of the main characters go by an

20. Hexogen is a kind of high explosive, RDX, believed to have been used in a number of bomb plots, and here refers to the explosive used in the 1999 bombing of the apartment houses in Moscow (www.3Dchem.com).

21. Aleksandr Prokhanov, *Gospodin Geksogen* (Moscow: Ad Marginem, 2002), 196. Citations from this work are given in the text with the notation "GG" and page number.

epithet rather than their actual name. For example, the Yeltsin figure is the "Idol" (*Istukan*), and the Putin figure is the "Chosen One" (*Izbrannik*). It is also a novel of quest in which a highly ranked, retired intelligence officer Beloseltsev (whose name means "white village," suggesting a racially and ethnically segregated concept of national self) is called back to service to help discredit the Yeltsin government and to install one of the secret police's own, the "Chosen One." Beloseltsev is a credulous hero, who does not condone or necessarily even understand all aspects of the restoration project of a secret brotherhood of former KGB agents, known as the Fund. Although he feels as if he has been floating aimlessly since the end of the Soviet regime, through his work for the Fund Beloseltsev regains some semblance of national pride. It is through his adventure that the reader experiences the process of national mythmaking. Much more so than Ivan in *The War*, Beloseltsev feels threatened by everything he cannot identify as Russian. He has long felt the weakness of his own position and is depressed at Russia's fallen status in the world. He identifies Russian strength with the secret police and bemoans the toppled statue of Dzerzhinsky, now stored away in the statue cemetery near the Moscow River. Strolling through Moscow, he has the impression that the "enemy" has occupied his beloved city and all its power centers (GG, 45). The Muslims from the Caucasus, whom he sees selling their fruits and vegetables at the market, particularly stand out as strong and self-assured, in contrast to doubting, weakened, impoverished Russians. Looking at these southerners, Beloseltsev feels "the inimical feeling of desecrated national pride" (GG, 97). He directly blames them for Russia's current position of weakness: "Having destroyed the 'evil empire,' having gnawed Russia to the bone, having wept to their hearts' content over the victims of the 'Russian occupiers' in Baku, the fiery clan of the Caucasus was not letting go of Russia" (GG, 97–98).

Just as in *The War* where Aslan points out the weakness of Russians as a nation, it is a Chechen, the Oxford-educated Vakhid, who in Prokhanov's novel articulates the ultraconservatives' position: "Russians have grown amazingly weak as a nation. They have lost the will to govern. Men don't want to wage war, and women don't want to have babies. With the support of America, Jews are running politics. The church is indifferent to the welfare of the people" (GG, 183). Throughout the novel Beloseltsev encounters a string of idiosyncratic Russian types, contemporary holy fools, who themselves are looking for paths leading to Russia's renewal. The first is the Old Believer Nikolai Nikolaevich, a holy-fool type with an apocalyptic mindset, who blames the Jews for many of the misfortunes of revolution and Stalinism (GG, 15) and believes that the Kremlin has been infiltrated by the Serpent. In his garage Nikolai Nikolaevich is building an airplane named

Gastello after the famous World War II suicide bomber Nikolai Gastello (GG, 211–215). His goal is to blow up Red Square and the Kremlin (GG, 217) in order to purify them of the Serpent and ease the entrance for the Chosen One.

Another strange figure is Doctor Dead, a biologist who, inspired by the nineteenth-century thinker Nikolai Fedorov, is working on ways to raise the dead. He has "visited the graves of Zoia Kosmodemianskaia, Aleksandr Matrosov, the 28 Panfilov guards," all of whom are "holy martyrs who gave their lives for eternal life" (GG, 311).[22] Doctor Dead believes that Lenin did not die for all eternity but his "ideal essence is waiting to return to the flesh" (GG, 311). Finally, Beloseltsev visits an ancient monk named Paisy who believes that Russians turned away from their tsar and took the wrong path (GG, 331). No one seems to have a good and realizable goal for Russia, and in this vacuum the secret police put their own plan into action.

Significantly Russia's current predicament is put in geographical terms along the north-south symbolic axis—Russia has become the new Africa, the postcolonial victim of the world's wealthy countries. As Beloseltsev's younger colleague Grecheshnikov puts it, "today's Russian life brings Africa to mind. 'Russian Africa' is what Swahili [a deceased intelligence agent] called it" (GG, 47). Beloseltsev's special knowledge of the Islamic world makes him useful in helping the Fund restore the Russian homeland to its former status. He has connections with leaders in the Muslim Caucasus. Beloseltsev's special knowledge can help the Fund misrepresent events in order to discredit those currently in power and regain their own control over their country.

Beloseltsev answers the call of his secret-police colleagues, in part because of his sense that his country is being victimized by two ethnic Others—the Jews and particularly the Chechens. Through him, the Chechen Other is villainized, creating an enemy against whom to focus Russian national will. Throughout the novel the most thoroughly and outrageously demonized are the Jewish oligarch characters, stand-ins for actual oligarchs Gusinsky and Berezovsky, who are viewed as the current power behind the Yeltsin regime. The other ethnic group, viewed as even more demeaning to ordinary Russians in their everyday life, are the Chechens. Both of these minorities

---

22. Zoia Kosmodemianskaia was a young partisan hung by the Nazis in the early part of World War II. Aleksandr Matrosov was a soldier who, according to Soviet propaganda, sacrificed his life so his unit could move forward against the Nazis. The 28 Panfilov Guards were young soldiers who resisted the Nazis and destroyed many tanks before most of them gave up their lives.

are rendered less than human through the narrator's constant attention to a sensuous vitality that preys on weak, susceptible Russians.

Prokhanov appeals to crude social prejudice, playing on the attitude that where there is smoke, there must be fire—if a thought gets repeated enough times, then there must be some truth to it. Although his Jewish-oligarch characters exert a great deal of influence at the highest levels, as Prokhanov depicts them, they are manipulated and finally destroyed by their bodyguards, who themselves are members of the Fund. In contrast, Prokhanov shows Chechens preying more directly on impoverished and defenseless Russians and thus suggests that they are a minority more insidious than the Jews. For example, the Chechen Akhmet takes advantage of street children, whom he presses into underage prostitution. The reader meets Akhmet from the point of view of the holy fool Nikolai Nikolaevich. Akhmet, Nikolai Nikolaevich tells us, is a "parasite, he deals in drugs....He gathers them [the children] in the evening. Dresses them up and sends them to the Azeris at the market, to the hotel for the night...And in the morning the gals and Lekha crawl back here all beat up, some of them drunk and some drugged up. They sleep it off in the garage....In the evening Akhmet comes and gets them again" (GG, 102–103). Akhmet beats the girls if they contract a disease, and bribes the police to keep them from paying too close attention. (At the same time, to complicate the picture, we find out that Nikolai Nikolaevich is buying explosives from Akhmet to blow up the Kremlin [GG, 217].) Through Nikolai Nikolaevich one also hears of ordinary Russians who themselves were nearly killed or had relatives killed by their Chechen neighbors in Chechnya (GG, 207).

As if these incidents were not enough, Prokhanov condemns the Chechens during Beloseltsev's adventures in Dagestan. Beloseltsev flies south to meet with an old Dagestani comrade to convince him not to take up arms against the Chechens. During an attack by Chechen militants, he witnesses a horrifying scene that Prokhanov could only have meant to dehumanize the Chechens. After the Chechen raid on the Dagestani village Beloseltsev witnesses an unspeakably bestial sex act—a Chechen soldier raping a corpse (GG, 250). Through these encounters with "ordinary" Chechens—business people, neighbors, soldiers—the reader is treated to seemingly "eyewitness" accounts of Chechen "deviltry." The point is clear—in Prokhanov's view, Chechens are less than human.

Toward the end of *Mr. Hexogen* Beloseltsev believes that it is the Chechens who want to blow up some apartment houses. He rushes to warn his Fund contact Grecheshnikov that Moscow is wired, and Vakhid is ready to kill again (GG, 370). Grecheshnikov's answer is, "Let them," at which point Beloseltsev understands that his own comrades from the Fund have set up this provocation to make it look like the work of Chechen militants. Grecheshnikov wants to bring on a crisis: "We are making history on a grand scale, we are breaking through this dead end, where traitors put us" (GG, 372). After trying to forestall the event, Beloseltsev is beaten unconscious (GG, 435).

Afterward, lying in the hospital (GG, 437), Beloseltsev retreats in his hallucinations to the mythic home in the north, traditional for Russian nationalists. He fantasizes about an anthropologist named Anya with whom he had once been in love, who is excavating an ancient Slav burial mound. They live in the house of a blacksmith for several days, swimming, rowing, and taking long walks. It is now that Beloseltsev feels revived and arrives at the conclusion that life is a process of "eternal rebirth" (GG, 455).

Victory for the secret police comes with the installation of the Chosen One and the initiation of a second war in Chechnya. This vision for Russia resembles Dugin's: both want to secure Russian control over Eurasia and to restore Russia to its earlier grandeur. Grecheshnikov explains: "That is why the great empires of the past stand higher than the great republics. They carried with them the idea of a united humanity capable of hearing and fulfilling God's idea. That is how today's loathsome, liberal Russia is worse and more depraved than the great Soviet Union, an empire so mindlessly lost by us" (GG, 426).

Balabanov's film and Prokhanov's novel give two clear examples of the demonization of the Muslim south in the Putin years. The geographical axis of Russian identity in these works has shifted from the traditional east-versus-west axis to the axis linking colonist north to colonized south. Symbolically, Russia allays its own suspicions that it might have become the postcolonial third world by physically crushing the southern, non-Christian Other within its national body and by asserting itself as a powerful northern country. In contrast, even in these strongly nationalist works, it is clear that the Russian self and the southern Other have, to some degree, become doubles. Both try to solve their problems through violence. Both disregard the middle ground of negotiation. Both are deceitful.

The overall effect of the Second Chechen War—the inability of the Russian government to confront the other, the patina of centralized power around Putin perpetrated by the obsequious television media—has been to encourage an isolationist mentality, to cause what Ryklin calls an "ever greater anxiety at the outsider's gaze" (VD, 179). In Ryklin's view, the second war in Chechnya is the "Trojan horse" (*koshcheevo iaitso*) of the current regime. The secrecy around it and its aftermath has undermined "public politics" and is "enslaving society" (SZK, 13). He mentions that in 2003, along with the controversial exhibit "Caution, Religion!," the Armenian curator

Arutiun Zulumian also opened another exhibit on "The Face of Caucasus Nationality." As a result, Zulumian himself was frequently harassed by the police. The attitude projected by the authorities is that: "it is dangerous to fraternize with alien people [*chuzhaki*]" (SZK, 92)

Chechnya has functioned as a site for the tremendous broadening in the Putin government of clandestine rule that Susan Buck-Morss in *Dreamworld and Catastrophe: The Passing of Mass Utopia in East and West* calls the "wild zone of power." She defines the wild zone as a "terrain" constructed by "democratic" regimes, "claiming to rule in the name of the masses," in which the "exercise of power is out of control of the masses, veiled from public scrutiny, arbitrary and absolute." Here is a "zone in which power is above the law and thus, at least potentially, a terrain of terror."[23] The wild zone functions in secret, outside the "normal and legal authority" of the civil state, which is accountable to voters. States, Buck-Morss argues, establish a "monopoly on violence," something completely inimical to the idea of a democracy: "the sovereign's legitimate claim to the monopoly of violence cannot be granted by the people...this power is not and can never be democratic."[24]

The Putin administration's expanded wild zone of power has done a great deal of damage, destroying anyone who challenges the official line, any notion of a loyal opposition, while maintaining the false front of what Ryklin has called "managed democracy." The "other south" of the Chechens has been used during the first years of the twenty-first century to rekindle age-old Russian xenophobia, to put Russians in a mood that is both isolationist and belligerent—in short, to separate the Russian national self from the Other (*chuzhak*) or, as Tolstaia puts it, a bit archaically, *chuzhenin*. The major effect in the near term has been to eviscerate hopes of tolerant, multicultural understanding of Russianness as citizenship.

One of the distinctive aspects of the post-Soviet reincarnation of the Caucasus conflict is its shift in Russian imagined geography—from being viewed as "oriental," that is, from functioning only on the traditional east-west symbolic axis (Russia is located between two ancient civilizations, European and Asian) to operating on the postcolonial north-south axis. As we have seen in a number of instances, one of the obsessions of the post-Soviet period has been the "third-world anxiety," the suspicion that Russia, the world's geographically northernmost country, is fundamentally a developing

23. Susan Buck-Morss, *Dreamworld and Catastrophe: The Passing of Mass Utopia in East and West* (Cambridge: MIT, 2000), 2–3.
24. Ibid., 10.

economy that exports raw materials rather than manufactured goods, thus ironically positioned at the southern end of the symbolic axis.

It is worth noting Putin's response to Politkovskaia's death because it gives us a good sense of the place that official Russian identity inhabits at present. In a comment made in Dresden on 10 October 2006, he remarked that the crime:

> of course, must not be, must not go unpunished. There might be a variety of motives [for it]. Yes, indeed, this journalist was a sharp critic of the current regime in Russia. But I think that journalists must know, at least the experts understand splendidly, the degree of her influence on political life in the country, in Russia, was extremely insignificant. She was known in journalistic circles, in civil rights circles, and in the West. I repeat, her influence on political life in the country was minimal. And the murder of this kind of person, the cruel murder of a woman, a mother, was by its very nature also directed against our country, against Russia, against the current regime in Russia. (ZCh, 876)

Putin responds in double fashion, which belies the larger struggle for identity. He first reacts defensively to Politkovskaia's death, insisting that she (and by implication the free press) enjoys no real power or influence among the Russian public. He then shifts to another discursive register, turning Politkovskaia's demise into a metaphor for Russia and her state of siege at the hands of her enemies. Putin, thus, implies that Politkovskaia's murderers were not Russian. These comments show that, on the one hand, Putin is at war with whatever free press has survived and the kind of tolerant social and national identity that a free press supports. On the other hand, he is concerned to build Russian identity by appealing to the opposing national archetypes of "Russia/we" and "not Russia/they," which deflect attention away from his possible complicity in the crime and toward an external enemy.

On considering the position of the south in Russian imagined geography, one comes away with the strong impression that what had been unthinkable to many in the 1990s has now happened. If after 1991 the drumbeat "We can't go back" reverberated throughout intellectual talk, then in the Putin era Russia has indeed "gone back," relying on age-old habits of rule by force and state control of the mass media, but this time supported by a statist-nationalist rhetorical offensive. Russian citizens again live in a country where, if they disagree with state policy, they have to defend themselves against the armed forces and police who are supposed to be defending them, their freedom, and their rights.

CONCLUSION

Until recently, Russia saw itself as Pluto in the Western solar system, very far
from the center but still fundamentally a part of it. Now it has left that orbit
entirely: Russia's leaders have given up on becoming part of the West and
have started creating their own Moscow-centered system.
—DMITRI TRENIN, "Russia Leaves the West" (2006)

W HO is a Russian? Where is Russian identity located? Why is Russia
in such trouble, as Petr Pustota quips in Pelevin's novel? And is there a solution? Was the end of the Soviet Union the catastrophe of the century that
Putin claimed it was? Or was it an opportunity to think differently about
being Russian? Since the early 1990s Russian public discourse has divulged
an obsession with the geographical ideas of center and periphery and with
the question of post-Soviet Russia's global status—whether as a center or a
periphery. While insisting that Moscow return to its former glory as a global
center, ultraconservatives of various stripes associate that center with one
of several peripheries, the "Russian" north. They typically want to seal off
the center from its vibrant and fractious southern and western peripheries,
thus running the risk of making the center itself into a periphery. Instead of
seeing the chance for renewal that dialogue between center and periphery or
a decentralized community might offer, they have symbolically isolated the
center and returned to authoritarian forms of identity.

Among the real social achievements of the 1990s were Yeltsin's broad definition of all citizens of the Russian state as Russians, no matter what their
ethnic heritage, and his efforts to curb the power of the secret police and to
promote civil freedoms of speech, association, and action, which fostered a
riveting debate about Russian identity.[1] Although the argument for a tolerant, multicultural concept of Russianness—which we have been associating

1. John B. Dunlop, *The Rise of Russia and the Fall of the Soviet Empire* (Princeton: Princeton
University Press, 1993), 55–56. Dunlop calls Yeltsin's ideal citizen the "supra-ethnic *rossiiskii
chelovek* [Russian citizen]" (56). See also Dmitri Trenin, "Russia Leaves the West," *Foreign
Affairs* 85, no. 4 (July–August 2006), 87–96.

with the symbolic periphery—has found many voices, it lacks social organization and strong leading proponents. Ryklin's and Ulitskaia's openness to other voices and to cultural hybridity has gained relatively little purchase for a number of reasons, among them, the inaccessibility of Ryklin's turgid post-structuralist prose and the tendency of critics to pigeonhole Ulitskaia as a "women's writer." Pelevin's play with neo-Eurasian and authoritarian political views has so far attracted no attention from critics. In the Putin years debate has dwindled as the fearlessly vocal loyal opposition—politicians (Starovoitova in 1998), journalists (Listyev in 1995, Politkovskaia in 2006 and Baburova in 2009), dissidents (Litvinenko in 2006 and Markelov in 2009), and artists (Alchuk in 2008), to name only the best known—met violent ends, likely at the hands of Russian security forces and their churls, who once again wield too much power.

Although the ultraconservatives, among them, the neo-Eurasianist Dugin and the popular ultranationalist Prokhanov, dreamed perfervid dreams of a new, Russocentric imperial state, a large number of prominent thinkers and writers thought creatively about Russian national identity, as a constructed space for many worldviews and cultural heritages rather than a primordialist, essentialist id-entity, realized through military and police brutality. Ryklin's idea of Moscow as a space with borders going through it offers a memorable image of a different society based on civil tolerance. Mamardashvili's centrifugal metaphor of identity as a multicentered and multiperipheried sphere, and Prigov's dismantling of imperial chauvinism also echo memorably. Ulitskaia's repeated attention to the spaces of the periphery and the borderlands of empires as places of insight and creativity rather than conquest provides an alternative to the overbearing centripetal force of the Russian state, of Moscow and its Kremlin inhabitants, with their imperial-national idea of Russians as first among putative equals. For these and other writers geographical regions of the west and the south represent the chance for multicultural openness, while the north and northeast represent dogmatic thinking.

Clearly there are at least two approaches to conceptualizing Russianness—the essentialist and the constructivist. In one view, Russians are ethnically Indo-European, speak "pure" Russian, adhere to the Eastern Orthodox confession, and swear loyalty to a Russia defined by a myth of the north, whether Dugin's Aryan-based Arctogaia or Prokhanov's Slav-based north. The other view broadly embraces as Russian anyone who is a citizen and welcomes the "hybrid" person who combines ethnic background with a broadly defined sense of citizenship. In contrast to both these views, Pelevin in *Chapaev and the Void* implied that Russia was in trouble because of imperial nostalgia and the too-great centripetal force of Moscow—suggesting that there was no solution leading away from the totalitarian past and into another kind of future. Such may be the case, given that the debate about Russian identity has now been truncated, and the possibilities for creative thinking about national selfhood have narrowed.

Since 2000 the debate appears to have been increasingly co-opted by various ultraconservative dreams, among them Dugin's dream of an authoritarian state ruled by the White Tsar and the secret police. If political satire, the canary in the mine of the social-cultural world, is any proof, then the ultraconservatives' vision of a north-oriented, isolated, dogmatic order certainly dominates over the vision of a tolerant civil society. Early on, we discussed Tatiana Tolstaia's *Slynx* (2000), in which power in a post-nuclear community that once was Moscow belongs to the slynx—rapacious, wildcat-like mutants, who control their fellow citizens through terror, very much like totalitarian secret police. Tolstaia associates the slynx, who makes people "mindless," with a mythical North with its "deep forests, full of storm-felled trees."[2] In a much different literary register Tolstaia confirms Ulitskaia's insight that the neo-authoritarians' Russian North could be associated with a closed, doctrinaire mentality.

In 2006 two satires of Dugin and neo-Eurasianism appeared—Viktor Pelevin's anti-imperial novel, *Empire V: A Story about a Real Superman (Ampir V: povest' o nastoiashchem sverkhcheloveke)* and Vladimir Sorokin's *The Day of the Oprichnik (Den' oprichnika)*. Duginesque neo-imperialism is embedded in the title of Pelevin's book, in the idea of the fifth empire. The title playfully links the notion of imperial succession with vampirism. The Russian realm is now part of a "fifth empire," referring at once to Rome the concept of Moscow as the Third Rome—also the concept of the Third Reich—and to vampires as rulers of an "empire" modified by the Roman number V. If Rome was the first great empire, Byzantium the second global empire, Hitler's Third Reich the third great empire, and the postcolonial, post-Soviet globalism the fourth—then the vampires' new universal empire is the fifth. When the "V" attaches to the front of the word empire, or, more effectively, the French-rooted Russian word *ampir,* pointing to "empire style" in furniture, clothing, and architecture, then we arrive at the Russian word *vampir.* Russia—and the universe—is ruled by an oligarchy of cultivated vampires who can read thoughts by sucking the blood of citizens and each other.

Pelevin makes fun of Dugin, combining Dugin's predilection for ancient religions and mythologies and his geopolitical vocabulary, borrowed from Mackinder, of Russia as the power center of the continental heartland. The term heartland is here realized as a metaphor for the "heart"—an underground power center that churns blood through the body, both corporeal and socio-political. It is the holiest of shrines where initiated vampires meet

---

2. Tat'iana Tolstaia, *Slynx,* trans. Jamey Gambrell (Boston: Houghton-Mifflin, 2003). 3.

their goddess Ishtar, here Ishtar Borisovna (her patronymic certainly making her the "daughter" of Boris Yeltsin). Traditionally in Sumerian culture the goddess of fertility and corporeal love, this Ishtar is by now nothing but a Wizard-of-Oz-like head.

Like the neo-Eurasianists and their Russian precursor Lev Gumilev, this Eurasianist world creates its own sciences. In this vampire world those sciences are "glamour" (*glamur*) and "discourse" (*diskurs*). The first has to do with image making and disguising, while the second has to do with control and power.[3] Pelevin has fun with Duginesque false etymologies, for example, the putative origin of the word *glamur*. *Glamur*, the vampire-mentor claims, has its roots in the Scottish word for sorcery (*koldovstvo*) and in the Latin word. grammar.[4] In the middle ages, the novel's protagonist Rama learns, being literate was also associated with occult practice. In the new, post-Soviet middle ages that Dugin wishes for, such is once again the case.

At the end of this strange novel, when Rama apparently dies and turns into a bat, flying over nocturnal Moscow, he produces *glamur* that parodies both the first lines of Pushkin's "Bronze Horseman" and the last lines of the Frenkel song "Cranes" that Serdiuk in *Chapaev and the Void* adores and seeks to realize in his own life. Having sacrificed himself to write his darkly prophetic vampire sonnet, "Prince of This World," Rama sings: "I love our empire [*ampir*]. I love its tortured glamour and its discourse hammered out in battles. I love its people. Not for the bonuses...but simply because we are of one red liquid—although, of course, from a different perspective. I look at the mighty towers, sucking black liquid from the vessels of the planet—and understand that I have found my place in the structure."[5] Once again, as in *Chapaev and the Void*, Pelevin here stresses the centripetal force of the Duginesque center and its focus on control rather than creativity.

While Pelevin's novel plays with various contradictory aspects of Dugin's cosmology and geopolitical theory, making them interact in a fantastic world, Vladimir Sorokin's salacious *Day of the Oprichnik* imagines the new Middle Ages through detailing a twenty-four-hour period in the life of a neo-medieval secret police agent. A spoof on Duginesque dreaming, it imagines a neo-medieval Muscovy in 2028. Postmodern in Dugin's high-tech-but-anti-modern sense of the word, this secret police bring to mind the barbaric *oprichnina*, the special personal army created by Ivan the Terrible

---

3. Viktor Pelevin, *Ampir V: povest' o nastoiashchem sverkhcheloveke* (Moscow: Eksmo, 2006), 271–272.

4. *Ampir V*, 57. It is difficult to know what Pelevin has in mind, perhaps the Anglo-Saxon word *galdre*, http://www.etymonline.com/index.php?term=witch.

5. *Ampir V*, 406.

in 1565 to crush political opposition among the boyars. Although nominally this Duginesque oprichnina serves a new "White Tsar," in fact, the head of the secret forces controls life in this isolated Russian space, brutally massacring anyone, who stands for anything other than Holy Russia, the tsar, and secret police power. Following neo-Eurasianist taste, which admires the Mongol heritage in Russian political life, the head of the oprichnina Boris Borisovich, is affectionately called "Batia." This nickname possibly has a double meaning of *batiushka* or "little father"—the obsequious term used by peasants for the tsar; and of "Batyi Khan," the Russian name for Batu Khan of the Mongol conqueror of the East Slavic lands in 1237–1238.

The security forces adopt a neo-Muscovite ideology, worshiping Holy Russia and ritualistically repeating pseudo-Orthodox prayer. The impoverished ideology of this regime becomes apparent in the lisping chatter of the holy fools at the Kremlin court who can do nothing but repeatedly lisp a few Duginesque words, such as "poweh" and "Euwasia, Euwasia, Euwasia."[6] It is in his satiric reconstruction of the beloved Slavophile concept of spiritual community (*sobornost'*) that Sorokin destroys any pretense of moral and political rectitude in this imagined regime. This brotherhood of secret-security barbarians have dismissed women as second-class citizens. Women cover themselves in the *sarafan,* stay at home, and are expected to be submissive to their husbands. In his political satire Sorokin has a predilection for depicting (male) power relationships as fundamentally homoerotic (see *Blue Lard (Goluboe salo),* 1999), and this novel is no different. *The Day of the Oprichnik* ends with a bestial, late-night homoerotic orgy in which older agents "bond" with younger ones, thus renewing their own vital energies.

In the new middle ages of 2028 innovative minds like Mikhail Ryklin are a thing of the past. Sorokin makes fun of Ryklin's too-great attachment to the mysteries of French and American post-structuralist discourse and his inability to express any idea simply and accessibly. We hear a Swedish radio discussion of the latest book by the Ryklin character, Rykunin, *Where Did Derrida Eat Lunch?,* with a most detailed description of the places where the French philosopher ate during his visit in post-Soviet Moscow. Another channel carries a twenty-fifth anniversary celebration of the art exhibit "Caution, Religion!" The central character Andrei Danilovich dismisses Ryklin and Moscow Conceptualist art as "polyps on the body of our healthy Russian art," embodied for him in Surikov's famous painting "Boyarinya Morozova."[7]

6. Sorokin, *Den' oprichnika* (Moscow: Zakharov, 2006), 171. See Dugin, "Russki orden."
7. Ibid., 144–145.

The real point of Sorokin's satire is to mock the post-Soviet secret police and their stranglehold on contemporary political life. *The Day of the
Oprichnik* ends with Andrei Danilovich's "comforting" thought: "As long
as the oprichnina is alive, Russia will be alive" (223). The secret police is
the new Russia, and Russia is the secret police. Moscow has returned to its
medieval look—there is no more mausoleum on Red Square; the walls of
the Kremlin are white; and instead of Felix Dzerzhinsky Lubianka Square
now features a statue of Maliuta Skuratov, the head of Ivan the Terrible's
oprichnina. Russia has sunk into a cult of violence and terror.

The imagined geography informing this new middle ages is isolationist.
Walls separate the neo-Muscovite state from the west and the south. The
Chinese, who have all the energy and enterprise, have adopted all previously
Russian manufacturing and have built a giant east-west road to link their
new Chinese settlements in Krasnoiarsk and Novosibirsk with China. The
neo-medieval Russian state lives on oil sold to Japan.

Beyond these satires, Eurasianist thinking has had a positive impact on the
popular reimagining of history. For example, the 2007 blockbuster film *Mongol* (dir. Sergei Bodrov), draws on Eurasianist ideas, working in a serious,
epic register. The movie shows a heroic medieval world at the dawn of the
Mongol state. Bodrov successfully popularizes a broadly Eurasianist picture
of the Mongol conqueror Genghis Khan, as the model of the great leader,
focusing on the early years of the Great Khan's life and his struggles to
unite his people. Toward the end of the film, Temudjin—the future Genghis
Khan—didactically conveys four social-political dicta clearly directed at
post-2000 Russian boys: 1) Never kill women and children; 2) Don't forget
your debts; 3) Always fight your enemies to the end; 4) Never betray your
khan. Clearly Bodrov is operating within the Eurasianist subtext that the
Mongol empire became the template for later Russian empires.

Importantly, the film appears to support historian and ethnologist Lev
Gumilev's theory linking national character and geographical environment.
Bodrov's work highlights the beauty of the heartland, the steppe, and the
Turkic-Mongolian peoples who live there. Implicitly, because the steppe is
a crucial aspect of Russians' sense of homeland, the film is certainly at least
as much implicitly about Russian empire as it is explicitly about the rise of
the Mongol empire.

Meanwhile, the Putin regime has also been participating in the game
of imagined geographies that has framed the post-Soviet identity debate.
Beyond manipulating the economic and political lives of Russia's smaller
neighbors, "poetically" the Putin team has realized geographical metaphor,
for example, through the horribly lame lyrics of the new Russian anthem,
adopted in December 2000, that are distantly reminiscent of "America the

Beautiful" and Woody Guthrie's 1940 song "This Land Is Your Land." The English translation goes something like this: "From the southern seas to the polar zone / Forest and fields spread out—our own! / You alone on earth! Are such a one / Guarded by God, our native land!"[8] In contrast to Guthrie's critical reminder that the United States belongs not just to the rich and powerful, this anthem just reconfirms the size of Russian territory and alleges its God-given right to remain whole.

A more recent move bespeaks Putin's worry about borders and his affirmation of an authoritarian identity, heralding the spies, who "protect" Russia from its (southern) enemies. On 11 December 2008, Putin anointed a 10,788-foot, unnamed north Caucasus mountain near the Georgian border the "Peak of Russian Counterintelligence Agents."[9] These attempts can only be interpreted as an effort to co-opt the discourse about Russian identity by highlighting the grandeur of the Russian state and emphasizing the police, who allegedly protect the Russian land. Putin's efforts, in turn, invite people to accept the lack of transparency of the government and the illegal use of force by the military and the secret police, as being necessary for their own security. Ignored here is the ongoing bullying of both Russian citizens and neighboring countries and the creeping closure of those very peripheries that might have at an earlier time have opened new, promising vistas for the future of a Russian civil society.

Since the 1970s Russian public intellectuals have frequently reauthorized the periphery as more than a mere backwater feeding the demands of the economic and political center. It is rather a place of creative intersections and productive challenges to the self-justifications of the center. In the present discussion we have seen the unique defensiveness of the Russian center, Moscow, and the differences in symbolic value assigned to its various peripheries. Clearly the southern and western peripheries are by far the most challenging for the center. It is these peripheries precisely that have functioned imaginatively as the sites of vital debate of issues surrounding Russian identity and cultural difference. To many sectors of Russian writing culture, Moscow's growing self-isolation from those peripheries means the closing-down of that debate and a return to recycled thinking, a move which once again puts Russia "on the edge."

8. See http://www.national-anthems.net/rs. It is curious to see that contemporary school notebooks often popularly sport maps of Russia or the Soviet Union—with the slogan "Born in the USSR." Another notebook tells us that, "I live in Russia and am proud of it."
9. http://en.rian.ru/russia/20081211/118812388.html.

INDEX